Human Rights and World Trade

This book provides an analysis of the political viability of basic rights and offers an in-depth investigation of the largest violation of human rights: world hunger.

Dr Gonzalez-Pelaez develops John Vincent's theory of basic human rights within the context of the international political economy and demonstrates how the right to food has become an international norm enshrined within international law. She then assesses the international normative and practical dimensions of hunger in connection with international trade and poverty. Using the society of states as the framework of analysis, she explores the potential that the current system has to correct its own anomalies, and examines the measures that can move the hunger agenda forward in order to break through its current stagnation.

Demonstrating the interaction between international relations and international political economy, this book will be of significant interest to IR theorists as well as human rights scholars and practitioners concerned with basic rights and the problem of hunger.

Ana Gonzalez-Pelaez is an independent researcher of international affairs based in London. She has worked in broadcast media, published in various academic journals, and served as a consultant to several human rights projects.

The New International Relations
Edited by Barry Buzan, *London School of Economics*
and Richard Little, *University of Bristol*

The field of international relations has changed dramatically in recent years. This new series will cover the major issues that have emerged and reflect the latest academic thinking in this particular dynamic area.

International Law, Rights and Politics
Developments in Eastern Europe and the CIS
Rein Mullerson

The Logic of Internationalism
Coercion and accommodation
Kjell Goldmann

Russia and the Idea of Europe
A study in identity and international relations
Iver B. Neumann

The Future of International Relations
Masters in the making?
Edited by Iver B. Neumann and Ole Waever

Constructing the World Polity
Essays on international institutionalization
John Gerard Ruggie

Realism in International Relations and International Political Economy
The continuing story of a death foretold
Stefano Guzzini

International Relations, Political Theory and the Problem of Order
Beyond international relations theory?
N.J. Rengger

War, Peace and World Orders in European History
Edited by Anja V. Hartmann and Beatrice Heuser

European Integration and National Identity
The challenge of the Nordic states
Edited by Lene Hansen and Ole Waever

Shadow Globalization, Ethnic Conflicts and New Wars
A political economy of intra-state war
Dietrich Jung

Contemporary Security Analysis and Copenhagen Peace Research
Edited by Stefano Guzzini and Dietrich Jung

Observing International Relations
Niklas Luhmann and world politics
Edited by Mathias Albert and Lena Hilkermeier

Does China Matter? A Reassessment
Essays in memory of Gerald Segal
Edited by Barry Buzan and Rosemary Foot

European approaches to International Relations Theory
A house with many mansions
Jörg Friedrichs

The Post-Cold War International System
Strategies, institutions and reflexivity
Ewan Harrison

States of Political Discourse
Words, regimes, seditions
Costas M. Constantinou

The Politics of Regional Discourse
Meddling with the Mediterranean
Michelle Pace

The Power of International Theory
Reforging the link to foreign policy-making through scientific enquiry
Fred Chernoff

Africa and the North
Between globalization and marginalization
Edited by Ulf Engel and Gorm Rye Olsen

Communitarian International Relations
The epistemic foundations of international relations
Emanuel Adler

Human Rights and World Trade
Hunger in international society
Ana Gonzalez-Pelaez

Human Rights and World Trade

Hunger in international society

Ana Gonzalez-Pelaez

Routledge
Taylor & Francis Group

LONDON AND NEW YORK

First published 2005
by Routledge
2 Park Square, Milton Park, Abingdon, Oxon, OX14 4RN

Simultaneously published in the USA and Canada
by Routledge
270 Madison Ave, New York, NY 10016

Routledge is an imprint of the Taylor & Francis Group

© 2005 Ana Gonzalez-Pelaez

Typeset in Sabon by
Rosemount Typing Services, Auldgirth, Dumfriesshire

Printed and bound in Great Britain by
Antony Rowe Ltd, Chippenham, Wiltshire

British Library Cataloguing in Publication Data
A catalogue record for this book is available from the British Library

Library of Congress Cataloging in Publication Data
Gonzalez-Pelaez, Ana, 1974–
  Human rights and world trade : hunger in international society /
Ana Gonzalez-Pelaez.
     p. cm.
  Includes bibliographical references and index.
  1. Food supply. 2. Hunger. 3. Human rights. 4. International
trade—Social aspects. 5. International economic relations.
  6. Vincent, R. J., 1943– I. Title.
  HD9000.5.G65 2005
  363.8–dc22

                                                    2004018464

ISBN 0–415–34939–7

Contents

List of tables   ix
Series editor's preface   x
Acknowledgements   xiii
List of abbreviations   xv

Introduction   1

1 The problem of hunger   6

Definitions 6
Statistics: size and shape of the problem 7
Causes of the problem 12
Introduction to international trade 21

2 Basic human rights: political origins   32

The basic rights discourse 32
Basic rights in Vincent 43
The right to food 50

3 Basic rights in international society: the right to food   53

The World Food Summit and plan of action 53
Poverty summits 61
World trade and the Doha Declaration 66
The degree of legalisation 69

4 International trade and the options for eradicating hunger   78

Theoretical background 79
Maintaining the current liberal trading system 85

*Maintaining the existing system while introducing
    reforms 92*
Radical change in the system 105
Anticipating Vincent's position 114

5   **Can international society eliminate hunger?**   115

Summary of the key points in the argument so far 115
World society 118
International society: solidarism–pluralism 128

6   **Conclusion: assessment of Vincent's basic rights project**   134

The viability of the basic right to food 134
Vincent's contribution to the English school 138

Notes   143
Bibliography   145
Index   167

Tables

1.1 Proportion of undernourished in the developing world   9
1.2 Rate of population growth   11
1.3 Extreme poverty   16
1.4 The relationship between extreme poverty and hunger   18

Series editor's preface

The persistence of mass starvation and chronic hunger is one of the most shocking and shameful features of the modern world. It is shocking because of the sheer volume of people who are every day either hungry or actually dying from starvation and it is shameful because it should be possible for the international society of states to make very substantial reductions in the number of people in the world who are hungry or starving. Although there are disagreements about how best to tackle the problem, it is beyond dispute that there is simply too little being done at this juncture to eliminate the hunger and starvation that exists around the world.

This book assesses the theory and practice of how international society has responded to the global problem of hunger. The focus is not on crisis or emergency situations caused, for example, by drought or civil war, when special circumstances make it difficult to feed people, but on situations where hunger is a routine problem that arises and persists primarily because of poverty. Ana Gonzalez-Pelaez investigates whether the international society of states considers that there is an international responsibility or duty to alleviate hunger and if so, what is being done to fulfil this duty and what can, in theory, be done to eliminate hunger.

This investigation into the problem of hunger builds on the work of John Vincent who is closely identified with the English school of international relations theorists who presuppose the existence of an international society of sovereign states where order is promoted by the existence of a complex set of international institutions. In his early work, Vincent focused on the problem of intervention and he strongly endorsed the norm of non-intervention that is intended to reinforce the sovereignty of the state. Vincent accepted the prevailing view within the English school, at that time, that the virtues of sovereignty and non-intervention are their capacity to preserve the distinctiveness or plurality of the states that constitute international society. Later, however, when Vincent's research focus turned to human rights, he began to question an undiluted pluralist perspective. He argued that there are some basic human rights that every state has a duty to observe. The emerging international consensus about the existence of these rights reflects a growing solidarity within international society. Vincent, therefore, was intent on accommodating a solidarist conception of international society.

Vincent died when he was at the height of his powers and his thinking about human rights was still at a formative stage. He insisted that all human beings have a basic right to both security and subsistence, but he privileged the right to subsistence. From his perspective, international society, as well as states and individuals, has an unequivocal responsibility to ensure that no one suffers from hunger. Gonzalez-Pelaez aims in this book to show that, in developing this argument, Vincent was taking English school thinking in a new and distinctive direction because he acknowledged the centrality of the international political economy in any attempt to understand what international society must do in order to eliminate starvation. The English school has often been criticised for failing to recognise the importance of economic factors in international relations. But such criticism ignores Vincent's contribution. Gonzalez-Pelaez wants, therefore, to highlight this dimension of Vincent's work, and then to follow through the implications of his thinking.

Although Vincent acknowledges the importance of the international political economy for understanding why hunger and starvation are endemic features of the modern world and that structural changes to the economy will be required to deal with the problem, his argument does not extend beyond this point. Before probing the economic dimension, therefore, Gonzalez-Pelaez identifies the scale of the problem and then looks at the wide range of commitments made by international society to eliminate hunger. A clear gap between theory and practice is exposed. The international society of states is committed, in theory, to massive reductions in the levels of hunger and starvation across the globe. In practice, although some progress is being made, without major new initiatives, there is no possibility of meeting the targets that have been set.

Gonzalez-Pelaez is well aware that there is a complex set of factors underlying the persistence of hunger, but in this book, she focuses specifically on the contested links between poverty, hunger and international trade. It is widely accepted that only by reducing poverty will the problem of hunger be successfully eliminated. But the link between trade and poverty is highly contested. Gonzalez-Pelaez argues that an analysis of the literature on international trade reveals three competing options for how to reduce poverty and hunger. One option is to maintain the prevailing liberal trade system, but she argues that this option is failing to meet the targets for the reduction of hunger set by the international society of states. At the other extreme, it is suggested that the liberal trading system should be abandoned. Gonzalez-Pelaez is also sceptical about this option because the proposed reforms are untested and involve too many unknowns. She favours the second option that involves making major reforms in the current liberal trading system and argues that this is the option that is most compatible with Vincent's position.

How likely is it that this second option will be implemented and that international society will make serious attempts to reduce significantly the existing, unacceptable levels of hunger? Gonzalez-Pelaez argues that Vincent was, at the end of his life, beginning to advance ideas that can be used to establish a framework that enables us to address this question. The framework draws on the familiar English school distinction between world society and international society and an intimation that the debate that has opened up in recent years between pluralists and solidarists rests on a false dichotomy. Vincent recognised that the complex world that we live in cannot be comprehended by focusing exclusively on the international society of states, or alternatively, on a world society made up of non-state actors. By the same token, international society does not have to be characterised as either pluralist or solidarist. Pluralists attach primary importance to the maintenance of sovereignty states, but there is no reason, in principle, why the significance attached to sovereignty cannot be strengthened, as international society becomes more solidarist, with states accepting an increasing number of shared values.

By the end of this book, Gonzalez-Pelaez does provide some grounds for optimism. There is no doubt that the international society of states has, in recent years, become increasingly committed to the goals of eliminating hunger and poverty. Vested national interests are still getting in the way of making the reforms to the international trading system that advocates of the second option believe are necessary to achieve these goals. But states in the developed world are facing growing pressure from activists within world society and they have, as a consequence, made some concessions. There are, however, no easy or immediate answers to the problems of poverty and hunger. Establishing a solidarist consensus that the international society of states has an unequivocal moral responsibility to eliminate poverty and hunger in all states is, nevertheless, an important and necessary first step.

Richard Little
University of Bristol

Acknowledgements

My first thank you goes to Barry Buzan, who introduced me to the most challenging intellectual experience that I have ever embarked on. From supervising my PhD thesis to co-editing this book, Barry's knowledge and enthusiasm have guided my journey. I am thankful for his commitment to my project and for the amount of work that he has invested in it over the years.

Richard Little has also played a crucial role in the process of putting this book together. He believed in its potential when it was far from its final shape and contributed a great deal to it. His generosity, with his time and his assistance, has been inexhaustible.

Talking about believing in the initial potential of this book, I must thank the publishers of this series, and in particular Heidi Bagtazo and Grace McInnes, who have given a structure to this process and contributed to it in different ways.

I would like to thank the members of the CSD department at the University of Westminster where I did my PhD and Masters in International Relations. It was an inspiring time that opened a new path for me. A particular acknowledgement here for the then director of the department Richard Whitman who examined my PhD thesis and gave useful insights on how to develop my research further.

Another intellectually inspiring source was the English school meetings. I am grateful to the different scholars with whom I have had motivating conversations and great laughs too. A particular thank you to Tonny Brems Knudsen for reading my initial outlines, to Tim Dunne for encouraging my project on Vincent and to Nicholas Wheeler for his email clarifications about the 'Silent Genocide' term.

In the practical chapters, I owe thanks to Anna Carla Lopez from FAO whose help was essential in accessing part of FAO's data. My acknowledgement also to Imelda Dunlop from the World Economic Forum and to Steve Suppam from the Institute for Agriculture and Trade Policy, who provided important sources of information. A thank you here to Julian Oran from the New Economics Forum; his long emails about agricultural trade issues have been excellent guidelines for my research. George Kent, Co-Convener of the Commission on International Human Rights, has also always been at the other side of the email to reply to any questions.

I would also like to thank the *International Journal of Human Rights*, and in particular Sarah Elvins, who have kindly allowed me to use in this book some ideas that I had earlier published in their journal in an article entitled 'R.J. Vincent and the Basic Rights Discourse' (Spring 2004).

I must bring in here my colleagues at Bloomberg Television, who were happy to exchange shifts with me so I could attend to my university commitments, especially Elizabeth Wootton. She has also patiently proofread parts of my work over the years and been there for me unconditionally.

Thank you also to other friends and family who were supportive of this book. I am aware that one line does not do justice to the value that their support has had along the way, and neither does the fact that I will not mention here all their names. Marion Goldstraw spotted the International Relations course that I later applied to and which meant the start of the journey that has led to this book. A warm thank you to Rowan Douglas, who has understood the value of this dream and shared its highs and lows with me on a daily basis. I would like to conclude this account with a special place for the members of my family that I grew up with: my sister Luci who taught me never to give up, and my parents, Jose and Maria Luisa, who instilled my desire for the pursuit of knowledge. Their economic help through different stages of my university life has also been crucial for arriving here.

Abbreviations

ACP	Africa, Caribbean and Pacific
ADB	Asian Development Bank
AGOA	African Growth and Opportunity Act
AoA	Agreement on Agriculture
BN	Basic Needs
CA	Committee on Agriculture
CAP	Common Agricultural Policy
CESCR	Committee on Economic, Social and Cultural Rights
CETIM	Centre Europe–Tiers Monde (Europe–Third World Centre)
CFS	Committee on World Food Security
CI	Consumers International
CSD	Commission on Sustainable Development
CTA	Technical Centre for Agriculture
DSB	Dispute Settlement Body
EBA	Everything But Arms
EC	European Commission
ECOSOC	Economic and Social Council
FAC	Food Aid Convention
FAO	Food and Agriculture Organisation
FIVIMS	Food Insecurity and Vulnerability Information and Mapping Systems
GATT	General Agreement on Tariffs and Trade
GDP	Gross Domestic Product
GMO	Genetically Modified Organism
GSP	Generalised System of Preferences
HCHR	High Commissioner for Human Rights
HIPC	Heavily Indebted Poor Countries
H-O	Heckscher-Ohlin
HR	Human Rights
IATP	Institute for Agriculture and Trade Policy
ICTSD	International Centre for Trade and Sustainable Development
IFAD	International Fund for Agricultural Development

IGC	Institute for Global Communications
IGO	International Governmental Organisation
ILO	International Labour Organisation
IMF	International Monetary Fund
INGO	International Non-Governmental Organisation
IPE	International Political Economy
IPO	International Progress Organisation
IWG	Interagency Working Group on Food Security
LDC	Least Developed Country
LIFDCs	Low-Income Food-Deficit Countries
MRAs	Mutual Recognition Agreements
NAFTA	North American Free Trade Association
NAM	Non-Aligned Movement
NFFC	National Family Farm Coalition
NFIDCs	Net Food-Importing Developing Countries
NGO	Non-Governmental Organisation
NICs	Newly Industrialised Countries
NIEO	New International Economic Order
ODA	Official Development Assistance
OECD	Organisation for Economic Co-operation and Development
S&D	Special and Differential Treatment
SPFS	Special Programme for Food Security
SPS	Sanitary and Phytosanitary Standards
TPRM	Trade Policy Review Mechanism
TRIPS	Trade Related Intellectual Property Rights Agreement
UNCTAD	United Nations Conference on Trade and Development
UNDP	United Nations Development Program
UNEP	United Nations Environment Program
UNESCO	United Nationsl Educational, Scientific and Cultural Organisation
UNHCHR	United Nations High Commissioner for Human Rights
UNICEF	United Nations Children's Fund (formerly United Nations International Children's Emergency Fund)
URAA	Uruguay Round Agreement on Agriculture
WSRG	World Society Research Group
WEF	World Economic Forum
WFFS	World Forum on Food Sovereignty
WPF	World Parliamentary Forum
WSSD	World Summit on Sustainable Development
WTO	World Trade Organisation

Introduction

This book analyses the political viability of the basic right to food in the society of states and assesses how this right is affected by the existing patterns of international trade. Famine kills more people than any other violation of human rights: 24,000 people die every day from the consequences of hunger. If this number of deaths occurred as a consequence of breaching civil and political rights, outraged calls for immediate action would echo across the globe. Instead, these deaths are often treated as a permanent, albeit unfortunate, feature of the system. Like the poor, the starving seem to be always with us. In total nearly 800 million people are hungry (FAO's 2003 figures) because their subsistence rights are not being met due to socio-politico-economic conditions at local, national and international levels.

Most of those who suffer undernourishment do so as a result of national and international structural failures, and only a fraction of the cases (67 million people) are attributable to man-made and natural disasters. Governments across the world have not only acknowledged the problem but also signed in 1996 an unprecedented set of legal commitments to eradicate starvation and malnutrition. Their biggest commitment is to halve the global number of hungry people by 2015. However, at the current rate of progress (a reduction of 2.5 million per year), it will take over a century to meet that deadline. The moral price of this delay is the loss of millions of lives.

The big question now is how to break the vicious circle that inhibits progress. The international response to this question will determine the viability of the project to end world hunger. In this book I focus on the international side of the right to food, and in particular on the connections between hunger and international trade (agricultural trade specifically). This side of the problem has triggered a heated discussion in public discourse. However, it is underdeveloped in academic discourse, where more systematic enquiry could help to widen the horizons of the policy debate.

I pursue this task within the theoretical framework developed by the English school, and in particular drawing on John Vincent's work on basic rights. Vincent developed a theory of basic rights that represents a substantial contribution to the human rights literature. He argued for the establishment of a core of basic rights as a way to create a common culture under the societies of the world while still respecting the principle of sovereignty. Such an enterprise requires the adoption of a universal benchmark below which standards should not drop. His normative objective was to establish guidelines for decision makers to realise those basic rights that 'everyone should enjoy regardless of political circumstances' (Vincent, 1986a: 14).

Vincent's basic rights initiative has two dimensions: the right to security and the right to subsistence, the latter meaning freedom from starvation. The first dimension reflects the concerns of his predecessors in the English school, especially Hedley Bull, and has inspired the section of the school that currently works on the dilemmas associated with humanitarian intervention. The second dimension questions the legitimacy of the international economic system. On this front, Vincent suggested the possible need to restructure the international economic system to meet the right to subsistence of the world's 'submerged 40 per cent'. However, Vincent left undeveloped his interest in the right to be free from starvation. This part of his basic rights programme has not been followed by the next generation of scholars either, despite the fact that Vincent gave it priority within his basic rights project.

By choosing to use Vincent's theoretical framework to analyse the political viability of basic rights, I demonstrate that his contribution is highly relevant both for human rights discourse and for the internal dialogue within the English school. In the analysis of human rights in international society, Vincent differentiates between routine and exceptional violations of rights. Routine violations (such as mass starvation) are the product of established structures. Exceptional violations, by contrast, are deprivations of a right at a specific point in time. They are usually the result of man-made crises that are dealt with by humanitarian interventions, although in the case of hunger the term also includes natural disasters.

Vincent developed his research in the pluralist–solidarist tension defined by Hedley Bull. Pluralism prioritises the importance of preserving sovereignty in the society of states by promoting a minimalist interaction of norms, rules and institutions. The solidarist current of thought, however, asks for a higher degree of integration in international society than the mere preservation of difference. As states share more values, the solidarists argue, the principle of sovereignty is strengthened. As far as traditional English school thinking goes, these two currents are opposed to each other, and Vincent became an advocate of solidarism through his human rights work. I suggest here that by incorporating elements of international political economy (IPE), he anticipated a different approach to the pluralist–solidarist dichotomy, one that favoured an understanding of international society where elements of solidarism and pluralism cohabit (see Chapters 2 and 6). This book points to new avenues of investigation, suggested by Vincent's theory, that need to be brought into the mainstream of English school thinking. In particular, it identifies a place for IPE and calls for a reassessment of the pluralist–solidarist debate.

I extend Vincent's theory by assessing the normative and practical dimensions of hunger at the global level in connection with international trade and poverty. These two factors are linked by levels of wealth and purchasing power, which have a direct impact on hunger. The capacity of people to fulfil the basic right to subsistence depends both on the availability of food and on the availability of the income to afford it; consequently, purchasing power determines access to food, especially for those who are not subsistence producers. I focus on the international dimension of poverty linked to the overall global trading system and to agricultural trade in particular. Within the global market, agricultural trade plays a significant role in the growth of developing countries, and its dynamics affect the way in which food is produced, distributed and priced. Although I am aware that hunger is a multidimensional problem, I concentrate on this particular facet, following Vincent, who took his argument into the terrain of permanent structural international reforms on the grounds of equality, while respecting sovereignty. International trade provides the arena that answers these concerns.

By the same token, the subject of this investigation will be the almost 800 million people suffering from chronic hunger in the developing world; this research does not include the more than 32 severe food emergencies that are affecting more than 67 million people as a consequence of man-made or natural disasters. Following Vincent's guidelines, this research concentrates on hunger as a permanent phenomenon within international society, and not on sporadic circumstances that can cause famine.

My line of enquiry operates at the state level, where Vincent also raised crucial questions. The argument is divided along two related analytical dimensions: normative and practical. This pattern is anchored in Vincent's defence of an essential relationship between theory and practice: 'Theory cannot be an intellectual exercise divorced from the requirement ultimately to deliver a position on policy' (Vincent, 1994: 30). The position is connected to his final identification with solidarism, which has a normative side that describes how states ought to behave and a practical one that looks at how they behave in practice: 'the central distinction becomes that between theory (policy) and practice (experience), a distinction akin to that between values and facts' (ibid.: 29). This normative–practical interaction has had a crucial impact on this research both for analysing the scope of basic rights in international society and for structuring the argument. The body of this book aims to extend Vincent's unfinished analysis of the right to subsistence. The conclusion is also based on his understanding of theory. I distinguish between how far the basic right to food has been fulfilled and the theoretical–normative commitment to this right. I also assess how the normative consensus on the basic right to food in international society will affect its future fulfilment. If theory and practice coincided, then hunger would be eradicated. However, the gap is still very wide and I analyse how it can be reduced. The conclusions answer the ultimate question posed in this book: is the basic right to food a viable political and economic goal?

This study of basic rights in the international landscape through the lens of the English school in general and Vincent's writings in particular, is divided as follows:

Chapter 1 surveys Vincent's foundational claim about starvation being 'the resident emergency' in international society and its connections with the international economic structure. First, I investigate the scale of the problem and outline its dynamics. Then I focus on international trade with special attention to agricultural trade and the debates surrounding it. The connection between hunger and international trade is made via poverty, a triad that has been accepted in the public discourse as one of the mechanisms that affect the number of hungry people.

Chapter 2 tracks down the political origins of basic rights in general and the right to food in particular. It provides an account of how 'basic rights' emerged in the political arena and highlights the features of the debate surrounding the term. This chapter has two objectives. In relation to the wider research, it sets out the conceptual framework needed to understand the background to Vincent's project. It locates Vincent within the English school and explains the relevance of this tradition of thought for research on basic rights and subsistence. In relation to human rights discourse, it puts forward a concise account of the political (not philosophical) origins of basic rights, which are often neglected. I explain the political emergence of basic rights in terms of the East–West and North–South ideological divisions that dominated the second half of the twentieth century.

Chapter 3 examines the practical implications of basic rights in international society through the problem of hunger and, therefore, the right to food. I analyse this within the international trade–poverty–hunger framework established in the previous chapter. I describe what governments have done, or have committed themselves to do, on all three fronts. These commitments have important consequences for my final assessment of the political viability of basic rights in international society and the relevance of Vincent's project for both foreign policy and English school thinking.

Chapter 4 assesses the three options that have been proposed to eradicate the problem of hunger: maintaining the current liberal system, keeping the existing system while introducing reforms within it, and carrying out a radical change in the system. After documenting and evaluating the consistency of each option, I point out that Vincent's claims for reform do not mean a radical reshaping of the system in favour of something unknown, but they do call for a series of normative and practical reforms along the lines of the second option. This turn in the argument sets the framework for the conclusions of the book along reformist lines.

In Chapter 5, after a thorough analysis of the practicalities of the right to food in connection with international trade and hunger, I come back to the conceptual dimension of Vincent's project, in particular 'world society–international society' and 'pluralism–solidarism'. This analysis helps to provide a deeper understanding of the potential for international society to eliminate hunger, and it sets the basis for the conclusions in Chapter 6. I structure this analysis around the crucial division between the normative and practical realms. This distinction breaks down the complexity of the problem and offers a manageable platform to study what has been achieved, what is left in relation to both, and what possibilities there are of a higher complementarity.

Chapter 6 threads together the arguments of the book in order to assess the political viability of basic rights. It determines both the final viability of a cross-cultural project on basic rights and Vincent's relevance. Based on the previous findings, I finish this research with a final assessment of Vincent's neglected contribution to the English school, focusing on the importance of international political economy.

1   The problem of hunger

This chapter examines the size and shape of the problem of hunger and provides the empirical evidence used in the subsequent chapters to assess the right to food in international society. The first section defines key terms involved in the hunger discourse. The second presents the global statistics on 'hunger' from the 1990s (with highlights from the 1980s and 1970s) and reveals the dynamics of the problem. The third section investigates the disputed causes of the problem, highlighting the debate that occurs on both national and international levels. Section four concentrates on how international trade can cause hunger, paying special attention to agricultural trade.

The analysis in this chapter provides the necessary background to assess John Vincent's claim that routine starvation arises from the existing structure of the international economic system and constitutes the 'resident emergency' of international society. His theory of basic rights develops on the basis of this claim, examined here in Chapter 2. A critical assessment both of the phenomenon of hunger and of Vincent's theory is made later in the book (Chapters 3, 4 and 5).

Definitions

There are several key concepts that are used in the language of food-related problems. These terms set out different analytical perspectives in the process of collecting statistics and organising the data obtained (definitions from FAO, 1999b: 11 and Parker, 2003: 1):

- *Food security* refers to people's ability to have economic and physical access to food that can be properly utilised to ensure adequate nutrition. 'Food security' suggests that people have enough to eat but it does not address who produces it or how.
- *Food insecurity* is characterised by a low level of food intake, which can be transitory (when it occurs in times of crisis), seasonal or chronic (when it occurs on a continuing basis).

- *Hunger or undernourishment* refers to an insufficient supply or, at worst, a complete lack of calories. It is a stage of chronic food insecurity in which food intake is insufficient to meet basic energy requirements on a continuing basis.
- *Malnutrition* is characterised by the lack or shortage of micronutrients (vitamins and minerals) in food that provides enough calories. It is a physiological condition resulting from inadequacy or imbalance of food intake or from poor absorption of food consumed. These micronutrients are vital for the functioning of cells, especially the nervous system. The lack of them in the first five years of a child's life can cause death, or disability for life.

Undernourishment and malnutrition are two sides of the same coin: the lack of food security and its devastating consequences for human survival and wellbeing. Statistics and different studies on this matter refer to 'hunger' or 'the hungry', meaning both groups. By the same token, in this book I also mean both undernourishment and malnutrition when using the terms 'hunger' or 'hungry'. Other relevant definitions are:

- *Vulnerability*, involving the presence of factors that place people at risk of becoming food insecure or malnourished.
- Based on these concepts, a new term has been introduced recently for practical reasons when calculating the state of food insecurity in the world: *depth of hunger*. This is a measure in calories of the 'per person food deficit' of the undernourished population within each country or area. Therefore, where the undernourished lack 400 calories a day, the situation is more dire than where the average shortage is 100 calories. The healthy average is calculated to be around 2,700 calories per day, although it varies depending on level of activity, age and gender (FAO, 14/1/02c: 1, 2).

The focus of this research will be the hungry in general. This terminology will help to determine the grade of undernourishment experienced by people in these circumstances.

Statistics: size and shape of the problem

This section begins by sketching the general background of the problem of hunger in absolute terms. Then I analyse the trends that these statistics display and establish the dynamics of hunger, considering both absolute and proportional figures (evolution of undernourishment in relation to population growth). The time frame for this study is mainly the decade of the 1990s to the present. Flashbacks into the 1980s and 1970s are provided in order to establish the dimensions of the problem at the time when Vincent wrote his work and their evolution since then.

Statistics on food security date back to the late 1960s as a preparation for the first hunger-related summit: the World Food Conference in 1974 (FAO, 1996b: 1–15). However, it is not until the 1990s that exhaustive data become available. The World Food Summit (1996) led to the creation a year later of the Food Insecurity and Vulnerability Information and Mapping Systems (FIVIMS), a complex data collection mechanism. It consists of networks of systems that assemble, analyse and disseminate information about the problem of food insecurity and vulnerability at both global and national levels. The Food and Agriculture Organisation (FAO) has an ongoing project for monitoring the nutritional status of populations worldwide. Its statistics are accepted by governments around the world and formed the basis for the World Food Summit in 1996.

This summit is the crucial date for international action against hunger where governments agreed on several commitments intended to halve the number of hungry people by 2015 (taking as a point of reference the global 818 million that there were in the developing world in 1990–92, the benchmark period used at the World Food Summit). The FAO's major contribution to the plan is *The State of Food Insecurity in the World*, published on an annual basis since 1999. The average annual decrease required to meet the 2015 target would have been 22 million per year since 1996 in absolute numbers, which differs dramatically from the trend maintained in the decade of the 1990s, where a 2.5 million reduction per year was registered (FAO, 2003: 6). This figure corresponds to an annual average established in estimate terms; this does not mean that the reduction has been constant. There might be years when it has reached higher or lower levels. There are no statistics that monitor the year-to-year variations in the hunger levels (Mernies, 2002).

Because the data collection system is itself still under development, figures can change dramatically from one yearly report to the next. The 1990–92 data were used as a benchmark for the 1996 summit and do not vary, but the figures after that have been constantly revised. Despite these continuous reviews of the numbers, the statistics provide a map of the areas of the world where the hunger spots are localised.

In these general terms, from 1990 to 1999 there was a net reduction of 20 million hungry people in the developing world, calculated on the basis of the reduction of 116 million that the best performing countries experienced and the 96 million increase that 47 countries suffered (FAO, 17/10/02: 8).

The causes of hunger are spread across different levels and their impact varies among countries. During the past two decades, the global per capita availability of food has increased despite a population growth of 1,600 million. The average energy supply rose from 2,410 calories in 1969–71 to 2,800 calories in 1997–99 in the world as a whole and from 2,110 to 2,680 calories in developing countries (FAO, 14/1/02k: 1). However, the absolute number of undernourished in the developing world only went down from 956 million in 1969–71 to 798 million in 1999–2001 (FAO, 2003: 6).

These figures contrast with another fact calculated by the FAO: at the present stage of development of agricultural production, the Earth could feed 12 billion human beings, providing food equivalent to 2,700 calories a day for every individual. And yet there are only 6 billion people currently living on the planet. On average 62 million die a year; out of those, 36 million die from hunger-related diseases (UN, 2001d: 5), of whom 9 million die from starvation itself (De Haen, 2002: 1).

Most of the victims live in the more than 80 nations classified as low-income food-deficit countries (LIFDCs), many of which cannot produce enough food to feed their population and lack the financial resources to import the extra supplies they need (CFS, 2002a: 3). By regions, Table 1.1 shows how the undernourishment map looks.

Asia has the largest number of undernourished people, 508 million, which is 16 per cent of the total population of the continent. Asia's number of hungry people in the 1970s was equivalent to 41 per cent of the population. Even when the region's population has increased during the past two decades by 800 million, the number of undernourished people was reduced to 16 per cent of the total population. Within that region, East and South East Asia are the best performers, while South Asia is one the three worst affected areas in the world, with 24 per cent of its population being hungry. The other two major hunger spots are Sub-Saharan Africa and the Caribbean (FAO, 2003: 31).

Table 1.1 Proportion of undernourished in the developing world

	Total population 1990–1992 millions	Total population 1999–2001 millions	Undernourished 1990–92 millions (%)	Undernourished 1999–2001 millions (%)
Developing world (total of regional figures)	4,050	4,638	818.5 (20)	799 (17)
Asia and Pacific	2,812	3,162	567 (20)	508 (16)
Latin America and Caribbean	442	504	58 (13)	54 (11)
Near East and North Africa	321	384	26 (8)	40 (10)
Sub-Saharan Africa	474	587	166 (35)	198 (33)

Source: Adapted from FAO, *The State of Food Insecurity in the World 2003*.

Looking at the number of victims in relation to the size of the population, *Sub-Saharan Africa* is at present the worst affected area in terms of percentage of the total population: 198 million people, 33 per cent of the total population, are permanently undernourished. Most of them suffer from 'extreme hunger', with an average daily intake of 300 calories less than the minimum quantity required for survival.

Therefore, and in relation to the definitions provided earlier, there are more chronically hungry people in Asia and the Pacific, but the depth of hunger is greatest in Sub-Saharan Africa. There, in 46 per cent of the countries, the undernourished have an average deficit of more than 300 calories per person per day. However, in Asia and the Pacific only 16 per cent of the undernourished suffer from food deficits this high (FAO, 2000b: 3, 4; FAO, 17/10/02: 31–5; FAO, 2003: 32).

When the number of undernourished people is viewed by areas (Table 1.1) there is a generally decreasing trend, considering that there has also been a substantial growth of population. However, these results benefit from the progress made in large countries. China registered a decrease in the number of undernourished people from 16 per cent of its total population in 1990 to 9 per cent in 2000, together with an increase of its total population by 90 million. Indonesia went down from 9 per cent in 1990 to 6 per cent in 2000, having also registered an increase in population of 20 million. Nigeria reduced its 14 per cent of undernourished people in 1990 to 7 per cent in 2000 while its population went up by nearly 20 million (FAO, 9/4/00j: 2–5; FAO, 17/10/02: 30, 31).

In proportional numbers, between 1990 and 2000 the number of undernourished fell in the majority of developing countries, although in some areas the decrease has not been sufficient to compensate for the population growth. In total, 61 developing countries achieved a proportional decrease during this period, although in 26 of them it was not sufficient to cover the population growth. That is the case in Angola, Chad, India and Mozambique, which, because of their high population growth, did not manage to reduce the number of undernourished significantly in absolute numbers despite their performance (FAO, 2001b: 1–3). For example, in India the absolute numbers of undernourished have increased by 18 million, although the proportional numbers fell from 25 to 14 per cent (FAO, 17/10/02: 8).

Table 1.2 shows the average rate of population growth by taking four years as an example; although the percentages have started to decrease, the trend is still not strong enough to determine the direction it will take.

In terms of the 2015 deadline, the picture is mixed and subject to individual country analysis. In the 1990s, 22 countries (including Bangladesh, China, Haiti and Mozambique) managed to achieve substantial progress in their traditionally alarming records.

Table 1.2 Rate of population growth (percentage)

	1980	1990	1995	1999
East Asia	1.50	1.59	1.27	1.10
South Asia	2.34	2.09	1.87	1.90
Sub-Saharan Africa	3.06	3.61	2.71	2.53
Latin America	2.22	1.85	1.67	1.10
World	1.73	1.78	1.43	1.36

Source: Adapted from 'Data for the Analysis of Poverty Reduction', World Bank
        (7/2/2002a).

However, and in terms of the region as a whole, improvement does not look as clear in *Sub-Saharan Africa*. This region is made up of the world's poorest countries, and rapid economic growth there is unlikely. Undernourishment is expected to decline from 33 per cent in 1998 to 22 per cent in 2015. High population growth has a negative effect and the number of hungry people could even increase. Some very poor countries in *Asia, the Caribbean and the Near East* share similar characteristics (FAO, 14/1/02c: 2). The prospective rate of population growth is calculated on the basis of the current patterns, although they could be altered by increased use of contraceptive methods in the developing world, changes in cultural patterns regarding fertility or the rising number of deaths from AIDS, which has reached epidemic levels in parts of Africa and Asia. Even then, estimates maintain that the world population will grow from 5.3 billion in 1990 to 8.9 billion in 2030, with the highest rate of increase located in the developing world (Thomas, 1997: 462).

* * *

In the light of the statistics just presented, it can be said that despite regional differences, hunger is a phenomenon found all over the developing world with higher incidence in parts of Africa, South Asia and parts of Latin America and the Caribbean. In absolute terms, there has been a reduction in the past two decades in the number of hungry people, considering that the population went up by over 1.5 billion. The general outlook by region is improving, helped mainly by large countries that have experienced a strong reduction. However, when looking at countries on an individual basis, the picture is mixed, with a rapid reduction in some of them and a slow reduction or none in others.

The net decrease amounts to 20 million (in the 1990s), which is not sufficient to meet the heads of states' commitment to eradicate hunger by 2015. In terms of proportional numbers, the growth of population tends to overshadow improvements in hunger reduction, especially in very poor countries. In fact, the annual rate of reduction would need to be accelerated to 26 million per year, more than 12 times the current rate. However, population increase is not the only determining factor. There are countries that have seen a substantial population growth and still reduced both the absolute and proportional numbers of undernourished.

Causes of the problem

This section outlines the major areas of dispute in the literature on the causes of hunger. The purpose of this survey is to highlight the main themes of the multidimensional debate in order to locate the route followed in the book. Each theme is highly contested both internally (arguments in favour and against) and externally (the priority they should be given in relation to the other causes involved). I sketch the main lines of the debate that frame the problem of hunger, before focusing on Vincent's approach, but I do not attempt to resolve these disputes or to take sides.

The account given here embraces both national and international causes of hunger, although in some cases there are no clear boundaries and they can overlap at various points. The factors considered here are overpopulation, food distribution, access to land and credit, discrimination against women, corruption, wars, external debt, poverty, developments in biotechnology, and world trade.

Overpopulation

The first school of thought in the debate about hunger places central importance on the relationship between human population growth and the food supply. It is known as the orthodox, nature-focused explanation of hunger and asserts that population growth shadows the increases in food production. This explanation identifies overpopulation as the cause of hunger and explores possible ways to reduce human fertility in the fastest growing section of the world, the poor of the 'Third World'. In particular, the most populous countries are Bangladesh, Brazil, China, Egypt, Ethiopia and Eritrea, India, Indonesia, Iran, Mexico, Nigeria and Pakistan. They account for half of the world's population and their rate of growth is expected to increase over the next decades, which will make the reduction of hunger very difficult (Thomas, 1997: 462).

Food distribution

Food distribution is the main factor for a second school of thought that opposes the previous approach. Its advocates construct their argument around the idea that there has been an enormous increase in food production since the Second World War, thanks to the development of seeds and agricultural technology. However, this increase has made little impact on the numbers of the victims of hunger. For this line of thought, the most important element is not per capita food availability, but the distribution of food, whether or not the person can establish an entitlement to that food (having the money to buy the food available in the market or having the land to grow food for their own consumption). Therefore, it is a question of people 'not having enough to eat rather than there not being enough to eat'. This pattern requires a close look at the social, political and economic factors that indicate how food is distributed and why the access to it is uneven (Thomas, 1997: 463). This food distribution argument is applicable both to the structure within the country where the subjects are its own citizens and to the international structure where the subjects are the countries themselves and the gaps among them. The poorest developing countries are short of foreign exchange and cannot afford to buy food from the world market, despite its availability (Kwa, 1998: 5).

Access to land and credit

A common denominator in theories of development is that access to land is a key element for the improvement of conditions in rural societies and has a direct effect on the access to food. Land ownership is related to the ability of rural people to provide for their own subsistence and to participate in the market. Several projects have been initiated in countries such as India, the Philippines and South Africa. However, these reforms are not always carried out successfully: in the case of India (West Bengal) there has been an 18 per cent increase in agricultural output, but Zimbabwe is struggling with declining production. The chaos in the land redistribution process in Zimbabwe coupled with corruption and violence is increasing hunger by wrecking the efficiency of a highly concentrated pattern of land ownership. Mugabe's regime has turned a country that exported maize to the rest of the region into an economy that cannot feed itself (Elliott, 2002: 10).

The concentration of land ownership in a segment of the population is criticised for being one of the engines of food insecurity. The lack of access to land for many people in agrarian societies is considered to deprive them of permanent access to adequate and sufficient food. This problem has promoted the Zapatista movement in Chiapas, Mexico, and the Landless Rural Workers movement in Brazil. In Brazil 1 per cent of landowners own 46 per cent of all farmland and 4.5 million peasant families have no land at all (UN, 2001d: 10). These examples demonstrate the unequal patterns of land ownership in developing countries. Among the Asian countries, land reforms have been extensively implemented in China and Taiwan, and to a lesser extent in India. However, in Central America very little progress has been made, with percentages of landless and near-landless agricultural households above 60 per cent. In Africa the rate is around 40 per cent (Thomas, 1997: 458).

In its 2002 report on food insecurity, the FAO has noted that developing countries where land was more equally distributed in 1980 have made more progress in reducing hunger during the past two decades. This has been the case in China, Indonesia and, to a lesser extent, in Thailand (FAO, 17/10/02: 27).

Discrimination against women

This aspect is linked to the particular interpretation given to social, economic and political rights in certain cultures. In many countries women do not have access to the ownership of land. Together with this, there are cultures where women suffer from the unequal distribution of food within households. This problem perpetuates undernourishment in these societies, since malnutrition can be a hereditary condition. Seriously undernourished mothers give birth to seriously undernourished babies (FAO, 2000b: 4). Other vulnerable groups are children, the elderly, the disabled, ethnic and religious minorities, indigenous populations, refugees, migrants, displaced persons and prison inmates.

Corruption

Corruption can take several forms and its social consequences in poor countries have direct repercussions on food security. The case of Chad has called attention to this problem: in November 2000 the government of Chad asked for international aid against a devastating internal famine. At the time, the World Bank handed over to the Chadian government US$25 million for an oil project that would help to combat poverty. The parliamentary opposition later accused the government of diverting the money into arms purchases and other corruption mechanisms (UN, 2001d: 23).

Another variation of corruption at state level is the case of the Democratic Republic of Korea in the early 1990s. International aid from the World Food Program and several non-governmental organisations (NGOs) was diverted by the army, the secret services and the government (UN, 2001d: 13).

Wars

In wartime, the supply of and access to food becomes difficult and, at times, impossible. Despite prohibitions by international humanitarian law, food is often used as a weapon. This happened, for example, in Sarajevo between 1992 and 1995 when the Yugoslav Federal Army and Serb militias besieged the city (UN, 2001d: 24). In wartime, food insecurity is also caused by other elements such as the destruction or abandonment of crops and government policies themselves. Governments use their resources mainly to buy weapons. For instance, during the 1994 famine that struck Ethiopia the Addis Ababa government was investing 46 per cent of the state's budget in arms. In Angola an escalation of the 15-year civil war has resulted in the displacement of more than 2.6 million people, the majority of them suffering from malnutrition (FAO, 21/1/02: 2).

In 1992, in Somalia, hundreds of thousands of children under five died of hunger or hunger-related illnesses. The same happened between August 1998 and May 2000 in the Democratic Republic of the Congo, where 1.7 million persons died (Marchal, 2001: 43).

In more general terms, the FAO has concluded that war and civil strife have caused food emergencies in 15 countries during 2001 and the first quarter of 2002 (FAO, 17/10/02: 22).

External debt

This refers to the structural adjustment programmes of the International Monetary Fund (IMF), which are criticised for aggravating under-nourishment and malnutrition in debtor countries. The debt of the 47 most indebted countries totals U\$422 billion, which is equivalent to 124 per cent of their gross national product (Worldwatch Institute, 2002: 2). Since 1990, gross domestic product growth in the 48 poorest countries in the world has been less than 1 per cent per annum. On the other side of the balance, the international financing institutions have also taken measures to help with fighting poverty: for example, the debt relief initiative of the World Bank and the IMF for the heavily indebted poor countries (HIPC) initiated in 1996. Under these initiatives, 26 countries have had their debt repayments cancelled on condition that the money saved is channelled to poverty reduction. However, half of these countries are still spending 15 per cent or more of their revenue in debt repayments, which means that they invest less money in public health than in debt relief (Elliott, 2002: 10).

Poverty

The United Nations Development Program (UNDP) estimates that at least 1.2 billion human beings live on an income of less than US$1 a day (World Bank, 2002a: 1). The figures on poverty could take different shapes: for example, over a billion people are not connected to a modern water supply system; some 2.4 billion people do not have acceptable sanitation arrangements; 4 billion cases of diarrhoea are recorded every year, 2.2 million of which are fatal (UN, 2001d: 11). Some voices claim that many poor people around the world do not get enough to eat because food production is geared to cash payment, which is linked to the previous point on food availability and entitlement to that food.

Poverty declined slowly in developing countries during the 1990s. The proportion of people living in poverty (those whose level of consumption fell below the international poverty line of US$1 per day) went down from 29 per cent in 1987 to 26 per cent in 1998. However, the number of poor remained almost unchanged at around 1.2 billion due to population growth (World Bank, 8/4/02a: 1–4).

Their distribution by region is set out in Table 1.3.

The reduction in global poverty is attributed to progress made in East Asia, especially in China. Since 1993 India has also shown signs of poverty reduction (World Bank, 2002a: 2). However, by regions the performance in Africa, Latin America and South Asia shows only moderate decline or increase.

Africa: In 1987, 47 per cent of the population was living below the international poverty line. By 1998, this rate had declined to only 46 per cent. With an average rate of 2.5 per cent population growth over the 1990s, Sub-Saharan Africa is today the region with the highest incidence of poverty in the world (ADB, 2000: 4).

Asia and Pacific: Poverty in the Asia and Pacific region is marked by magnitude and diversity. Close to 900 million (75 per cent) of the world's poor live in this area (including Central Asia). Within the region, East Asia and China have performed well in reducing poverty over the past decade. Although some progress has been made in South Asia, the depth of poverty there reaches similar levels to Sub-Saharan Africa, but on a much larger scale as more than half a billion people are in poverty in South Asia. The countries in the Pacific have a higher per capita income (ADB, 2000: 6).[1]

Latin America and the Caribbean: The level of poverty decreased in Latin America and the Caribbean during the first half of the 1990s. However, during the second half of the decade economic growth in most countries was insufficient to reduce the absolute number of poor people. As a result, in 1997, the incidence of poverty in Latin America remained 3 per cent higher than in 1980, with around 70 million more people living below the poverty line of $2 per day (ADB, 2000: 9).

Table 1.3 Extreme poverty (Number of people living on less than US$1 a day; millions)

	1987	*1990*	*1998*
East Asia and Pacific	417.5	452.4	267.1
(excluding China)	114.1	92.0	53.7
Eastern Europe and Central Asia	1.1	7.1	17.6
Latin America and Caribbean	63.7	73.8	60.7
Middle East and North Africa	9.3	5.7	6.0
South Asia	474.4	495.1	521.8
Sub-Saharan Africa	217.0	242.3	301.6
Total	1,183.0	1,276.4	1,174.9

Source: Adapted from 'Income Poverty: Latest Global Numbers', World Bank (8/4/2002a).

The data given above show the scale of poverty, a situation that is likely to continue at current levels for the coming years if policies do not achieve faster growth in combination with an equitable distribution of the benefits. These policies need to be spread across different levels: 'macroeconomic stability, sustained structural reforms, prudent and transparent use of public resources, improvements in the provision of public services and infrastructure to the poor, actions to reduce vulnerability and development choices' (World Bank, 8/4/02c: 42).

The poor are divided into two big groups: the rural poor and the urban poor. The *rural poor* encompass smallholders, landless labourers, pastoral nomads and fisher people. Inefficient production and lack of access to credit, seeds, fertilisers and marketing limit their food production. In poor farming communities hunger tends to occur seasonally between harvests, when the previous one has been consumed and the new one has not been gathered yet. Other factors that affect their access to food are the degradation of land and soil from misuse or overuse or climate change, which can take the form of natural disasters. The *urban poor* suffer from low income that does not allow them to purchase the food available; in the worst case, they have no income at all.

In both rural and urban cases, poverty creates a situation of vulnerability that places people at risk of becoming food insecure or hungry. In the case of the rural poor, insecurity can come from two sources: land-related problems (no land ownership and insufficient production) and lack of income to purchase food from the market. In the case of the urban poor, food insecurity depends exclusively on the level of income that will allow them to buy available food. Since entitlement to food depends in most cases on having money to purchase the products, hunger and poverty are intrinsically related. Even in the rural scenarios where people could have direct access to grow their own food, entitlement is given by factors such as land ownership or adequate production environment. Therefore, in these cases, lack of land or inadequate conditions are also an expression of poverty. The connection between poverty and hunger happens also at the macro level, as is reflected in the statistics collected in this chapter. The three areas with the highest incidence of starvation are those with the highest levels of poverty. Table 1.4 compares the two phenomena in those three areas (excluding China and India).

Regarding medium-term poverty projections (2015), these three regions are expected to register the slowest reduction of people in extreme poverty, because prospects for immediate and rapid economic growth are limited (World Bank, 28/8/02: 2, 3). These calculations are parallel to those on hunger reduction, which attribute to these three areas the highest probable incidence of undernourishment in 2015.

Table 1.4 The relationship between extreme poverty (less than US$1 day/1999) and hunger (2001)

	Poverty (millions)	% of total population	Hunger (millions)	% of total population
Sub-Saharan Africa	300	46	195	33
South Asia	490	38	307	22
Latin America and Caribbean	77	21	54	11

Sources: Adapted from World Bank, 'Global Economic Prospects and the Developing Countries 2002' and FAO, 'The State of Food Insecurity in the World 2003'.

Developments in biotechnology

On this topic there has also been an intense public debate. First, there are concerns about the effect of modified organisms on the human body. From the angle of the right to food, 'accessibility' implies access to food free of harmful substances, and Genetically Modified Organisms (GMOs) can be argued to present risks to human health. A GMO is the result of a process of 'introducing, rearranging or eliminating specific genes through modern molecular biology techniques' (FAO, 14/1/02e: 1). With regard to developing countries, there is also the danger that field testing of these substances is being carried out in countries lacking policies on GMOs. Voices in favour of GMOs view them as a way to reduce both food shortages and the use of agricultural chemicals. The counter-argument is that the world does produce enough food (previous point) and that in any case GMOs would not help the hungry masses in developing countries, since they require high levels of technology. This technology is in the hands of big corporations and oriented to the export market, not available to the local people.

Another crucial debate flows from the issue of patents protected by the WTO. International patents are held by Northern multinationals; they also benefit from universal protection and trade-related aspects of intellectual property rights, which deprive poor farmers of access to the production mechanism (Moser and Shiva, 1995). The Trade Related Intellectual Property Rights Agreement (TRIPS) protects the rights of rich corporations but easily allows the knowledge of indigenous communities to be patented by others. Patents affect not only the area of GMOs, but also the commercialisation of biotechnology. Modern biotechnology makes it possible to breed plants faster and in a more controlled way than before. This knowledge owned by a few powerful corporations is protected by the TRIPS, which means that developing countries cannot easily gain access to technology (FAO, 14/1/02e: 5).

The GMO debate also affects the field of food aid, as has been intensely debated in the Johannesburg Summit (August 2002). The polemic came from Zambia, which declined a US$50 million aid package from the US

Department of Agriculture because of provisions that it would have to accept GMO commodities (Esipiu, 2002: 3). The controversy, named 'eat GM or starve' (ibid.: 1), highlighted the dilemma of facing mass starvation in the present or risking possible side effects of genetically modified food later. There is no straightforward answer to this scientific and economic battle. While Zambia has rejected the GMO aid offer, Malawi accepted it to overcome the starvation affecting 2.5 million people in the summer of 2002. In the meantime, the European Union has strict regulations regarding imports of GM food, a fact that worries environmentalists and some African governments: 'with thousands of tons of genetically modified seeds being donated to the region ... some of it may be planted by local farmers, letting the GM genie out of the bottle and potentially shutting the export market in the European Union' (Johnson, 2002: 1).

World trade

This issue is mentioned across a variety of studies on the right to food. It refers to the impact of international trade on the food situation of poor countries and is both complex and contradictory. The argument centres on the debate about whether free trade in agriculture would actually help or worsen the problem of hunger. There is disagreement about this between liberals, who think it would help, and anti-liberals, who think it would make matters worse, since it could destroy the fragile local self-sufficient markets in developing countries and could damage the national agricultural infrastructures in developed countries.

There are other concerns of security surrounding this argument, such as the transmission of diseases if the trade barriers were to be opened. However, some voices claim that these worries disappear for those products that are of interest to the richest countries. These arguments have moved into a new dimension after the WTO conference in Doha (November 2001) where governments made an effort to identify the causes of concern and agreed on a plan of action beyond the polemics (thoroughly reviewed in Chapters 4 and 5).

International trade has consequences for the economies of developing countries, and therefore for the right to food. In fact, in Commitment 4 of the World Food Summit (1996) states acknowledge the effects of trade on food security: 'We will strive to ensure that food, agricultural trade and overall trade policies are conducive to fostering food security for all through a fair market-orientated world trade system' (FAO, 1996e: 19).

* * *

So far, I have described the different elements in the debate about the phenomenon of hunger. Some of the causes clearly operate at the national level (such as the topics of corruption, population growth, distribution of land), others at the international level (external debt, biotechnology and market access) and others, such as poverty, combine international and national factors. The survey shows how hunger is a complex phenomenon where each element contributes to a larger, more complicated agenda that extends across scientific, political and economic terrains.

Vincent, however, did not discuss what should be done about hunger along these multiple dimensions; he focused on the international responsibility for the problem regardless of cause and looked specifically at what international society can do about it without infringing on sovereignty. He suggested the possibility of having to restructure the international economic order to meet the right to subsistence of the 'submerged 40 per cent'. Although Vincent did not expand on these statements any further, two clues define the move that I make in this research. First, the drive in his basic rights project is to respect, or even strengthen, sovereignty. He does not intend to overthrow the current system, but to 'add to its legitimacy' by pursuing a solidarist project through the introduction of basic rights. Second, when referring to what international society can do about the problem of hunger, his argument follows the terrain of permanent structural reforms that will benefit the 'submerged 40 per cent' on the grounds of equality. International trade is the arena in which his basic right to subsistence can be tested on both of these fronts. Within this context, I will look in detail at agricultural trade, given its relevance for the economies of developing countries.

Agricultural trade is the most pressing structural problem for these economies because it is the most restricted area in the international markets, while it employs more than 60 per cent of the population in low-income countries and about 73 per cent of the poor in developing countries live in rural areas (World Bank, 2003: 103). That is the reason why 'agriculture is crucial to their survival and to the global fight against poverty' (Green, 2002: 3). Other subjects that intervene in the international domain (aid, debt relief, international commodity policies and biotechnology expansion) sometimes overlap with elements of international trade. However, it is not the purpose of this research to assess the capacity of aid (including debt relief) offered by the richest part of international society when helping countries to overcome short-term crises. The summary of the possible causes of hunger is necessary to make a final assessment of Vincent's project (Chapter 6) by putting his statements on international responsibility into perspective.

Here, the connection between international trade and hunger will be made via poverty, because, as shown, a correlation exists between areas with the highest levels of poverty and those with the highest levels of hunger: a reduction of poverty levels implies a reduction in the levels of hunger. However, the cause–effect relationship between the two is reciprocal: poverty causes hunger and hunger causes poverty. Poverty causes hunger by not allowing access to food (through lack of purchasing power and/or lack of access to productive land). Hunger causes poverty by limiting physical and mental capability resulting in lower productivity and lack of economic progress (FAO, 1996a: 2). The relationship is a vicious circle and the most commonly debated way to break it is to start by tackling poverty; the reduction of poverty has proven to cut down the numbers of undernourished. The latest FAO report emphasises this connection: 'Most of the widespread hunger results from grinding, deeply rooted poverty... [and only] between 5 and 10 percent of the total can be traced to specific events: droughts or floods, armed conflict or political, social and economic disruptions' (FAO, 17/10/02: 12). Poverty acts as the intervening variable linking international trade and hunger.

The connection between trade and poverty is accepted by the practice of international society, as I will document in the next section and expand in Chapter 3. The report produced by UNCTAD in 2002 clearly establishes this link and concludes that the incidence of poverty in most underdeveloped countries is so high because 'international trade and finance relationships are reinforcing the cycle of economic stagnation and poverty' (UNCTAD, 2002: 1). The Cairns Group, which accounts for one-third of the world's exports in agriculture, asserts that 'the costs of agricultural trade distortions are rising hunger, losing out on global prosperity and unstable markets' (Cairns Group, 2002: 3).[2]

Introduction to international trade

This section describes the international structure of trade. It is divided into two parts. First comes an assessment of the current world trade framework with special emphasis on the position that developing countries occupy (its history will be set out in Chapter 4). Second, it focuses on the role of agriculture in international trade. This section provides a background for the next two chapters.

World trade issues

The policies of trade liberalisation are embodied in the WTO, which came into existence in 1994 with the Marrakesh Agreement following the Uruguay Round of Talks. It replaced the General Agreement on Tariffs and Trade (GATT), which applied only to goods. Multilateral agreements sponsored by the WTO have created a new framework for international trade, furthering global integration (Castells, 2000b: 114). The WTO core consists of a set of principles that reflect the elements associated with globalisation: free trade, open markets and tariff reductions. It works on the principle of multilateral trade negotiations, where some sectors gain and others lose, and it acts as a mediator in disputes between trading partners. The WTO provides a forum for trade rule-making, protects trade opportunities, fosters transparency in the trading system and enforces rules through a dispute-settling mechanism (Lengyel and Tussie, 2002: 491). For the first time ever, the Uruguay Round of Talks introduced the Agreement on Agriculture; among other topics, governments committed themselves to reducing national support of their products and opening up their markets.

The Uruguay Round started a reform programme under which Third World countries could establish a commercial relationship with the rest of the international market. The passage from the GATT to the WTO marked a turning point for trade policies in developing countries (Lengyel and Tussie, 2002: 485). They are divided into two types: *Least Developed Countries* (LDCs)[3] made up of 49 countries, and *Net Food-Importing Developing Countries* (NFIDCs) comprising 18 states. In the context of the new policy, aid was dramatically reduced: from 22 per cent in the 1980s to 2 per cent in 1998 for NFIDCs and from 64 per cent in the 1980s to 23 per cent in 1998 for LDCs. The Third World countries saw an immediate rise of 15 per cent in their import bills. The Marrakesh Decision tried to implement remedies in the form of assistance to protect developing countries heavily dependent on food aid and concessions. It called for donors to 'establish a level of food aid commitments sufficient to meet the legitimate needs of developing countries during the reform program' (Clay and Stokke, 2000: 93). It diverted this responsibility into the Food Aid Convention (FAC). WTO ministers asked for the FAC to look after the needs of developing countries during the implementation of the agricultural liberalisation agreed in the Uruguay Round.

The FAC tries to create a safety net for poor countries that guarantees aid regardless of the fluctuations of the market. 'Donors fix their food aid budgets in fiscal terms, so that when international prices increase, the volume of food aid tends to decline' (Clay and Stokke, 2000: 94). The FAC looks at this motion and works in favour of fixing a permanent floor where aid would always be available independently of the circumstances of trade. However, this safety net still depends directly on the donors meeting their minimum commitments. As an example, in the years 1996/97 most of them had not fulfilled the promised amounts, which had already been reduced after 1994's change of strategy. Since 1999, the concept of aid has come under further criticism. From the initial reductions of permanent aid amounts, the whole strategy of the FAC was reviewed. In the 1999 convention there was a change of objectives, from permanent structural aid to an emergency-need focus. This approach seems to transfer the weight of meeting the regular needs of the world's poorest countries into the permanent economic structure, leaving aid available only in exceptional circumstances. This change hints at the recognition of the responsibility of international society for the elimination of poverty/hunger, and in particular, the identification of international trade as an area where this responsibility should be exercised.

The developments through trade are surrounded by controversy, given the gap between developed and developing countries. For example, even when developing economies become partners in international trade, the differences are overwhelming. Exports of manufactured goods from developing countries increased from 6 per cent in 1965 to 20 per cent in 1995; even if there is a substantial margin of growth, it still leaves 80 per cent of the world's trade in the hands of developed countries. During the period between 1990 and 1998, more than 62 per cent of the increase in total world trade was represented by trade between advanced economies (UN, 2001c: 3).

Developing countries' per capita income increased by less than 1 per cent per year during the 1990s, compared with more than 2 per cent in industrial countries. This absolute number, within the developing group, varies if those countries affected by political conflicts are excluded, in which case the per capita income rose by 1.5 per cent a year during the 1990s, about 1 per cent faster than in the 1980s. These figures match a growth in the exports of these countries by 6.4 per cent a year during the 1990s, about 2 per cent higher than in the 1980s (World Bank, 8/4/02f: 1, 2).

It must be noted at this stage that the statistics on poverty and trade vary among sources, and even among official sources such as the UN, UNCTAD, World Bank, WTO. Their common denominator is a correlation between economic growth and trade (both positive and negative), and that is what the numbers collected here try to show, even if their precision can be contested.

Critical voices complain that liberalisation has progressed only in selected areas that give Northern countries more access to resources of the South, weakening the domestic economies of developing countries and promoting food availability through trade, while also debilitating development self-sufficiency. On this line, the growth of GDP has been criticised for not registering the real impact on developing societies at large; while a minority became wealthier, the mass of the population saw little change. Critics of these patterns of distribution insist that liberalisation has resulted in increasing economic differentiation between and within countries.

In this context of international trade and developing countries, two dimensions, internal and external, intervene in the final configuration of the economic gap between the rich and the poor.

Internal dimension

As indicated earlier, there is a substantial difference in the performance of countries affected by *conflict*. Ten of the low-income countries have gone through some kind of armed conflict or political shock during the 1990s. The average per capita figure in the low-income countries (mainly located in Sub-Saharan Africa) declined during this period, but if the countries in conflict are excluded, the rest of the low-income countries grew by 1.5 per cent, which is higher than their record in the 1980s but lower than that of the middle-income countries.

Diversification: The exporting activity of the low-income countries (excluding those in conflict) grew 3.5 per cent slower than that of the middle-income countries, mainly because world trade in the products that Sub-Saharan Africa exports increased less than the rest of international trade. These countries have been unable to adapt their traditional markets to the newly required diversification (World Bank, 8/4/02f: 2).

Exporting infrastructure: The exporting infrastructure includes high administrative costs, weak service, lack of reliable communications, limited access to credit and expensive transport. For example, countries in Africa usually absorb all, or most, transport expenses incurred in gaining access to external markets. Their net freight and insurance payments in 1990/91 were 3.9 billion, which equals the 15 per cent of the total value of the exports of the region. This figure is even higher if we look only at the 10 landlocked African countries, where those payments in 1990 were 42 per cent of their total exports (World Bank, 8/4/02f: 17). Together with these internal difficulties, other obstacles to international trade come from outside, and include quality standards imposed by the governments in importing countries. Many exporting countries lack both the technological capability to meet the industrial countries' requirements and the financial means to retaliate when quality standards are used to discriminate against their products (World Bank, 8/4/02e: 1).

Internal tariffs: This is another side of the process of market liberalisation. Despite progress made in this area, tariffs remain high in many developing countries, at around 15 per cent. This percentage came down from 32 per cent in the first half of the 1980s (World Bank, 8/4/02f: 17).

The *unequal distribution of wealth within countries*: Liberalisation is criticised for having benefited the elites of developing countries, who enjoy rich lifestyles and consumption patterns while large segments of the population experience no significant improvement in their standard of living.

External dimension

Together with the internal impediments, developing countries confront other obstacles in the international arena.

The *quality control measures* just mentioned have, on many occasions, faced criticism due to the political connotation they can acquire. They have been criticised for their protectionist dimension, since they demand technical requirements, testing, certification and labelling to which developing countries have no easy access. The polemic that has surrounded this topic led the way for the Agreement on Sanitary and Phytosanitary Standards (SPS), which provides that 'trade restrictions can be imposed only to the extent necessary to protect life or health, that they must be based on scientific principles and that they cannot be maintained if scientific evidence is lacking' (World Bank, 8/4/02e: 5).

However, this agreement has not ended the controversy, since the scientific community is sometimes unable to determine the risks until the damage is already evident. In the middle of this process, the exporting countries are disadvantaged, unable to fight the disputes due to their lack of a competing technological and financial infrastructure. Their disadvantages grow further when they are unable to meet the international standards for the marketing of a product set by the Mutual Recognition Agreements (MRAs). Since differences in standards among countries are a feature of the international market, the MRAs establish a general consensus about the level required. This means that producers coming from outside the MRA face higher entry costs than the producers from the countries that signed the agreement. In fact, the costs involved in complying with all the standard agreements 'are likely to be equal to an entire year's development budget in some least developed countries' (World Bank, 8/4/02e: 8).

Therefore, product standards have a crucial role in restricting trade and the number of disputes over this issue has increased since the second half of the 1990s. Their highly political implications have been criticised by different voices, since 'governments and firms in more advanced countries can establish strategic standards that shut out developing country firms or that alter the terms of competition or the terms of trade in favour of domestic firms' (World Bank, 8/4/02e: 7).

Other international factors that limit the growth of exports in developing countries are the *import restrictions and export subsidies* in industrial countries. Reference to 'industrialised' countries in the context of international trade policies often implies the Quad countries: Canada, the European Union, Japan and the United States. In these countries the average importing tariffs range from 4.3 per cent in Japan to 8.3 per cent in Canada (World Bank, 8/4/02f: 18). These tariffs limit developing countries' capacity for growth; an example of this relationship has been provided by a World Bank study, which reports how least developed countries that have received high preferences for their exports to Quad countries in the post-Uruguay period have grown by about 8 per cent per year on average, outpacing growth of LDC exports that have received medium or low preferences (World Bank, 2002b: 54).

However, the average tariff for general imports is still high, and much more so for products where developing countries have a comparative advantage. The products with high tariffs in Quad countries are:

- Major agricultural food products, such as meat, sugar, milk, other dairy products and chocolate. In this sector, tariff rates often exceed 100 per cent.
- Fruits and vegetables. For example, shelled groundnuts incur a tariff of 550 per cent in Japan and 132 per cent in the United States.

- Food industry products, including fruit juices, canned meat, peanut butter and sugar confectionery see rates exceeding 30 per cent in several markets.
- Tobacco and some alcoholic beverages.
- Textiles, clothing and footwear may have tariff rates of between 15 per cent and 30 per cent.

This list (World Bank, 8/4/02f: 18) shows the radical position that agriculture takes in international trade. This sector is not only highly protected by tariffs, but also by agricultural subsidies in the industrial countries.

Between 1997 and 1999, the average annual value of subsidies was about 60 per cent of total world trade in agriculture, and almost twice the value of agricultural exports from developing countries (World Bank, 8/4/02f: 20). These measures, which range from 3 per cent in New Zealand to 76 per cent in Switzerland, have also a high cost for the countries that apply them. Estimates calculate that subsidies equal 1 to 3 per cent of national income, being a burden on public finances (OECD, 1998: 38).

These external measures have a clear impact on the developing world, especially on the poorest countries, since their economies are primarily agricultural and it is in this sector that they have more room for growth. Although there are a series of internal factors that intervene in the development of their markets, external elements such as trade restrictions and subsidies have an adverse impact on growth: 'Policy reforms and investments in rural areas are unlikely to yield significant improvements unless the demand for many of these products can be expanded through exports to world markets' (World Bank, 8/4/02e: 21).

According to the World Bank, more than half of the world's workforce is engaged in agriculture. Given the relevance of agricultural trade for economic growth, and therefore for the reduction of poverty and hunger, the next section will look closely at its international dimension.

Food trade and agricultural policies

Due to the essential role of agriculture in developing economies, my argument now concentrates on the controversy surrounding this area of international trade. Studies on the subject have corroborated that countries that have developed their agriculture (such as China, Indonesia, Malaysia and Thailand) have all experienced a radical decline in rural poverty and have improved food security (FAO, 1996f: 1–17). Achievements on this front require a broad-based economic strategy with access to both national and international markets.

On the international front, the WTO has seen the need to reform agriculture in order to create an equal trade system. Up to 1995, GATT rules were ineffective for disciplining agricultural trade; in fact, the agricultural sector was dominated by export and domestic subsidies and import restriction. The 1986–1994 Uruguay Round addressed this problem and countries signed the Agreement on Agriculture (AoA) as the basis for initiating a process of reform of trade in agriculture: 'Having agreed that in implementing their commitments on market access, developed country members would take fully into account the particular needs and conditions of developing country members, by providing for a greater improvement of opportunities and terms of access for agricultural products of particular interest to these members, including the fullest liberalisation of trade in tropical agricultural products' ... 'having regard to the agreement that special and differential treatment for developing countries is an integral element of the negotiations, and taking into account the possible negative effects of the implementation of the reform programme on least-developed and net food-importing developing countries' (WTO, 1994: 1).

This document marks the introduction of agriculture into multilateral trade reforms and focuses on three main topics: market access, domestic support and export competition.

Market access sets a minimum level of imports that member countries must purchase from the international market to meet their agricultural needs. This area includes also all the regulations regarding tariffs.

Domestic support measures are aimed at reducing the amount of money that producers receive from their national governments. The AoA asks for a cut of 20 per cent in developed countries. These measures apply mainly to the highly trade-distorting mechanisms: the so-called 'amber box', which supports production directly. However, there are a series of exemptions through which countries have managed to keep their high levels of subsidies, especially the EU, Japan and the US. They are mainly classified in two types: Green Box and Blue Box. The Blue Box administers direct payments to farmers aimed at limiting production. The Green Box includes all the support policies that do not pay for production directly, such as disease control, infrastructure development, disaster relief, early retirement policies for farmers, financed research and development and environmental protection. This long list allows a wide range of flexibility with policies that can have a very clear impact on the productivity levels and, as a consequence, have trade-distorting effects. In fact, the total use of Green Box measures has grown since the Uruguay Round: the EU, Japan and the US account for 90 per cent of all domestic subsidies in the world (CI, 2001: 14).

In the *export competition* area, the AoA focused on the trade-distorting subsidies given by the governments of wealthy countries to exports in order to make them more competitive in the international market. This is the less trade-distorting mechanism, since only 5 per cent of agricultural exports by OECD countries have been facilitated by export credits. In 1998 the US accounted for half of the export credits in agriculture and the other half was used by Australia, Canada and the EU (FAO, 1/9/02: 11).

These points suggest that even if in theory agriculture was liberalised as the result of the Uruguay Round, significant trade barriers remain. The tensions surrounding the differences within the WTO members boiled over in December 1999 when 135 of its members met in Seattle. Seattle shook the basis of the liberalisation process by illustrating that international trade relations were the subject of strong criticism both inside and outside the WTO. The discussions collapsed due to several factors: lack of political will to push further liberalisation in the EU and the US; strong disagreements over the scope of agricultural liberalisation; opposition of many developing countries to including on the agenda issues such as labour standards and dissatisfaction of developing countries with the agenda-setting process. This failure called to the surface governance-related problems within the international trade mechanism, such as the rule-making process, participation of developing countries and transparency of the WTO (Lengyel and Tussie, 2002: 488). The last point relates to the 'green room' mechanism accused of operating with a 'democratic deficit'. The 'green room' is the name given to the process used by GATT/WTO to carry out consultations. It involves a group of 25 to 30 countries, both developed and developing. However, its problem lies in the fact that there is no objective basis for determining the composition of the group (ibid.: 491).

The dissatisfaction with the WTO was not only expressed indoors; it provoked in the streets the now-called 'Battle of Seattle' with violent reactions coming from tens of thousands of protesters led by environmentalists and labour union members. They accused developed countries of hypocrisy and used the WTO as the focal point for a diverse set of anxieties about the dilemmas of international trade (Moon, 2000: 110). Because the Ministerial Conferences are the WTO's highest-level decision-making body, Seattle became a major focus of concern. The WTO started a campaign to improve its image both internally and externally, and prepared itself for the next major challenge: the Doha ministerial meeting in November 2001. After the failure of Seattle, the organisation could not afford another collapse. A series of negotiations preceded the meeting and developing countries' concerns became the centre of attention, with agriculture being the main topic on the agenda.

Since February 2000 agriculture has been the object of a series of negotiations structured in several phases. The first one ended in March 2001 and was devoted to general consideration of proposals, including those of developing countries. Altogether, 126 member governments (89 per cent of the 142 members) submitted 45 proposals and three technical documents that contained their starting positions for the negotiations (WTO, 12/4/02a: 5).

The second phase (from March 2001 to March 2002) focused on all issues of policy reform set out in the first phase. The discussions were by topic and included more technical detail than the first round, which made the negotiations more complicated. In the middle of this phase, the Doha ministerial conference took place and the previous negotiations were subsumed in a broader round of multilateral trade talks. This new round launched in Doha considers agriculture as a 'single undertaking' and is structured in three more phases of negotiations. So far every deadline has been missed, including the test that the negotiations faced in the fifth ministerial meeting in Cancun (September 2003).

The ongoing negotiations use Article 20 as their basis and the November 2001 Doha Ministerial Declaration as their mandate. Article 20 says WTO members have to negotiate to achieve progress in the reform of agricultural trade, which should be done on the basis of 'substantial progressive reductions in support and protection'.

The Doha ministerial meeting concentrated on the structural difficulties that the least developed countries face in the global economy. The ministers committed themselves to negotiations aimed at improvements in market access, reduction of all forms of exports subsidies and cuts in trade distorting domestic support (WTO, 2001b).

The negotiations try to establish a balance between agricultural trade liberalisation and governments' individual interests. They work on reductions in tariffs, domestic support and export subsidies. A crucial element present in these negotiations is the provisions for Special and Differential Treatment (S&D) that Article 20 has expanded into agriculture. S&D treatment, introduced in 1979, 'constitutes a set of rights and privileges that apply to developing countries and least-developed country members and from which industrial countries are excluded' (Oyejide, 2002: 504). In relation to agriculture it includes non-trade concerns, such as environmental protection, food security, structural adjustment, rural development and poverty alleviation. However, in operational terms the S&D treatment has been translated into preferences offered by industrial countries on an individual basis to specific developing and least developed countries (ibid.: 505).

Underlying the Doha objectives is the idea of some countries to bring agricultural trade under the same rules as trade in other goods (WTO, 12/4/02a: 1–4). However, other countries reject the idea on the basis of the non-trade concerns mentioned above. Most countries agree that agriculture is not only about producing food, but also has other functions specified under the non-trade concerns. However, the question the WTO faces now is whether trade distorting subsidies or subsidies outside the green box are needed to help agriculture to play its many roles. Some countries insist that all the objectives should be achieved through 'green box' subsidies, which in principle do not distort trade. Other countries say that the non-trade concerns are closely linked to production. They apply in the case of plantations, for example, which are promoted to prevent soil erosion; while protecting a non-trade measure, the production increases and affects trade. Countries such as Japan, the Republic of Korea and Norway focus on the need to tackle agriculture's diversity as part of non-trade concerns. Several countries maintain that any economic activity (such as manufacturing) is subject to non-trade concerns; however, it is not in the interest of the WTO's richest members to address those issues in relation to agriculture.

The next task is to produce target figures, formulas and other procedures on which countries' specific commitments will be based. The deadline for this comprehensive draft of commitments was the Fifth WTO Ministerial Conference in September 2003 in Cancun, Mexico, although it was not met (WTO, 12/4/02a: 3).

When ministers of the 146 WTO member states arrived in Cancun they needed to reach consensus in five areas: agricultural subsidies, industrial tariffs, market access, investment and competition rules, and special help for developing countries. However, the final aim of the meeting, especially for developing countries, was to correct and prevent restrictions and distortions in world agricultural markets (WTO, 21/1/02c: 1–3). 'The need was for the WTO's wealthiest and most advanced members to open their markets more fully to the products of the poorest and least developed nations' (WTO, 2000d: 3). Weeks earlier, on 14 August, the EU and the US had reached an agreement in which they admitted the importance of this issue and renewed their commitment to open the markets. This was considered a valuable step in the tense political environment created after the fallout from the Iraq war. However, in Cancun both giants pushed to divert the talks into matters of investment and competition, but developing countries insisted on focusing on agriculture and they formed an unexpected block organised by the G-20, a coalition centred on heavyweights such as India, China, Egypt and Brazil (Sharma, 2003: 1). The most powerful players of the WTO on issues of agriculture, the US and the EU, found a developing world united in its members' claims against rich nations, despite differences in their own agendas (Koppel, 2003: 3–6). The lack of compromise provoked the collapse of the talks for a second time, although not as disastrous as the breakdown in Seattle. The channels of negotiation set in the Doha Round are still open, and developing countries consider this a success on the basis that 'no deal is better than a bad deal'. In the meantime and despite the disappointment, developed countries insist on their commitment to continue the negotiations and strengthen the multilateral trade system (Becker, 2003: 4–7).

Despite the setback that this entails for the principles of the WTO in general and the disadvantages for the interest of the different members, a positive message that seems to have been taken from Cancun is the emerging shift in the power dynamic at the WTO, with a stronger developing bloc, led mainly by Brazil, China and India. Voices of hope have pointed to the potential of the events at Cancun to establish a more transparent and balanced system (Lilliston, 2003: 1).

After this breakdown at Cancun, the way in which the WTO as an institution responds will be critical. Therefore, attention has turned back to the negotiations carried out at Geneva. These negotiations revolve around the three pillars of the AoA, which are addressed in this order of priority: export subsidies and restrictions, market access, and domestic support – a sequence against which developing countries have already expressed their discontent. They ask for domestic support to be given priority, since it has implications for market access issues (FAO, 1/9/02: 6). It is important to note that at the top of the negotiation priorities is the less trade-distorting measure used by developed countries (which affects only 5 per cent of OECD exports) which is consequently the easiest one on which to reach an agreement, in order to claim that progress has been made.

Chapters 3 and 4 will further assess the link between starvation and trade that has been postulated in this chapter in order to examine how international society has responded to the persistence of mass starvation. First, Chapter 2 will sketch the theoretical background of the right to food by turning to John Vincent's theory of basic rights that prioritises the elimination of starvation.

2 Basic human rights
Political origins

This chapter sets out the key elements involved in the basic rights debate within the human rights discourse, starting with a general account of basic rights, followed by a detailed review of Vincent's position. The main focus is on the trajectory of Vincent's thinking on the subject and not on the discourse of basic rights itself. Vincent's work on basic rights cannot be detached from the theoretical framework within which he operated: the English school of International Relations. Therefore, this chapter includes a section on this tradition of thought in order to show how his argument agrees, differs or innovates by reference to this wider picture. Finally, the chapter introduces the specific right to food within the basic rights context.

The basic rights discourse

This section highlights the main components of the basic rights discourse in order to understand the background to Vincent's project. The analysis is divided into two parts: first, a brief survey of how the concept emerged in the political arena; second, an account of the debate surrounding the term, with special attention to the contribution of Shue, whose work inspired Vincent's.

Emergence of basic rights

This section recounts when the concept of basic rights appeared in the political arena and under what historical circumstances. It does not develop a theory of basic rights or explore its philosophical consistency.

Basic rights are a set of rights, within the wider human rights discourse, whose enjoyment is essential to the enjoyment of other rights. 'When a right is genuinely basic, any attempt to enjoy any other right by sacrificing the basic rights would be literally self-defeating, cutting the ground from beneath itself ... basic rights specify the line beneath which no one is to be allowed to sink' (Shue, 1996: 19).

The term can be traced back to its origins as a moral idea through a study of the conception of the individual from the Greek Stoics to the

Middle Ages and the Renaissance. However, it is not until the French Declaration of the Rights of Man (1798) that the definition of fundamental principles appeared in a legal framework. This declaration adumbrated the modern idea of basic rights through natural rights theory, according to which rights are defined on the basis of humanity, and not according to membership of a particular political community. The natural rights (or rights of man) tradition protected fundamental areas that political agreements should not modify: life, property, safety and resistance to oppression (Vincent, 1986a: 14, 15).

Together with this declaration there were other landmarks such as the British Bill of Rights (1689) and the American Bill of Rights (1791), whose influence on the idea of basic rights should not be underestimated. Although these examples promoted developments within countries, 'concern by one country for the welfare of individuals inside another country met many obstacles' (Alston and Steiner, 1996: 116). Even if these declarations were limited to the national realm and subject to particular political environments, other events started to take place slowly in the international arena: in the nineteenth century, European and American states abolished slavery and the slave trade on the basis of protection of human dignity. States began also to pursue agreements to make war less inhumane, to safeguard prisoners of war and civilian populations (ibid.: 114).

Although these declarations and treaties are a precursor of the principle of basic rights, the parallelism is not exact. The earlier declarations were designed to safeguard a minimum standard of human dignity. This concept of the rights of man evolved into the general human rights framework. With the atrocities of the Second World War and the Holocaust, human rights (earlier called natural rights) became a subject of international political awareness. In 1948 the UN Human Rights Declaration 'established a standard of civilized conduct which applies to all governments in the treatment of their citizens' (Dunne and Wheeler, 1999: 1). 'Basic rights' emerged as a term once the human rights standards were established in 1948 and represented a specific discussion inside the wider human rights discourse.

There is no record of when the term 'basic rights' was first used in the post-1948 political arena. I argue here that the two central and interlinked events in the twentieth century that promoted the growth of this concept were the Cold War and the New International Economic Order.

East–West ideological division of the Cold War

In 1967 the UN Human Rights Declaration was divided into two sets of rights corresponding to the rivalry that the Cold War had created: civil and political rights promoted by the West, and economic and social rights promoted by the Communist world. This division was a product of the

Cold War ideological conflict. While the West criticised the Soviet Union for not respecting civil and political rights, the Soviet Union defended itself by praising its own record on economic and social rights and attacking the West for not protecting them. The disputes created a struggle in the political discussion about which rights should be given priority and where human rights were most respected. Throughout the Cold War, the Western world emphasised the basic civil and political rights of individuals (freedom of expression, assembly and religion and political participation), while the Soviet Union stressed the importance of basic economic rights for international peace and security (Shaw, 1997: 198).

As a consequence of these ideological disputes, the debate moved in different directions and provoked a growing interest in the classification of human rights. Some Western liberal voices took the distinction just presented further and established three generations of human rights. First: civil and political rights; second: economic, social and cultural rights; third: collective rights such as the right to development, to a clean environment and to one's own natural resources (Baehr, 1996: 8).

Connected with the above idea of classifying human rights, a discussion about protecting a specific number of rights as the minimum standard was developed. This attempt to institute hierarchies has created a variety of terms: fundamental rights, elementary rights, suprapositive rights, principal rights and basic rights, which are treated as synonyms with 'basic rights' being the most widespread.

North–South divide: Basic Needs versus New International Economic Order

I have now outlined the historical trajectory of one part of the story underpinning basic rights, developed after the UN Declaration and associated it with the ideological division maintained during the Cold War. This struggle provoked a desire in the international political arena to prioritise rights. Another event was taking place simultaneously in international politics: decolonisation, with the subsequent claims for a New International Economic Order. This new infrastructure generated a debate about basic needs. Although this discourse proliferated in the 1970s, it had already been framed by the UN Human Rights Declaration in 1948 and was rooted in the industrial revolution of the nineteenth century. The following paragraphs provide a historical account of basic needs and its links to basic rights.

With the abuses of the industrial revolution, the concept of basic needs entered social policy in Europe through the social reform movements in the nineteenth century. The industrialising nations introduced child labour laws, minimum wages and maximum hours of work, compulsory education, public health, social security and disability allowances. Initially these changes were seen as charity rather than entitlements, until later in the century when the language of rights replaced that of charity. In the late nineteenth century in Britain, Booth and Rowntree laid the conceptual foundations of basic needs. Rowntree carried out a study of the 'basket cost' for the minimum maintenance of households of different sizes, ages and sex composition. Those with insufficient income to meet the basket cost were considered to be below the poverty level (McHale and McHale, 1977: introduction, x–xx).

After the Second World War, most industrialised countries had established a legal framework of welfare. In 1948 the UN Declaration of Human Rights elevated the meeting of basic needs to the rank of global entitlement, specifically in Article 25: 'Everyone has the right to a standard of living adequate for the health and well-being of himself and of his family, including food, clothing, housing and medical care and necessary social services, and the right to security in the event of unemployment, sickness, disability, widowhood, old age or other lack of livelihood in circumstances beyond his control.'

In 1954 the UN published a report on the 'international definition and measurement of standards and levels of living'. It consisted of a list of 12 elements that tried to create an international catalogue for analysing an acceptable level of living: health, food and nutrition, education, conditions of work, employment, savings, transportation, housing, clothing, entertainment, social security and human freedoms (UN, 1954: 1–8). In 1964 the ILO adopted a resolution concerning minimum living standards. These are the conceptual and political origins of 'basic needs', although an international political movement parallel to the New International Economic Order failed to emerge until the 1970s.

As decolonisation progressed in the 1950s and 1960s, attention centred on Third World development, with the US and the Soviet Union competing to win allies. The latter promoted a state-sponsored method while the former favoured a market-based approach, coupled with the support of the World Bank and the IMF. Most new countries joined the Western liberal order, which gave them a place in the international trade system developed under the auspices of the GATT. After surveying the dynamics of the first two decades of development, however, a feeling of unrest started to grow, based on the idea that the periphery was strongly disadvantaged within the international economic system while the core of wealthy countries was getting richer through its economic activities with the Third World. This understanding was initially portrayed by dependency theorists who observed how developed countries imported cheap raw materials, converted them into manufactures and exported them back into the periphery. The concerns grew into the developing countries' campaign for a New International Economic Order (NIEO) promoted mainly by the Non-Aligned Movement (NAM) and UNCTAD (Little and McKinlay, 1986: 95). The demands for a NIEO can be formally dated to the Algiers conference of Non-Aligned Countries in 1973 (Cox, 1981: 413). This package was adopted by the UN General Assembly (Resolution 3201 S-VI) in 1974 as the Declaration and Programme of Action on the Establishment of a New International Economic Order: 'Our united determination to work urgently for the establishment of a new international economic order ... which shall correct inequalities and redress existing justices, make it possible to eliminate the widening gap between the developed and developing countries' (UN, 1974a).

It was a macro-economic approach that, among other measures, demanded improved terms of trade between the periphery and the core, more control by the periphery over the world economic circle, and increased trade between the periphery countries themselves (Galtung, 1991a: 287). The demands developed in the context of the doctrine of self-determination, which had promoted, first, liberation from colonisation, then freedom from racial oppression and now a claim for economic and social independence (Vincent, 1986a: 83). NIEO advocates insisted on a collective approach to deals between industrialised and developing countries at the global level; but its emphasis was on fairness among nations, not within nations.

The failure to address the equality of individuals encouraged a Basic Needs (BN) movement that saw the NIEO as a political tool that would benefit even further the rich elites of Third World countries. Based on the ILO's list of minimum standards, Basic Needs started as a movement at the non-governmental level, and it was echoed by voices coming from places such as the Aspen Institute and the Center for Integrative Studies. It built on a development theory that gave priority to producing, first, what is essential to meet human needs. The urgency of establishing a connection between a development strategy and basic human needs spread quickly among different writers and working groups. By the mid-1970s it became a theory widely held by some economists in international agencies, including UNESCO, UNICEF, the OECD, the World Bank and many Western governments (Alston, 1979: 1). In 1976 the ILO approved a proposal to include basic needs in development planning: 'that the development planning should include, as an explicit goal, the satisfaction of an absolute level of basic needs' (ILO, 1976: 31). In 1977 the World Bank issued a paper entitled 'Basic Needs' which supported this strategy of development (McHale and McHale, 1977: xvi). For the first time there was an insistence on relating international economic arrangements to the meeting of basic human needs: food, shelter, clothing, healthcare and education (World Bank, 1977: 4) and not strictly to GDP growth.

In its radical shape, the BN doctrine bypasses the state by promoting justice among individuals: 'it is a claim for transnational or cosmopolitan justice and not for international justice' (Vincent, 1986a: 86). The previous two decades of development had focused on overall figures of economic growth and the particular situation of people had not been considered. There was a growing concern at the beginning of the 1970s about basing the development strategy on increases of production and GDP without addressing who was getting the benefits.

The World Bank's 1977 paper intensified the new line of concern: 'Economic growth appears to have done very little for the poorer of the Third World's growing populations' (McHale and McHale, 1977: 77). By establishing the individual as a priority, without altering the existing economic infrastructure, the Basic Needs movement appealed to liberal economists (Vincent, 1986a: 84–5).

Both NIEO and BN radically criticised each other's ideological understandings and practical approaches: representatives of the NIEO saw in the BN a Western ideological movement that prioritised the individual and legitimised the injustices of the international economic system. BN advocates attacked the collectivist approach of the NIEO, arguing that it did not apply to the post-colonial economic order and that their claims would benefit only the elites of those countries. In particular, 'they were adamantly opposed to the NIEO policy strategies most of which entailed large-scale discriminatory and interventionist techniques' (Little and McKinlay, 1986: 94).

By the beginning of the 1980s it was clear that the proposal for a New International Economic Order had not been successful. However, elements of the NIEO demands survived through time and filtered themselves into the negotiating table of the Uruguay Round in the 1990s through requests such as that for a more equitable trade system.

The Basic Needs approach received strong criticism from the NIEO for disguising a new way of legitimating external intervention on individual protection grounds while not doing anything about the problems of the economic structure itself (Galtung, 1991b: 292–5). It was also attacked for trying to offer an alternative to the human rights framework set by the Human Rights Declaration and reinforced by the Covenant on Economic, Social and Cultural Rights. In this context, liberal economists had started to use basic needs as a concept separate from human rights, which established the list of food, water, healthcare and so on as a set of elements needed to assess in the strategy of development that focused on the individual. Paradoxically during these years the promotion of human rights expanded, although the focus was more on the Western prioritisation of civil and political rights, while economic rights were neglected or left to the 'basic needs' approach which eliminated the entitlement–duty-bearer polemic intrinsic to rights (explained further in Vincent's section).

The term 'basic needs' was preferred over 'human rights' by liberal economists, because basic needs seemed to offer more practical advantages. It has been considered an economists' tool, since its vagueness allows room for shaping the principles according to contextual economic exigencies. In fact, the Basic Needs Declaration lists 'adequate food' but does not enter into the details of its realisation (Alston, 1979: 30, 59). However, in terms of the right to food, the Covenant on Economic, Social and Cultural Rights not only recognises it but also specifies the measures that need to be taken by states, both individually and through international cooperation, in order to ensure an equitable distribution of world food supplies (Articles 2 and 11).

This belief in the neutrality of basic needs has been rejected from different angles: 'the idea that human beings have basic needs is not different from the assertion that they have human rights which impose correlative obligations ... the doctrine of basic needs does not displace or transcend an older conception of human rights; what it does do, and this is its strength, is to hammer away at that aspect of the right to life, the right to subsistence, which has been neglected' (Vincent, 1986a: 88, 90).

But just as the New International Economic Order did not achieve its objectives, Basic Needs failed as a new approach to development, because it did not acknowledge the rights framework established in 1948 as well as its juridical significance. It ignored the role of the Third World states as duty-bearers in relation to their own citizens and as subjects of right in relation to the wider international economic system. However, this political movement increased awareness about the minimum requirements for a life of dignity and dissolved itself in the basic rights dialogue that took place in the 1980s and still continues. Although neither political movement succeeded as an end in itself, both enriched the dialogue sustained in subsequent years.

This review of the history of basic rights shows that while the nineteenth century represented the national struggle to protect a minimum standard across classes, the twentieth century addressed the same issue but within countries. These will be further discussed in this chapter through the analysis of the trajectory of the right to food.

So far this chapter has examined the historical origins of basic rights. The concept evolved in the international political arena within the post-1948 human rights framework. It was a consequence both of the conceptual disputes of the Cold War and of the ideological tensions behind the North–South divide. The former reflected the rivalry between two different political agendas that adapted the human rights discourse to their own interest. The latter was a dispute between the Third World's campaign for economic self-determination based on a collective approach and the First World's protection of the existing economic system while placing emphasis on individual rights. The tension was expressed in the dispute between the New International Economic Order and the Basic Needs approach to development.

While the campaign for a NIEO did not succeed, the liberal economic BN movement also fell through, not only as an alternative to the NIEO, but as a consistent theory in itself. Its major conceptual problem was its separation from the rights approach that had been established in 1948 and its focus on the individual as the subject of development while ignoring the inequalities of the international economic system at state level. During its short history, the BN approach went from being a call for a transformation in development strategies to merely identifying a list of minimum needs to be taken as guidelines without altering the pillars of the system (Seddon, 1982: 13–14).

However, the BN movement did highlight the importance of subsistence that had been neglected by the liberal approach and that was embodied in later discussions of basic rights. The doctrine of Basic Needs reflected 'First World' recognition that their defense of the basic right to life is as much about providing subsistence as about protecting security: 'The doctrine of basic human needs reminds us of what we have in the past been inclined to forget; that the right to life has as much to do with providing the wherewithal to keep people alive as with protecting them against violent death' (Vincent, 1986a: 90).

Therefore, this idea had already entered liberal thinking by the time the Cold War ended. It dissolved itself in the human rights debate as the idea that our basic needs make us recipients of basic rights: 'Rights imply needs' (Jonsson, 1996: 7). It is important to note here that the Basic Needs concept can be approached from a perspective that relies on philosophical pillars, for which there is a solid literature available (for example, reference could be made to the work of Maslow, O'Neill and Sen). However, my objective here is to highlight its political relevance for the basic rights discourse. I work on the generally accepted grounds of the public discourse that a relationship exists along the lines of rights being the means and the satisfaction of needs being the end (Galtung, 1994: 70). In fact, in the UN doctrine on the subject (which is the framework relevant to this research), basic needs and human rights require each other; they are indivisible. More specifically, this means that 'basic rights are social guarantees against threatened deprivations of some basic needs' (Shue, 1996: 18). Even if there are reasons for arguing that this relationship is not straightforward and not all needs are matched by a corresponding right, the survival need for food is unquestionably protected by a matching right. This makes it possible to associate need with the framework of claim and accountability provided by the existence of rights and their presence in international law (more on this in the next sections).

The political discourse on basic rights that followed in the 1990s promoted this connection through international agreements and developments in international law. 'Basic rights' is now a term used frequently across political discourse and refers usually to the right to be free from hunger and poverty. It has overcome the ideological problematic of the 'Basic Needs' movement by introducing an international framework that encompasses both the relations among states (rich and poor) and those among states and individuals (focus on the individual as the subject entitled to, for example, freedom from starvation). In terms of the general background to basic needs dialogue, basic rights are 'basic in the sense that when the right is violated, the consequences are fundamental in terms of deprivation and destruction of basic human needs' (Galtung, 1994: 71).

This does not mean, however, that there is ideological consensus about what forms the 'basic rights' discourse. There is no agreement on the validity of separating a group of rights considered 'basic' from the general human rights discourse. The next section addresses these aspects at the levels of both political and academic discourse in order to determine how the term is used in this book.

The basic rights debate

I do not address here the different arguments that justify or oppose the concept of human rights. Instead, I work on the basis of the regime that developed from 1948 and, within that framework, assess the particular idea of basic rights under Vincent's guidelines.

The basic rights discussion is now spread across academic and public discourses. In the public discourse, the term 'basic rights' seems to cover several kinds of rights depending on the context in which it appears (a war report, an economic plan, a human rights campaign, a summit focusing on a certain subject). In that way, we obtain 'basic right to equal concern and respect', 'basic personal rights', 'basic right to freedom', 'basic right to nutrition'.[1] Baerh (1996) has noted that the list of basic rights in the public discourse encompasses the right to life and personal integrity (which includes freedom from slavery, servitude, torture and any act that violates human dignity), the right to freedom of religion and expression and the rights to food, clothing and medical care (Baehr, 1996: 10). Public discourse is attracted to the term by the advantages it offers for policy making, being more manageable than considering the whole human rights discourse at once. The classification of basic rights has become prominent from the 1980s onwards in an effort to extract a core of rights from the lengthy list of the Universal Declaration and the Covenants. However, the list just mentioned includes a wide range of very different types of rights, whose nature and features vary enormously. This tendency to consider many rights as basic rights runs the risk of provoking inflation of terms by loss of significance. To distil this list implies facing the historical controversies between civil-political, economic-social and collective rights.

The previous section has already discussed the ideological complexity behind these divisions, which do not help the task of delimiting the exact boundaries of basic rights. In addition, there is no agreement on the idea of talking about basic rights rather than promoting the whole human rights discourse. The World Human Rights Conference in Vienna in 1993 registered this concern by indicating that all human rights, including the right to development, are universal, indivisible, interdependent and inter-related. The Vienna conference was the first global human rights meeting held after the end of the Cold War, and it had the participation of 171 states

(UN, 1993: 1–3). Therefore, it was significant that the summit insisted on overcoming the 'either/or' approach and emphasised the interdependence between the two historical divisions (Simmons, 1995: 39).

In any case, the language of basic rights persists within the overall human rights discussion and its presence is linked to the foreign policy arena, where it permits a manageable agenda for international action on behalf of human rights.

In the academic discourse there are also disagreements about what to locate in the basic rights cluster, and even about the validity of basic rights itself. The following examples illustrate how the hierarchy of basic rights varies in academic discourse: Ajami (1982) selects survival, protection against torture, protection against apartheid and food. Bedau (1979) includes life, liberty, property, security, freedoms of speech, press and assembly, and protection against arbitrary arrest and detention. Matthews and Pratt (1985) choose subsistence, protection against torture, protection against arbitrary arrest and detention, and protection against extrajudicial execution. Reiter, Zunzenegui and Quiroga (1986) select life, protection against disappearance, protection against torture, protection against arbitrary arrest and detention. Shue (1996) adopts security, subsistence and liberty.[2]

While this approach debates what is basic and what is not, an opposing line of thought questions the utility of the term. Jack Donnelly justifies this reaction and argues in line with UN discourse: 'All human rights are basic rights in the fundamental sense that systematic violations of any human right preclude realising a life full of human dignity' (Donnelly, 1989: 41). However, Donnelly modifies this conceptual reservation about 'basic rights' by acknowledging the policy-making advantages of setting boundaries around the most important human rights abuses within the systematic violations of the lengthy list of rights (ibid.: 43). But he does not confront the theoretical problems involved, nor does he provide the grounds for establishing a list of basic rights linked to foreign policy.

However, a few years earlier Henry Shue did confront the problem. As explained earlier, this section concentrates on Shue's discussion, since Vincent adopted it as the conceptual foundation of his basic rights project. Shue develops his theory in *Basic Rights*. His discussion is anchored in the idea that 'basic rights need to be established securely before other rights can be secured' (Shue, 1996: 20). Shue argues that this does not mean that other rights are less valuable, but that if choice has to be made between basic rights and other rights, basic rights ought to prevail: 'Intrinsically valuable rights may or may not also be basic rights, but intrinsically valuable rights can be enjoyed only when basic rights are enjoyed' (ibid.).[2]

In defining the boundaries of basic rights, he first sets out 'security rights', meaning the right to be free from murder, torture, mayhem, rape or assault. He justifies this choice by following the route of the previous statements. According to that, no one would be able to fully enjoy other rights protected by society if threatened with murder; therefore, this right is basic, not because its enjoyment is more satisfying than any other range of rights, but because its absence stops people from exercising other rights. The same line of reasoning applies to his other basic right, the right to subsistence, which in his understanding encompasses the right to 'unpolluted air, unpolluted water, adequate food, adequate clothing, adequate shelter and minimal preventive public healthcare' (Shue, 1996: 23). Shue is aware of the danger of this list becoming overcrowded and losing its meaning as 'basic' while creating disputes about where to draw the boundaries. In the event of this controversy, he asserts 'by a right to subsistence I shall always mean a right to at least subsistence' (ibid.). On this ground he sees the right to subsistence being just as vital as physical security; therefore, failure to deal with it would cancel the enjoyment of all other rights. A crucial point in Shue's theory is the connection between subsistence rights and security rights, considering them 'inherent necessities', that is, the enjoyment of security and subsistence is an essential part of the enjoyment of all other rights, which means exercising that particular right without suffering the loss of physical security or subsistence. In this sense, he insists that these two rights are not means to an end but are an essential part of the enjoyment of other rights.

Later in his argument Shue invokes the liberty discourse, selecting two rights as basic on the basis of the previous reasoning: social participation and social movement. However, these rights do not assume priority in his argument, since his 'primary purpose is to try to rescue from systematic neglect within wealthy North Atlantic nations a kind of right that deserves as much priority as any right: right to subsistence' (Shue, 1996: 65).

He believes that the 'rights to liberties' have already received substantial attention in North Atlantic theory and practice but to the detriment of the right to subsistence. While he still maintains the interdependence between security and subsistence rights, the bulk of his argument concentrates on the latter and he concludes that subsistence rights form the substance of basic rights: 'Prevention of the deficiencies in the essentials for survival is, if anything, more basic than the prevention of violations of physical security' (Shue, 1996: 25).

Before concluding this section, attention must be drawn to one of the most debated features of the controversy raised by the dispute over prioritising between subsistence rights and security rights at the basic level: starvation and torture. Those who prioritise starvation claim that people cannot enjoy the right to be free from torture if their basic subsistence rights are not met, because they would die. The counter-argument suggests that enjoying subsistence rights is pointless if one is going to live under inhuman conditions of torture. There are two responses to this line of argument. First, freedom from torture cannot override the need to be free from hunger. Second, central to the theme of this book, freedom from torture is irrelevant in the context of the 800 million people who are hungry because their subsistence rights are not being met as a consequence of socio-politico-economic conditions at the local, national and international levels. Confronted by the routinisation of hunger, torture is not an issue.

The approach to the concept of basic rights used here focuses on the international structural problems of hunger, rather than on other specific cases. The philosophical debate about the internal relationships among basic rights must be assessed at a different level when research involves, for example, cases where hunger is used as a weapon by governments employing policies of discrimination. The next section extends the guidelines developed in this section in the context now of Vincent's work.

Basic rights in Vincent

Vincent's project provides the framework for the book, and this section presents the key elements that constitute his basic rights argument. First, I sketch in general terms the tradition of thought in which Vincent worked. Second, I concentrate specifically on the basic rights dimension of his writings, using direct quotations in order to portray the precise character of his views on the subject. The analysis carried out in the remaining parts of the book refers back to these statements, extending their normative and practical implications (Chapters 3, 4 and 5) and then evaluating them critically (Chapter 6).

Vincent and the English school

Vincent worked within the tradition of thought articulated by the English school. Initiated by Butterfield and Wight with the purpose of 'extending the frontiers of thought about international politics' (Dunne, 1998: 91), the English school intellectual discourse remains significant in a world where 'neither liberalism nor realism is plausible by itself' (Buzan, 1999: 7). It is concerned about both 'the analysis of the history of international relations and the moral implications of current and future developments in the international arena' (Little, 1999: 20).

International society is the central plank in English school dialogue and is defined as 'a group of states which not merely form a system in the sense that the behavior of each is a necessary factor in the calculations of others, but also have established by dialogue and consent common rules and institutions for the conduct of their common interest in maintaining these arrangements' (Bull and Watson, 1984: 1). This definition reflects a key element in English school thinking: that agents are socialised by the international structure (Dunne, 1998: 10), and it combines the mechanical side of systems – units interacting – and a socially constructed side – the establishment and maintenance of rules and institutions (Buzan, 1999: 4).[3]

A series of questions about international society has been posed from inside and outside the English school. They concern the distinction between international system and international society, the history of both, the institutions of international society and the role of individuals in the society of states. The link between individuals and international society is central for this study. English school thinkers have tended to consider individuals and non-state subjects in the context of *world society*, which has conflictual and constitutive connections with international society. The scope for morality, order or justice in international society varies with different authors, and the degree of their commitment to these elements depends on the position taken within another crucial debate: *pluralism–solidarism*.

Pluralism and solidarism were distinguished by Bull who followed a pluralist theory of international relations, with states aiming for interstate order despite their different understandings of justice. In a pluralist approach, where there are as many versions of the 'good life' as there are states pursuing it, states are capable of agreeing only on some minimum principles, such as the recognition of sovereignty and non-intervention (Wheeler, 1992: 467, 469).

This understanding contrasts with what Bull calls solidarism. By a solidarist understanding of international society, he has in mind a states system that is ideologically homogeneous so that 'states are united not by a formula that allows different political, social and economic systems to coexist, but by determination to uphold a single kind of political, social and economic system' (Bull, 1977: 239). Pluralism presupposes 'a lower degree of shared norms, rules and institutions and solidarism a higher one' (Buzan, 2004: 49).

Although Bull became an advocate of pluralism, his writings are suffused with concerns for the more solidarist side of things by questioning the room for morality, justice and the provisions for enforcement. He explores these aspects through the lens provided by cosmopolitan human rights and a concern for democracy. He ignores the economic dimension, and he anchors his solidarist interpretation in political and social elements, particularly attached to collective security (requiring a suspension of the norm of non-intervention) and human rights.

The practice of placing human rights at the centre of solidarism has persisted in English school literature that followed Bull, starting with Vincent. Vincent, now seen as a herald of solidarism, did not follow a straightforward trajectory. His two major works, *Nonintervention and International Order* (1974) and *Human Rights and International Relations* (1986) mark two sides of evolution of his thought. *Nonintervention* follows a pluralist direction under the influence of his mentor, Bull. He defends the norm of non-intervention, although recognising that it places 'order between states before justice for individuals within them' (Vincent, 1974: 344). From the perspective of states, 'the observance of a general rule of nonintervention can be regarded as a minimum condition for their orderly coexistence' (ibid.: 331). He even rules out the possibility of humanitarian intervention as an exception to the principle, since defending a particular human rights principle would undermine order between states.

At this first stage Vincent works on the basis of a 'thin' international society where 'states are bound together by mutual acknowledgement of their separateness' (Vincent, 1974: 331; Dunne, 1998: 165). His initial concerns with order are rooted in Bull's work (from which he inherited the tension between sovereignty and the global community of mankind), and his views on international society are historically framed by the division of the Cold War. However, Vincent later (1990b) amends his initial position and engages in a thorough critique of Bull's conception of order. This marks the start of the solidarist phase of his career, best exemplified in *Human Rights and International Relations* (1986a).

His writings have now become a benchmark for the human rights thinking in the English school and provide the foundations for this research. Between these two phases, there is a process of evolution when Vincent concentrates on the culture and theory of international relations. Towards the end of this process, following Wight's line, Vincent recognises that international society has to make room for moral considerations. States were no longer seen to be distinguished by their 'separateness'; a growing concern with human rights forced Vincent to consider other possible aspects of sovereignty. Still committed to the idea of states as containers protecting collective identities, he hinted at a new approach to the principles of international society: 'There lies a countertheme of human rights consolidating the state rather than transcending it ... we might extend a cautious welcome to both the penetration of the state and to its strengthening itself in response' (Vincent, 1986a: 150–2).

Looking back to the start of his intellectual trajectory, Vincent's basic position remains unchanged: state sovereignty and a mutual acknowledgement of autonomy. But his understanding of this position has changed. In place of the emphasis on separation, the state is seen to operate within a 'thicker' international society, one that strengthens sovereignty by opening the state instead of insisting on separateness. Vincent now concentrates on the solidarist elements that troubled Bull: he starts with human rights and then narrows them down to a specific concern with basic rights. However, his work is beset by questions that had worried his predecessors and that continue to form the core of the pluralist and solidarist debate.

Most writers in the international society tradition are pigeonholed according to the position they adopt in the debate between pluralism and solidarism. However, there is now a reaction against this polarisation. Wheeler (1992) and Dunne and Wheeler (1996) have broken the division by exploring the solidarist tendencies in the writings of Bull, traditionally classified as pluralist. Knudsen (1999) argues that the two positions are not mutually exclusive in the context of humanitarian intervention and that combinations of pluralist and solidarist elements are possible in international life.

Buzan (2004) has also reassessed the polarisation of the English school and sees pluralism and solidarism as ends of a spectrum that marks degrees of difference rather than contradictory positions (Buzan, 2004: 49). At the pluralist end of the spectrum, international society is thin, and at the solidarist end it possesses a thicker texture within which 'a wider range of values are shared and where the rules will not be only about coexistence, but also about the pursuit of joint gains and the management of collective problems in a range of issue-areas' (ibid.: 59). It follows that 'solidarism initially builds on pluralism to become pluralism-plus, but can then develop into a variety of thicker versions' (ibid.). The number of values shared and the type of values (coexistence or cooperation) are central factors in the pluralist–solidarist distinction (ibid.: 143–5).

Vincent's approach to basic rights through the right to subsistence offers new insights on the pluralist–solidarist debate that have been overlooked until now. With his introduction of the economic sector, Vincent highlights the routine violations of human rights in the system, and moves beyond these exceptional situations that trigger the need for humanitarian intervention. The legitimacy of the whole international economic system, and not just that of a government, is thereby opened to examination. By moving the argument into the realm of international political economy, Vincent anticipates a new route to solidarism, circumventing the polarisation with pluralism and emphasising their complementarity in the economic sector. This point is examined further in the next section in the context of basic rights, and in Chapter 5 in relation to the overall theme of the book.

Vincent's basic rights project

Vincent's basic rights project lies at the heart of his understanding of international society. His discussion of basic rights, however, belongs to the last part of his career, and many elements remain incomplete. His position rests on two foundational claims: that there is a subject who has entitlements, and that to possess a right implies the existence of a duty-bearer against whom the right is claimed (Dunne and Wheeler, 1999: 3). Vincent asserts that all basic human rights precipitate three duties: a duty to avoid depriving others of their rights, a duty to protect others from deprivation of their rights and a duty to aid others deprived of their rights. The duty-bearer can be an individual, a responsible nation or an exploitative company, and the duty varies according to circumstances: for example, providing aid in a natural disaster or ensuring that others are not deprived of their right in a monopolistic market (Vincent, 1986a: 11). Introducing basic rights in international society presupposes the existence of duty-holders, which in Vincent's right to food would be the international economic system. Basic rights cannot guide international action if there are no duty-bearers.

Vincent was attracted to what he saw as the 'apolitical' quality of basic rights: 'They seek what is basic to our humanity, not to our membership of this or that political community. Or to put it in another way, they establish the values that all political communities should start by providing for' (Vincent, 1986a: 14). This idea underpins his major project: 'to construct a common floor under the societies of the world and not a ceiling over them; from the floor up is the business of several societies' (ibid.: 126). Vincent's floor metaphor allows him to escape the problem of relativism and provides for both unity and diversity: 'This means that we cannot act to impose our own conception of liberty on foreign communities. Instead we should reach out with those communities for a conception of basic human rights which is neutral with respect to the main political and economic divisions in the world' (ibid.). This take on universalism depends on a particular reading of natural law, where individuals share the same essential nature (subsistence and security) and where the naturalist tradition is a 'fecund place for thought' (ibid: 53). However, he hints at what will be his final position on the subject, as discussed further in 'Modernity and Universal Human Rights' (1992). In this posthumous article, Vincent accepts the idea of promoting consensus by establishing a 'global cosmopolitan culture ... where global values are being worked out in an exchange between the cultures' (Vincent, 1992b: 286).

Building on Shue's contribution, Vincent concludes, 'the basic right that has shaped the argument of this book has been the right to life, in the sense of a right to subsistence and a right to security against violence. Such a right is basic in the sense that the enjoyment of it is essential for the enjoyment of other rights' (Vincent, 1986a: 125).

Splitting the right to life into two basic rights opens the way to the two issues central in Vincent's work: 'security rights' underpin his discussion on humanitarian intervention; 'subsistence rights' form the base on which rests the right to 'freedom from starvation' as the 'most pressing issue' in international society. Shue also defended the complementarity and interdependence of both rights and took subsistence rights as the prior basic right.

The same trajectory is followed by Vincent: 'At the basic level it is true to say that economic and social rights (the right to subsistence) and civil and political rights (the right to security) are interdependent if something resembling a minimally satisfactory human life is going to be lived' (Vincent, 1986a: 90). This resolves a possible clash with the human rights argument that asserts that civil-political rights and economic-social rights are interrelated and interdependent. Vincent builds on interdependence overcoming the ideological rivalries between West and East–South: 'Neither of them need to expect to be taken seriously on their version of human rights unless they meet these basic rights first' (ibid.: 150). For Vincent (ibid.), 'basic rights ought to be met; the plight of the global poor is the worst offence against these rights'.

However, across his argument on basic rights it is clear that Vincent prioritises the right to subsistence, which he initially defines in broad terms: 'the right to subsistence [includes] food provision, supply of potable water, maintenance of public health and education' (Vincent, 1986a: 145). Later comments indicate that hunger is his main concern: 'to say that the problem of starvation is the most pressing rights issue does not mean that torture or genocide have less of a claim ... but starvation is, so to speak, the resident emergency, and it is reasonable that seriousness about human rights should be tested by reference to it' (ibid.). He takes the right to be free from hunger as the point of reference to build a common floor under the societies of the world while avoiding the difficulties of liberty discourse: 'It is a proposal about how progress might be made on basic rights in international community without running into insurmountable ideological obstacles along the way' (ibid.: 150). For Vincent, 'it is simply that subsistence might make a more workable international programme, a more neutral undertaking for international society than liberty' (ibid.: 148).

Therefore, Vincent tightens Shue's argument further in order to select the 'basis of basic rights'. Shue includes in the right to subsistence elements such as clothing, shelter and health care, which can be subject to discussion about how basic they are in terms of survival. That is what makes Vincent's project unique, in the sense that he tries to reduce ideological implications to the bare minimum. This does not contradict his initial theory about the right to security and the right to subsistence being interrelated at a basic level, but it complements it in the sense that his basic right to subsistence is basic not only to non-basic rights but to other basic rights as well. Therefore, the enjoyment of such a basic right is necessary for the enjoyment of all rights, including the other basic rights on his list. These would be the other aspects involved in the right to subsistence (adequate housing, clothing and health care) and the right to security. It is on his innovative understanding of the basic right to subsistence (specifically the right to food) that this book builds.

Together with Henry Shue's writings, Vincent also took into account the wider political discourses on the subject, citing Henry Kissinger who stated in 1974 that 'all governments should accept the removal of the scourge of hunger and malnutrition ... as the objective of the international community as a whole' (Vincent, 1986a: 146). Vincent acknowledges the magnitude of this project, suggesting that 'it might require a radical shift in patterns of political power in order that resources can reach the submerged 40 per cent in developing countries' (ibid.: 145). He does not extend the actual policy implications of this statement any deeper than suggesting that 'what is required is the bringing together of financial aid from the North to fund the programme, with provision for making allocative decisions and the monitoring of performance' (ibid.: 146). This is a massive project which he compares with the elimination of the slave trade.

Crucially, however, Vincent (1986a: 127) sees this as a project for international society, 'for it may be that, in regard to the failure to provide subsistence rights, it is not this or that government whose legitimacy is in question, but the whole international system in which we are all implicated'.

Vincent puts the responsibility to do something about starvation squarely in the international arena; however, he does not analyse possible national causes of the problem. He goes as far as making the following statement: 'the duty to aid the deprived should be above the explanation of their predicament, and the political appeal to do so should be based on this obligation in order that cooperative enterprise to meet human needs can start with generosity of spirit rather than mutual recrimination' (Vincent, 1986a: 147). His normative recommendations request deeper commitment from the United States: 'The United States ... cannot rely for the elimination of hunger on gunboats ... it must act in as wide a coalition as possible ... allies in the coalition might take the lead on particular initiatives, but it is the commitment of the world's largest economy that might make a difference' (ibid.: 146, 147).

From these extracts, several conclusions may be drawn:

- Initially Vincent defines the basic right to subsistence in broad terms. However, further analysis of his writings establishes starvation as his main concern, which he chooses as the base for his normative statements on what should be the priority for creating a more solidarist international society.
- Even if 'hunger' comes across as his priority, he does not expand on the causes of the problem. The practical implications of eliminating hunger are reduced to the few quotations collected above.
- It is clear that he refers to starvation as a routine phenomenon in many developing countries, which he calls 'the South' or the 'Third World', towards whose cause he orients his argument: 'This book has taken a right to life as basic, and has to this extent signed up with the Third World.'
- His normative approach suggests the need for reform at the international level and assumes the responsibility of the richer countries (pointing the finger at the United States in particular). However, he does not identify the possible types of reform necessary to satisfy the right to food on international grounds, nor does he consider the programmes that international society has already implemented to address the lack of food in some parts of the world.
- Vincent's basic rights project is innovatory in the sense that it tries to eliminate the ideological implications of the liberty discourse in order to see whether it is possible to agree on a universal common floor by focusing on the basic right to food. The acceptance of this right has consequences at several levels, and he focuses on the responsibility of

'whoever has the power to do something about it' by implying reforms in the international economic system and questioning its legitimacy.

The next section examines the status of the basic right to food in international society.

The right to food

The right to food is firmly established in international law through a series of instruments, both directly and indirectly. Tomasevski (1987) has compiled a chronological list of over a hundred international instruments that relate to the right to food in some way. However, only the following constitute benchmarks for the structure of contemporary international law:

- *Universal Declaration of Human Rights*, 1948: Article 25 affirms that 'everyone has the right to a standard of living adequate for the health and well-being of himself and his family, including food'. From this point, the right to food evolved from being a subject of philosophical and political speculation to acquiring a place in international law.
- *International Covenant on Economic, Social and Cultural Rights*, 1966, deals with the right to food more comprehensively than any other treaty by talking specifically about 'the fundamental right of everyone to be free from hunger' in Article 11. It has been ratified by 147 states (as of July 2003). Alston (1984) identified the reasons why this instrument has pre-eminence over other international right to food norms: it represents a codification of the earlier version contained in the Universal Declaration of Human Rights; it is more specific than other relevant international legal norms; a large number of states have signed it, which means accepting the obligation to take steps to achieve the realisation of the right; its content was largely shaped by the FAO, the most important international food agency; and finally, it established a mechanism to monitor state parties' compliance with their obligations. In addition, is the only right in both covenants that is stated to be 'fundamental' (Alston, 1984: 29, 32).
- *International Covenant on Civil and Political Rights*, 1966: General comment no. 6 on Article 6 states that 'states parties are required to take positive steps to reduce infant mortality and to increase life expectancy, especially in adopting measures to eliminate malnutrition and epidemics'. It has been ratified by 149 states (as of July 2003).
- *Convention of the Rights of the Child* declares that 'States parties must take appropriate measures to combat disease and malnutrition, including through the provision of nutritious food and drinking water' (Articles 24 and 27). It has been ratified by 192 states (as of July 2003).
- *Universal Declaration on the Eradication of Hunger and Malnutrition:* This declaration was adopted by the first World Food Conference held

in Rome in 1974. The declaration states that 'it is a fundamental responsibility of Governments to work together for higher food production and a more equitable and efficient distribution of food between countries and within countries' (para. 2). Since then, there have been several world food conferences where states renewed their commitment to eliminate hunger and malnutrition. The most significant commitment on this subject came through the World Food Summit in 1996, attended by 185 countries represented by their head of state or deputy. Moreover, 24 UN agencies, 55 other IGOs and 790 NGOs took part in the summit. It ended with the *World Food Summit Declaration and Plan of Action*, where the participants signed seven commitments related to food security, including a 'fair world trade system'. Their biggest challenge was to set 2015 as the date by which the number of hungry people would be reduced by half (400 million).

Stemming from the World Food Summit Plan of Action, a process for further defining the right to food and its correlative state obligations has been launched. The objective draws on the foundations of the covenant and has registered substantial progress in recent years. The FAO and the High Commissioner for Human Rights (HCHR) have carried out three expert consultations to clarify the content of the right. The first two (1997 and 1998) contributed to the elaboration of the General comment no. 12 adopted by the Committee on Economic, Social and Cultural Rights (CESCR). These general comments are authoritative interpretations of rights prescribed by the CESCR in its role of monitoring the implementation of the International Covenant on Economic, Social and Cultural Rights. General comment no. 12 gives a legal interpretation of the right to food, which was missing until its introduction in 1999.

The third consultation took place in 2001 and focused on the links between poverty and hunger, calling for the eradication of poverty to eliminate hunger. In 2001 the Commission on Human Rights appointed its first special rapporteur on the right to food, who has since then submitted reports to the Commission on Human Rights and to the General Assembly; one of the points stressed in such reports is the need to review international trade obligations to ensure that they do not jeopardise the right to food (Robinson, 2002: 7). At the moment, General comment no. 12 is the most authoritative legal interpretation of the right to food. Work is being done on further development of the legal mechanism through the elaboration of a code of conduct, which will describe with precision both the content of the right and the corresponding state obligations in the Covenant on Economic, Social and Cultural Rights. The code of conduct is intended to fill in the legal gaps regarding the impact of intergovernmental policies on the right to food (such as those of the IMF, World Bank or WTO). The decision to negotiate such a code, at the moment only in draft form, came from the state members of the FAO and the UN (Windfuhr, 2002: 13). The idea behind it originated during the preparation for the World Food Summit, and its main mission is to strengthen the final documents of the WFS in order to meet the 2015 deadline (Braun, 2002: 1–2).

Chapter 3 assesses how binding these agreements are. Here they provide the international context in which a rights-based approach to hunger has been created in international society. This approach defines the role of states and other actors in the attempt to reduce hunger and malnutrition, but it does not stipulate all policy measures. It primarily determines the minimum standards of state behaviour (Windfuhr, 2002: 2). In contrast to other rights in the general human rights discourse, there is a wide consensus across international society about the content of this right. The need to meet it is neither contested nor subject to cultural variations. The controversial points around this right are connected to its implementation, but not to the content itself.

Within this context, the *right to food* is defined as the 'right to have regular, permanent, free access, either directly or by means of financial purchases, to quantitatively and qualitatively adequate and sufficient food corresponding to the cultural traditions of the people to which the consumer belongs, and which ensures a physical and mental, individual and collective, fulfilling and dignified life ["Food" covers not only solid foods but also the nutritional aspects of drinking water]' (UN, 2001d: 7).

General comment no. 12 specifies that the core content of this right is the availability and accessibility of food, which establishes a set of state obligations at both national and international levels. At the national level, the comment stipulates that the right to food imposes on states an obligation to ensure that the right is fulfilled. At the international level, states are required 'to recognise the essential role of international cooperation and to comply with their commitment to take joint and separate action to achieve the full realisation of the right to food' (Robinson, 2002: 5).

These advances in the rights-based approach to the basic need of food answer Vincent's concern that 'what would make a difference is the acceptance of the basic needs as a doctrine of human rights imposing correlative obligations, and not merely as an option in the strategy of development' (Vincent, 1986a: 150). While this chapter has clarified the origins of the basic rights discourse and Vincent's contribution to it, the next chapters will assess whether it is normatively and practically viable as a project in international society.

3 Basic rights in international society
The right to food

This chapter expands on the previous one by studying the practical implications of basic rights in international society, specifically through the problem of hunger and, therefore, the right to food. This investigation uses international society as the framework of analysis and is structured around the international trade–poverty–hunger triad established in Chapter 1. The assessment of these three interrelated areas contributes to the final conclusions on the viability of Vincent's basic rights project in international society. This chapter, therefore, describes what international society has done, or has committed itself to do, regarding international trade, poverty and hunger. Analysis of the practical side of what international society is doing to deal with hunger will be provided in Chapter 4.

The first section examines the commitments embraced by states at the World Food Summit in 1996 and its evolution. The second focuses on summits dealing with the international dimension of poverty and the commitments signed by states. The third looks at international trade and, in particular, the agricultural policies established in the Doha Declaration.

The chapter concludes by analysing how legally binding these agreements are in international society and offers a critical assessment of the level of commitment implicit in them.

The World Food Summit and plan of action

The World Food Summit was held in 1996 in Rome, with the participation of heads of state and high-level representatives from 185 countries and the European Union at the invitation of the Food and Agriculture Organisation of the United Nations. It was a response to the continued existence of widespread undernutrition and a re-evaluation of the two previous international meetings on food issues held in 1974 and 1992. The first, the World Food Conference, was crucial to establishing the priority of the right to food in the international context. This event took place in the political context of the New International Economic Order (examined in Chapter 2). Governments attending the conference had proclaimed that 'every man, woman and child has the inalienable right to be free from hunger and malnutrition in order to develop their physical and mental faculties' and they set as a goal the eradication of hunger within a decade. However, lack of policy making and funding ensured that the goal was not met (FAO, 2002d: 1).

Twenty-two years later, governments, together with representatives of intergovernmental and non-governmental organisations, gathered to renew their global commitment at the highest political level to eliminate hunger, with a short-term plan to reduce the number of undernourished to half the level in 1996 (800 million) by 2015. The summit concluded with the publication of two major documents, the *Rome Declaration on World Food Security* and the *World Food Summit Plan of Action*. Their common objective was to achieve food security at the individual, household, national, regional and global levels. 'Food security exists when all people, at all times, have physical and economic access to sufficient, safe and nutritious food to meet their dietary needs for an active and healthy life style' (FAO, 1996e: 3). Given the many factors that have repercussions on food security, states made the following commitments on both national and international fronts (ibid.: 2, 3):

1   We will ensure an enabling political, social and economic environment designed to create the best conditions for the eradication of poverty and for durable peace.
2   We will implement policies aimed at eradicating poverty ... and improving economic access by all to sufficient, nutritionally adequate and safe food.
3   We will pursue participatory and sustainable food, agriculture, fisheries, forestry and rural development policies and practices, which are essential to adequate food supplies at the household, national, regional and global levels.
4   We will strive to ensure that food, agricultural trade and overall trade policies are conductive to fostering food security for all through a fair market-orientated world trade system.
5   We will endeavour to prevent natural disasters and man-made emergencies and to meet transitory and emergency food requirements in ways that encourage development and a capacity to satisfy future needs.
6   We will promote use of public and private investments to foster human resources, sustainable food and rural development.
7   We will implement, monitor and follow-up this plan of action at all levels in cooperation with the international community.

Each of these seven commitments embraced a plan of action in which governments specified how to achieve the commitment and the degree of their support for it. Since my argument concentrates on the international dimension of hunger, and in particular on the international trade–poverty–hunger triad, I focus on Commitments 1 and 4 which highlight these areas. Commitment 1 highlights the international dimension of poverty and hunger, and Commitment 4 relates specifically to international trade.

Commitments 1 and 4

Commitment 1: 'We will ensure an enabling political, economic and social environment designed to create the best conditions for the eradication of poverty and for durable peace.'

Under this commitment governments have drawn the following objectives as their basis for action. These objectives involve, 'as appropriate, the partnership with all actors of civil society' (FAO, 1996e: 6).

OBJECTIVE 1: To prevent and resolve conflicts peacefully and create a stable political environment, through respect of all human rights and fundamental freedoms, democracy, a transparent and effective legal framework, transparent and accountable governance and administration in all public and private national and international institutions, and effective and equal participation of all people, at all levels, in decisions and actions that affect their food security' (FAO, 1996e: 6).

OBJECTIVE 2: To ensure economic conditions and implement development strategies ... for sustainable, equitable, economic and social development. This objective intends to promote national and international policies for development and establish legal mechanisms that enhance access of the poor to resources' (FAO, 1996e: 7).

OBJECTIVE 3: To ensure gender equality and empowerment of women, promoting equal gender opportunities for education, training and division of labour.

Commitment 4: 'We will strive to ensure that food, agricultural trade and overall trade policies are conductive to fostering food security for all through a fair market-orientated world trade system.'

In this commitment states acknowledge that trade is a key element for achieving world food security: 'trade has a major bearing on access to food through its positive effect on economic growth, income and employment' (FAO, 1996e: 19). Given this key role of trade, Commitment 4 of the World Food Summit insists that all members of the WTO follow both the undertakings of the Uruguay Round and the Marrakesh Decision on Measures Concerning the Possible Negative Effects of the Reform Programme on Least-Developed and Net Food-Importing Developing Countries. The commitment incorporates the following objectives, which are also based on governmental action 'in partnership with all actors of civil society, as appropriate'.

OBJECTIVE 1: 'To meet the challenges of and utilize the opportunities arising from the international trade framework established in recent global and regional trade negotiations.' This responsibility is given to WTO members and the international community more generally.[1] 'Members of the WTO will pursue the implementation of the Uruguay Round Agreement, which will improve market opportunities for efficient food, agricultural, fisheries and forestry producers and processors, particularly those of developing countries' (FAO, 1996e: 20).

Under this objective, the international community agreed to look at the following points (FAO, 1996e: 20):

(a) To assist countries to adjust their institutions and standards both for internal and external trade to food safety and sanitary requirements.
(b) To promote financial and technical assistance to improve the agricultural productivity and infrastructure of developing countries, in order to optimise the opportunities of the international trade framework.
(c) To encourage technology transfer to developing countries, so that they are in a position to take advantage of the new market opportunities.

OBJECTIVE 2: 'To meet essential food import needs in all countries, considering world price and supply fluctuations and taking especially into account food consumption levels of vulnerable groups in developing countries' (FAO, 1996e: 20). This objective creates the following commitments:

(a) Exporting countries should reduce subsidies on food exports according to the Uruguay Round Agreement.
(b) Countries should administer all export-related trade policies and programmes with a view to avoiding disruptions in world food and agriculture import and export markets.
(c) WTO members should fully implement the Decision on Measures Concerning the Possible Negative Effects of the Reform Programme on Least-Developed and Net Food-Importing Developing Countries. This decision is intended to help least developed countries and net food-importing developing countries to meet short-term difficulties in financing essential food imports while adjusting to the global trade structure.

OBJECTIVE 3: 'To support the continuation of the reform process in conformity with the Uruguay Round Agreement, particularly Article 20 of the Agreement on Agriculture' (FAO, 1996e: 20). Under this clause, governments commit themselves to supporting the reform process agreed in the Uruguay Round and to working towards solutions that improve the developing countries' access to markets and food security.

* * *

These commitments provided a framework for specific objectives and actions. However, there were no proposals for creating new institutions or drawing additional resources. There was an implicit understanding that 'the world has the capacity to feed its population adequately today and in the future and that most of the international institutional arrangements for this are in place ... instead, the main concern was how to generate and sustain the political will to translate the commitments into the required actions' (FAO, 4/6/02: 3).

Follow-up

The Rome Declaration (World Food Summit 1996) was resumed by the participants in a clear statement: 'We consider it intolerable that more than 800 million throughout the world and particularly in developing countries do not have enough food to meet their basic nutritional needs. This situation is unacceptable' (FAO, 1996e: 19).

However, the most important element of this affirmation is the challenge of translating it into practical actions in order to reduce the large number of hungry people. The plan of action involves national, regional and international cooperation at governmental level as well as throughout all sectors of society. The monitoring mechanism, within the United Nations system, is managed by the Committee on World Food Security (CFS), which was established as a result of the World Food Conference in 1974. It receives reports from three sources: national governments, UN agencies and inter-agency coordination, and other relevant international institutions (FAO, 1999a: 4).

The summit, although organised by governments, also allowed the participation of representatives of IGOs and NGOs: 'In total, 10,000 participants from spheres that had helped to influence public opinion and provided a framework for bringing about important changes in policies and programmes needed to achieve food for all' (FAO, 2002e: 2).

In the summit preparatory process, NGOs were involved at the national, regional and international levels through various kinds of governmental consultations. Moreover, NGOs around the world wrote several declarations that were submitted to the secretariat for consideration at the summit. Parallel to the World Food Summit in November 1996, several influential meetings took place in Rome and their declarations were considered at the summit. These included meetings of the NGO Forum, the International Youth Forum and the Parliamentarians' Day, which is formed by parliamentary groups from all corners of the world. At the national level, before the summit 150 countries established national secretariats or World Food Summit committees to coordinate their contributions to the summit process. Therefore, in preparing for the World Food Summit, consultations took place among governments, IGOs, INGOs, NGOs and the private sector (FAO, 2002e: 6–8).

The World Food Summit apportioned the commitments among governments, international organisations and 'civil society'. The declaration states that governments should cooperate actively with one another and with United Nations organisations, as well as with financial institutions, intergovernmental and non-governmental organisations, and the public and private sector, on programmes directed towards the achievement of food security for all (FAO, 1996e: 2). There is clear interaction here between international society and world society (discussed further in Chapter 5).

As part of the plan of action, the Special Programme for Food Security (SPFS) created by the FAO before the summit has been given a central role. It works in the area of agricultural development and especially in low-income food-deficit countries (LIFDCs), where it aims to increase food production and availability. However, the SPFS has not been able to cover all the low-income food-deficit countries; for the programme to work properly, another US$900 million would be required. The FAO's director has insisted that 'the budget allocated to the Organisation to assist the 815 million hungry people in the world is equivalent to just 40 cents a year for each undernourished person' (Diouf, 2001a: 3).

Another crucial initiative launched at the request of the World Food Summit was the creation of the Food Insecurity and Vulnerability Mapping Systems (FIVIMS). The FIVIMS is a network to identify the food insecure people, and provide information on where they are located and why they are food vulnerable, in order to target accurately an effective action against hunger.

According to the trend followed since the summit, projections indicate that the goal of halving the number of hungry people by 2015 will not be achieved. In 1990–2000, 61 developing countries registered a proportional decrease in their figures of undernourished and 35 countries cut down their absolute numbers. However, none of these groups has claimed any specific change arising from the summit's resolutions in their reports to the CFS (FAO, 17/10/02: 8). Since 1990 the downward global trend has stood at an annual average of 2.5 million people. In fact, on an individual country basis the post-1996 picture is rather mixed, with rising levels of hunger in certain areas (mainly in parts of Africa) and falling levels in others. As a consequence, critical voices insist that 'what is needed is not more debate or scholarly treatises but a renewed determination on the part of governments, backed by international bodies and civil society, to implement the straightforward measures which they endorsed at the WFS five years ago' (FAO, 4/6/02: 8).

In June 2002 the 'World Food Summit: Five Years Later' was held with the aim of reviewing the achievements made since 1996. Most progress was made in the definition and institutionalisation of the right to food. Several expert consultations took place to delimit the national and international dimensions of the right to food (examined in Chapter 2). The consultations resulted in the adoption in 1999 of General comment no. 12 on the right to adequate food by the CESCR, together with the elaboration of the voluntary code of conduct, which describes the national and international obligations of states regarding the right to food.

Moreover, the commitment to halve the number of hungry people by 2015 was reinforced by the Millennium Summit on poverty, the G-8 Summit in 2001, the UN General Assembly in 2001, the International Conference on Financing for Development in 2002, the Johannesburg Summit also in 2002 and the WTO ministerial meetings.

However, in terms of the practicalities of the commitment, the results are far below the level required to meet the 2015 deadline. In June 2002 the Committee on World Food Security published its assessment of the progress made over the previous five years. However, there is no evidence that this progress occurred as a specific response to the World Food Summit. Nevertheless, the CFS celebrated the beginning of a new round of multilateral trade negotiations launched at the WTO ministerial conference in Doha (discussed later in this chapter). The CFS also observed significant changes in preferential trade arrangements between developed and developing countries, such as the creation of major trade agreements (CFS, 2002b: 15–17). The next paragraphs will concentrate on the two major global trade giants, the US and the EU.

In the first place, President Clinton signed the African Growth and Opportunity Act (AGOA) into law in May 2000. The aim of this act is to offer incentives to African countries to build free markets and open their economies. It gives to the qualifying countries access to the US markets by reinforcing African reforms. A subcommittee of the trade policy staff committee determines which countries are eligible and which products come into the scheme of zero tariff. Amongst other requirements, countries must show determination and progress towards establishing a market-based economy, efforts to combat corruption, political pluralism, protection of human rights and elimination of barriers to US trading and investment (AGOA, 2002: 1, 2). This last point has been criticised for serving US interests: for example, preferences for African garments are tightly linked to reverse preference for American fabrics (Bhagwati, 2002: 28). As of December 2001, 35 Sub-Saharan countries were approved by President Bush to form part of AGOA. These countries, which are already part of the Generalised System of Preferences (GSP), count on duty-free treatment for more than 1,800 products in addition to the standard GSP list (ibid.: 1). However, in its five-year progress report to the Committee on

World Food Security, the US did not highlight other agreements achieved during the period under review (CFS, 2002g: 9).

The second trading agreement between developed and developing countries was the Everything But Arms (EBA) agreement approved by the Council of Ministers of the European Union in 2001. The agreement gives 100 per cent access to EU markets to the world's 48 poorest countries. This liberalisation of import restrictions applies to all products except arms. The agreement came as a result of the failure to start new world trade negotiations in Seattle in 1999 due to the embargo imposed by developing countries, whose delegates felt excluded from the benefits of liberalisation. Duty and quota elimination for nearly all products took effect in March 2001. Three exceptions to the rule relate to products that the EU considers sensitive and needing time to adjust: sugar, rice and bananas. The integration of these products into the EBA agreement will be done gradually, leading to the total elimination of tariffs by September 2009 at the latest. However, to compensate for the delay in the liberalisation of these products, the EBA agreement provides for the creation of duty-free quotas for sugar and rice (EU, 2001a: 1–3). This agreement has been criticised for its repercussions on other developing countries that currently obtain preferences on their exports to the European Union, such as non-LDCs from Africa, the Caribbean and the Pacific (known as the ACP group); their exports to the EU are expected to fall following the implementation of EBA, since the products from LDCs will become more competitive (UN, 2001c: xviii). On the other side of this argument, the World Bank has carried out a study that shows that even if all Quad countries were to open their markets to LDCs for tariff-peak items only (i.e. those subject to a tariff exceeding more than 15 per cent), the exports of other developing countries would decline by only 0.1 per cent, while the LDCs' exports would increase by around 11 per cent (World Bank, 2002b: 60).

In its five-year progress report to the CFS, the EU mentions the Coconou Agreement signed in June 2000 between the ACP and the EU as a step forward regarding Commitment 4. The primary objective of this agreement is to foster 'the gradual integration of the ACP states into the world economy ... aiming at enhancing the production, supply and trading capacity of the ACP countries as well as their capacity to attract investment' (FAO, 2002e: 33). The negotiations started in September 2002 and are scheduled to finish in 2008 with the removal of all barriers to trade between the ACP and the EU. It is too early to assess the viability of this partnership.

Another measure included by the EU in its progress report is the Euro-Mediterranean policy set out in the Barcelona Declaration of 1995 and adopted by the European Council in June 2000. This economic area is made up of 27 members, the EU (then with 15 member states) plus Morocco, Algeria, Tunisia, Egypt, Jordan, Syria, Lebanon, Israel, the Palestinian Authority, Turkey, Malta and Cyprus. It is a reciprocal agreement between the EU and its partners that provides for the gradual removal of trade restrictions within a period of 10 to 12 years (FAO, 2002e: 35).

Even if these steps have been adopted in the five-year period that followed the summit, it is difficult to assess the influence that the commitments of the World Food Summit had in the process. For example, the idea for the EBA initiative stemmed from the WTO Ministerial Conference held in Singapore in 1995 (FAO, 2002e: 31) and was implemented as a result of events in Seattle in 1999. Although it entered into force in the post-WFS years, it originated before then. The same is true of the ACP agreement: the EU had a special system of trade relations with these countries since 1975; the new project, however, does enhance those trade relations.

Nevertheless, in the introductions to the reports to the CFS, countries insist on their commitment to hunger reduction and their seriousness about the objectives included in the WFS Declaration. The other two countries within the Quad group, Canada and Japan, have not registered any new achievements in their progress report regarding Commitment 4. Canada reasserts the Doha Declaration, saying that it plans to 'continue on work related to the WTO agriculture negotiations, ... in terms of contributing to better understanding of the needs of developing countries' (CFS, 2002d: 47). Japan simply reports 'Due and steady implementation of Agriculture Agreement of WTO' (CFS, 2002f: 13). Progress reports from other countries take the same form.

Poverty summits

The agreements regarding poverty adopted in international society usually form part of a larger agenda on development policies, now known as the Summits on Sustainable Development. The agreements are designed to promote the 'integration of environment and development in order to fulfil basic needs, improve living standards for all and better manage ecosystems for long-term sustainability' (UN, 28/8/02: 1, 2). This agenda was initiated in 1972 at the United Nations Conference held in Stockholm that stressed in its declaration the need 'for a common outlook and for common principles to guide the preservation and enhancement of the human environment' (UN, 1972: 1).

However, it was not until the 1990s that a series of similar agreements demonstrated a commitment to the problem of poverty. The benchmark is Agenda 21, the Declaration on Environment and Development signed in Rio de Janeiro (June 1992) by 178 governments. Chapter 3 of the agenda specifies the objectives and basis for action regarding the reduction of poverty, which includes measures at the international and national levels (UN, 1992b: 1–4). The agenda insists on the role of trade liberalisation in the process and calls for wider access to markets for developing countries 'to improve their economic structures and improve the standard of living of their populations through sustained development' (UN, 1992c: 2). Agenda 21, although general in its approach, nurtured a series of international meetings and declarations that have developed in international society since then.

In 1995, at the World Summit for Social Development held in Copenhagen, 117 heads of state or government pledged, among other objectives, to eradicate poverty. The summit produced the Copenhagen Declaration based on 10 commitments and a programme of action to achieve them. On poverty the countries stated: 'We commit ourselves to the goal of eradicating poverty in the world, through decisive national actions and international cooperation, as an ethical, social, political and economic imperative of humankind' (UN, 1995b: 5).

The programme of action was divided into two spheres: national and international. At the national level, governments committed themselves to:

(a) formulate or strengthen national policies and strategies to reduce overall poverty in the shortest term possible by a target date to be specified by each country in its national context;
(b) focus the policies to address the causes of poverty and to provide basic needs for all. These efforts include the elimination of hunger and malnutrition;
(c) ensure that people living in poverty have access to productive resources as well as to public services;
(d) ensure that national budgets are oriented to meeting basic needs and targeting poverty.

At the international level, governments committed themselves to:

(a) ensure that the international community and international organisations assist developing countries to achieve the goal of eradicating poverty;
(b) encourage international donors to support policies for the attainment of the specific efforts of developing countries and to meet basic needs for all;
(c) focus attention on countries in which there are substantial numbers of people living in poverty (UN, 1995b: 5, 6).

These commitments were followed by a programme of action in both national and international domains. Although no general solution to tackle poverty could be provided, governments insisted it should be done through country-specific programmes backed up by an international supportive environment. There was a general agreement that the solution to poverty does not depend simply on anti-poverty programmes, but on changes in economic structures also (UN, 1995c: 3).

In the formulation of strategies for the eradication of poverty, developed countries acknowledged their responsibility in the development project and the need to narrow imbalances in order to benefit all countries, including developing countries (UN, 1995c: 5).

The programme of action also included radical commitments to be met by the year 2000. Among them, the following have been selected according to the interests of this research:

- reduction of malnutrition among children under five years of age by half of the 1990 level;
- reduction of mortality rates of children under five years to 50 to 70 per 1,000 live births;
- achievement of food security through an adequate food supply at both national and international levels;
- provision of access to safe drinking water in sufficient quantities.

These aims were not met, and the failure created a wave of severe criticism around the commitments established at the summit. In the words of Juan Somavia, Director General of the UN International Labour Organisation, 'five years have brought little to cheer about' (Associated Press, 2000: 2).

In an attempt to address growing criticisms in world society, the commitments were renewed five years later under the *United Nations Millennium Declaration* (2000). World leaders decided that the first 15 years should concentrate on a substantial reduction of poverty. On this occasion, governments insisted on the need to address the special requirements of developing countries, which include 'an open, equitable, rule-based, predictable and non-discriminatory multilateral trading and financial system' (UN, 2000: 6). However, the biggest commitment in this declaration was to halve, by the year 2015, the number of the world's population whose income is less than US$1 per day (1.2 billion at the time of the declaration). The declaration also reiterated the commitment made at the World Food Summit to halve by that same year the number of people who suffer from hunger (UN, 2000: 7). The *Human Development Report* (UNDP, 2001) has evaluated this deadline and arrived at the conclusion that half the countries for which data are available will not achieve the poverty reduction goal, unless substantial changes are implemented straight away. Of the 81 countries examined, 11 (including large countries such as China and India) are on track to meet the deadline, while 70 are behind (UNDP, 2001: 25).

Another key stage in the international consensus on the elimination of poverty was the 2001 *UN Conference on Least Developed Countries* held in Brussels. The conference produced a declaration in which 193 governments renewed the Millennium goals. In particular, they adopted a programme for the decade 2001–10 that includes development assistance, debt cancellation and private investment in the 49 LDCs. A significant outcome of this programme was the priority given to international trade. Governments insisted that a non-discriminatory multilateral trade system is essential for LDCs to benefit from the global economy; at the same time, they stated that the accession of these countries to the World Trade System should be facilitated. Under the commitment on trade, 'development partners aim at improving preferential market access for LDCs by working towards the objective of duty-free and quota-free access for all LDC products in the markets of developed countries' (UN, 2001b: 7).

In terms of these international agreements, poverty and hunger were clearly connected in the Millennium Declaration. A year later, the Brussels Declaration added the explicit role of international trade in the reduction of poverty and hunger. It should be noted here (although the point will be expanded in the next chapter) that the impact of the liberalisation of markets could be measured on two fronts: opportunities and risks for the poor. In a balanced relationship between trade and the poor, trade helps to reduce poverty by constructing an environment in which there are more opportunities for the poor to earn a living. However, this relationship is more complex and can be divided into four areas (ADB, 2001: 1–4).

Prices of goods and factors of production

Trade liberalisation affects consumption and income patterns. It lowers the prices of imported goods, which can have positive implications for the poor by making cheaper food available to them. This trend also carries negative effects for the domestic economies, since local producers may be pushed out of the market by an incapacity to compete with imported products. However, trade liberalisation can also result in higher demand for certain products that the country produces, expanding the export-oriented industry and creating new jobs that benefit the poor.

Government revenue

Trade liberalisation can reduce government revenues by eliminating tariffs; as a consequence, the money destined for social services and anti-poverty programmes shrinks. By the same token, trade liberalisation can have positive effects on government revenues by an expansion of the market.

Economic growth effects from trade

Trade liberalisation can lead to higher growth rates and have a quantitative impact on the income of the poor. They can gain from growth in employment in expanding sectors, such as agriculture, or other sectors that are part of the infrastructure required for the exporting activity. A study made by the World Bank insisted on this connection between trade and poverty. In fact, it asserted that 'reshaping the world's trade system and reducing barriers to trade could accelerate medium-term growth and reduce poverty around the world ... expanding trade could increase annual GDP growth by an additional 0.5 per cent and by 2015 lift 300 million out of poverty in addition to the 600 million calculated with normal growth' (World Bank, 2002c: 2). The key to this growth would be the establishment of further reforms in agricultural trade that bring down barriers which block the foodstuffs produced by the poor.

However, employment opportunities for the poor do not necessarily come together with expansion of the exporting sectors, since the new job opportunities could require a set of skills that the poor do not offer. At the same time, small-scale local producers are exposed to the risk of falling into poverty if they cannot compete with the incoming products.

Costs of transition and exposure to shocks

Trade liberalisation means that export products must comply with certain international standards that require investment in infrastructure and the conversion of traditional means of production into more sophisticated ones. This brings a short- to medium-term process of adjustment with high costs, while the benefits are seen only in the long run. The poor are not able to afford these standards and their survival in the market depends on the existence of aid measures that cover the adjustment period. Trade liberalisation also makes the economy dependent on external flows, which can bring large revenues in good times and the opposite in times of crisis.

Because trade is a double-edged sword, the 193 governments gathered in Brussels in 2001 asserted the need to advance the development dimension of trade, in particular in the area of LDCs (UN, 2001b: 2) and they prepared the grounds for the Doha meeting held later that year. The Doha Declaration (reviewed in the next section) lay at the centre of the Monterrey Conference in March 2002, which prepared the ground for the Johannesburg World Summit on Sustainable Development (August 2002). While Agenda 21, together with the series of summits that followed, identified poverty as a central problem for international society, Johannesburg focused on what to do about it: 'how to bring about the necessary changes in state policy; how to use policy and tax incentives to send the right signals to business and industry; how to offer better choices to individual consumers and producers; how, in the end, to get things done' (Annan, 2002: 10). But Johannesburg did not move forward the agenda on how to deal with global poverty; it simply renewed the commitment to halving the number of people in poverty and hunger by 2015. In the Johannesburg Commitment governments declared that 'the most pressing challenges of our time remain poverty, underdevelopment, environmental degradation, and social and economic inequalities within and among countries' (UN, 2002b: 2). However, 'few of the 72 leaders at the summit offered new money or concrete plans to close the widening gap between rich and poor states but there were many urgent pleas for action to save the planet from disaster' (Vidal, 3/9/02: 4).

World trade and the Doha Declaration

The Doha Declaration was the product of the fourth ministerial meeting held after the creation of the WTO. Following the collapse of the previous meeting which took place in Seattle in 1999, many expectations were raised by the Doha encounter. During three years of preparations all WTO members engaged in extensive consultations in order to avoid the differences between delegations that Seattle had failed to bridge. Several informal ministerial meetings and frequent bilateral consultations were carried out to address North–South, North–North and South–South problems (Schott, 2002: 1–3). Although Cancun is the latest ministerial meeting, it did not produce a declaration because the talks fell through. Hence the Doha Declaration is the most recent commitment made by states and it is the one on which agricultural negotiations are being built. Moreover, the final ministerial statement approved in Cancun insisted on the sense of urgency to work on the points agreed on in Doha and it renewed the commitment to implement them 'fully and faithfully' (WTO, 14/01/04: 3–5).

Building on the ongoing discussions held in Geneva under Article 20 of the Agreement on Agriculture, the Doha Declaration launched a new round of negotiations scheduled to end in January 2005. They combine four objectives: introducing substantial improvements in market access, reducing (with a view to phasing out) all forms of export subsidies, cutting down trade-distorting domestic support and establishing a differential treatment for developing countries. The declaration recalled the long-term objective of establishing 'a fair and market orientated trading system through a programme of fundamental reform ... in order to correct and prevent restrictions and distortions in world agricultural markets' (WTO, 2001b).

The declaration acknowledges a need for a differential treatment for developing countries to enable them to meet their needs in food security and rural development. During the implementation of the reforms suggested, the least developed and net food-importing developing countries are over-exposed to the consequences of the internationalisation of the markets, such as the lack of availability of foodstuffs from external sources on terms and conditions they can afford. In the process of opening the markets, this group of developing countries is disadvantaged because of undeveloped infrastructure that does not allow them to compete in international terms. Special and differential treatment has been recommended along the following lines:

(a) Review of the level of food aid established by the Committee on Food Aid under the Food Aid Convention and initiation of negotiations aimed at agreement on a level of food aid capable of meeting the needs of developing countries during the reform programme (WTO, 6/1/02: 1). At the moment, the levels met in practice are not enough to cover these needs. Aid includes also technical and financial assistance to these countries to improve their agricultural infrastructure.

(b) Review of agricultural export credits. It has been recognised that 'in case of short-term difficulties in financing normal levels of commercial imports, net food-importing developing countries may be eligible to draw on resources of international financial institutions' (WTO, 6/1/02: 2).

(c) In the Doha Declaration, WTO members committed themselves to the objective of duty-free, quota-free market access for products from LDCs. This objective admits that integration of the least developed countries into the global trading system requires efforts by all WTO members (WTO, 2001b: 2). In this context, the committee established a WTO list of 19 least developed and net food-importing developing countries (as of July 1999): Barbados, Botswana, Cuba, Cote d'Ivoire, Dominican Republic, Egypt, Honduras, Jamaica, Kenya, Mauritius, Morocco, Pakistan, Peru, St Lucia, Senegal, Sri Lanka, Trinidad and Tobago, Tunisia, and Venezuela.

* * *

Data on the EU and the US, the two major global trading partners, help to reveal the framework that justified the commitments made at Doha. Europe is the largest importer of farm products and the largest market for the developing countries. These are some typical statements published by the European Commission (EC, 2002: 1–2):

(a) The EU is the world's biggest importer of goods from least developed countries. In 1999 the EU took 55 per cent of total LDC exports to the Quad countries.

(b) LDCs count on duty-free access to the EU market for everything but arms. In the US 52 per cent of LDC exports are duty free, in Japan 49 per cent and in Canada 45 per cent.

(c) Since the Uruguay Round developing country exports to the EU have risen by, on average, 15 per cent per annum.

(d) The rate of growth in developing country agricultural exports to the EU has doubled since the creation of the WTO. Developing countries account for 42 per cent of EU imports.

Nevertheless, the EU is still targeted as being the largest user of agricultural protectionist measures. Its work in this area reduced the expenditure on export refunds to 9.4 per cent of the total value of agricultural exports in

1998 compared with 55 per cent in 1992 (CA, 2000: 1). In the EU the total market support (including export subsidies) has fallen progressively from 91 per cent of total support before 1992 and is expected to reach 21 per cent by 2006 (EU, 10/12/01a: 5). Besides the reductions, the EU has a ceiling of €69 billion for agricultural protection (Economist, 11/5/02: 93).

At the moment, the agricultural policy of the EU consumes half of the overall annual budget, but only 4 per cent of the EU's population work in agriculture. This amounts to €40 billion per year, in addition to other indirect measures that protect Europe's agricultural structure such as price supports and tax breaks: in total, €104 billion in aid in 2001. These figures overshadow other plans such as the EBA or the fact that the EU has the biggest of all aid budgets to developing countries.

The US, another major trading partner within the WTO, has recently established bilateral preferential trade liberalisation measures: the African Growth and Opportunity Act, the Andean Trade Preference Act and the Caribbean Basin Trade Partnership Act. In terms of agriculture, the US has signed the WTO's reform plan aimed at ending high tariffs, trade-distorting support and excessive support subsidies (WTO, 10/12/01t: 1–5). However, the country faces strong criticisms in the area of international trade for promoting free trade principles only in sectors that benefit the US economy.

The United States is the world's biggest exporter of agricultural products. Three-quarters of these exports go outside the NAFTA area; for example, 40 per cent are destined for Asia (WTO, 21/1/02c: 1–3). The opening of markets has allowed an increase of 55 per cent in the expansion of US goods and services exports since 1992, to a total of $958.5 billion in 2000 (WTO, 2000d: 4).

The US ceiling for agricultural protectionism is $19.1 billion, considerably below the European Union figure, but it has traditionally assigned $50 billion to agricultural support (Economist, 13/7/02: 35), still much lower than the EU. However, the new farm bill approved by the House of Representatives and the Senate will (according to May 2000 data) increase government spending on agriculture by 80 per cent over the next 10 years, which means an additional $82 billion. These subsidies will help the biggest crops in the US (soya beans, corn and wheat) with effects that will severely distort trade and which are contrary to the Doha Declaration (Economist, 11/5/02: 93). The new US bill will have direct repercussions on Europe's own process of liberalisation: the EU will not open up its agricultural policies if the US is doing the opposite. This backsliding questions the commitments signed under the Doha Declaration and damages the confidence of the developing countries in the international trade system.

Therefore, the road to Doha's aims is very long and the success of its plan of action depends not only on WTO general agreements but on the national and regional politics of the most powerful members.

* * *

The review of the three arenas (hunger, poverty and trade) undertaken above reinforces the argument established in Chapter 1 about choosing the route to hunger via the relation between international trade and poverty. Vincent's call for international society to introduce permanent structural reforms to tackle starvation is parallel to the measures agreed by states across the spectrum. In the next section I will analyse the depth of the commitments that these international agreements portray.

The degree of legalisation

How legally binding are the commitments to reduce hunger? Using the model developed by Abbott *et al.* (2000, 54: 3), legalisation provides a set of three dimensions along which institutions vary: obligation, precision and delegation. Obligation indicates that states or other actors are bound by a rule or commitment. Precision relates to the degree to which a rule specifies unambiguously what is expected of a state, or other actor, in a particular set of circumstances. Delegation identifies the extent to which states, or other parties, grant authority to third parties (courts, arbitrators, administrative organisations, and so on) to implement their agreements (ibid.: 410–15).

All three dimensions are subject to variation: obligation goes from 'expressly nonlegal' norm to 'binding rule'; precision starts by 'vague principle' and escalates up to a 'precise, highly elaborated rule'; delegation has 'diplomacy' at the soft end and 'international court and domestic application' at the other end. Each dimension can vary from high to low (e.g. low level of obligation, high level of precision and low level of delegation) and evolve through time (Abbott *et al.*, 2000: 404). These dimensions display consistency independently of each other, although their combination indicates the degree of legalisation of any agreement and determines its position in the soft law–hard law spectrum. In this context, 'hard law refers to legally binding obligations that are precise and that delegate authority for interpreting and implementing the law', and 'soft law begins once legal arrangements are weakened along one or more of the dimensions of obligation, precision and delegation' (Abbott and Snidal, 2000: 422, 423).

The authors of this model consider 'softer' variants to be of equal interest to hard law depending on circumstances. Contrary to the realist denial of the merits of soft law, they see several advantages in this form of international law: it is easier to achieve than hard legalisation; it offers more effective ways to deal with uncertainty in processes where the impact of the agreement is not clear; it facilitates compromise between actors with different interests and values; and finally, it is dynamic and initiates a process that may evolve over time (Abbott and Snidal, 2000: 423).

The Doha Declaration

According to this scheme, the WTO is based on a system of legally binding agreements that score highly on all three dimensions: states are bound by international trade regulations (obligation), the rules specify the requirements (precision), and there is a third party in charge of settling the disputes, the so-called dispute settlement mechanism embodied by a panel of corporate lawyers (delegation). However, even though the main WTO agreements constitute hard law, others agreements, such as the Doha Declaration, take on the character of soft law when assessed along the dimensions of obligation, precision and delegation.

Obligation

Doha is essentially an agreement that sets the terms for negotiation and does not require that these terms are met. 'Each participating country will determine the maximum level of obligation that it will undertake in each area and the minimum level of obligation by other countries that it deems sufficient to produce a reciprocal package of agreements' (Schott, 2002: 5).

Precision

The final declaration is not as firm as it might look at first glance. The language used is subject to interpretation, since a further explanation of the terms involved is not provided. For example, 'fair and market-orientated system' means something different for the EU and for a developing country. It can accommodate advocates of further liberalisation ('market orientated') and their opponents ('fair'). Another example: in the statement referring to agricultural subsidies, the declaration affirms the commitment to negotiate reductions, 'with a view to phasing out, of all forms of export subsidies'. A week later and during the European Voice conference on the 'Future of European Agriculture', the EU Agriculture Commissioner Franz Fischler calmed the European farmers' distress by insisting that there was no commitment to negotiate the elimination of export subsidies. Similarly, the statement about 'substantial reductions in trade-distorting domestic support' is open to various interpretations. Developed countries have interpreted this statement in relation to the green and blue boxes, which give them ample room for manoeuvring (Agritrade, 2002: 4–5). The three commitments to move on domestic support for agriculture, export competition and market access are subject to further interpretations and conditions. For example, Fischler has insisted that the EU is ready to introduce changes in those areas as long as the EU's trade partners take similar measures, but bearing in mind that 'every democratic society has the right to choose its own agricultural policy; what is important in an international context is to limit its trade distorting effects' (Fischler, 2001: 2).

However, these issues create some pressure and eventually change the shape of things, even if they do this slowly. In the controversial preparations for the Cancun ministerial meeting, the EU reached in June 2003 what has been considered the most radical reform deal on the CAP so far. It de-couples subsidies from production, a measure accused of producing unnecessary mountains of excess food which are then dumped into the international markets, damaging producers in developing countries where there are no subsidies. This reform has been criticised for not introducing any major change since it maintains the old level of subsidies (all the way to 2013) while simply redistributing them under other labels. However, it does symbolise a noticeable change in the sense that it needed to overcome a strong opposition among the EU members. It ended a confrontation between pro-reform countries such as the UK, Germany and the Scandinavian states against others such as France, Spain and Ireland which had traditionally shown a strong resistance to Fischler's de-coupling proposal (Bridges, 2003: 1). At least this demonstrates an internal success in relation to a goal that looked very difficult to achieve and provides testimony that external international agreements put a certain degree of pressure on delivering changes.

The issue of domestic support for agriculture has created a crucial debate between the US and the EU, which became more intense in the run-up to the Doha ministerial meeting. Fischler criticised the new US farm bill by maintaining that it does not fit with the liberalisation doctrine that the country had promoted in the Geneva negotiations. The US replied with the figures for total producer support pointing out that in 1999 the EU's amount was US$114.5 billion, twice as much as the US level ($54 billion) and exposed how the EU took advantage of the green and blue boxes to increase its agricultural aid (CTA, 2002b: 5). These data show a weakness in WTO rules pointing to their inability to regulate domestic support for agriculture, where no action has been taken despite an increase in agricultural support programmes. This example also reveals the gap between rhetoric and practice among the richest participants in agricultural trade.

Agricultural trade, therefore, is not subject to the same level of regulation as other forms of trade. The Doha Declaration establishes the basis for new negotiations but does not provide a firmly defined commitment from the participants. WTO provisions on special and differential treatment do not carry the same weight as other commitments and are usually subordinated to other WTO principles. For example, the principle of non-discrimination is given more authority when considering trade arrangements than the right of developing countries to special and differential treatment (CTA, 2002b: 5).

Delegation

The WTO has two mechanisms that follow the implementation of the rules, the Trade Policy Review Mechanism (TPRM) and the Dispute Settlement Body (DSB). The Trade Policy Review Board conducts periodic surveillance of the practices of the members and constitutes a forum where members can question each other's actions. However, the board only has the capacity to bring to light violations within the system, and cannot even investigate them. That mission belongs to the DSB, which can initiate action only when one member files a complaint against the practices of another member. If differences are not resolved in consultations between the two parties, the DSB appoints a panel of three to five experts. The panel report recommends how the violator should rectify its action; the report can be taken to an appellate body, whose recommendation will be final unless the entire WTO membership unanimously opposes it. If the charged member does not obey, the DSB will authorise sanctions to be defined by the state making the complaint, which usually implies raising tariffs against the guilty member (Moon, 2000: 107). The practice of this mechanism is highly contested, due to its implications for sovereignty and to the strong political element involved when choosing the members of the panel, who may have direct interests in the case analysed.

Moreover, this mechanism works only in relation to the binding rules, such as specific ceiling levels of tariffs, particular subsidy outlays for agriculture and services, regulations limiting market access and non-discriminatory treatment of foreign firms (OECD, 1998: 84). However, none of those apply to the commitments made in Doha regarding the improvement of market conditions to developing countries. In fact, in the ministerial meeting at Cancun the influential leaders reaffirmed phasing out the subsidies but did not establish any commitments to end those subsidies that are important to the EU and the US, confirming that the Doha Agreement is not subject to the delegation mechanism of the WTO.

The World Food Summit

At the World Food Summit, heads of state and governments reaffirmed the right of everyone to food. In the commitments of the plan of action that followed the summit they ensured an enabling political, economic and social environment for meeting the right to food and eliminating hunger. However, the achievements are not in line with the commitments, and certainly the reduction of hunger is not happening at the level required to eradicate it by 2015. Questions must be raised about the legalisation of the agreement. Applying the Abbott *et al.* (2000) model, we obtain the following picture:

Obligation

At first sight, 'obligation' seems to be a strength of the World Food Summit Declaration, which attracted 186 states and produced a unanimous understanding of both the basic right to food and the pressing need to eradicate hunger. They adopted the global goal of reducing hunger by half by 2015. Further consultations following the summit contributed to the elaboration of General comment no. 12 of the UN Committee on Economic, Social and Cultural Rights. This comment gave a specific legal framework to the right to food and now constitutes the most authoritative legal interpretation of this right. According to the comment, states are obliged to respect the right to adequate food, to protect the access to productive resources, to use the maximum resources available to meet the right to food and to implement it through fair international trade agreements (Windfuhr, 2002: 8). Another addition to the mechanism of obligation is the plan to create a code of conduct for the right to food; it stems from the World Food Summit Plan of Action and has already received the support of several governments in Latin America and Europe. This further move towards a new international regulation would intensify the degree of responsibility of the different actors involved and not only that of the state; in the case of international trade, intergovernmental organisations and the corporate sector would also incur responsibilities. However, acceptance of the code of conduct is voluntary. Despite this progress in defining the legal dimension of the right to food, the level of obligation it imposes has been made clear by a post-World Food Summit statement by the United States: 'The fundamental right to be free from hunger is a goal or aspiration to be realised progressively that does not give rise to any international obligations … the United States does not recognise any change in the current state of conventional or customary law regarding rights related to food, even if it accepts the right of everyone to have access to safe and nutritious food' (FAS, 2001: 1).

Precision

Considering that this feature measures the degree of clarity in the rule, the declaration does not specify clearly what is expected of a state. In some areas, the text is totally unambiguous and strongly oriented towards policies improving the position of disadvantaged groups with respect to their right to food. However, in other parts, such as the commitment on macro-economic policies, it can be understood to mean that the current development system is experiencing a level of success that will eventually benefit the poor on a wider scale. This is a serious ambiguity considering that the major debates on development hinge upon the question over the current system. The same thing happens in the section on international trade and particularly agricultural trade. Some parts of the text ask for open agricultural markets to improve national standards by developing competition with foreign producers. Other parts ask for the support of marginalised producers, which would mean the intensification of protectionist measures for small farmers in developing countries (Windfuhr, 2002: 4).

Delegation

This dimension measures the extent to which states delegate authority to designated third parties to implement agreements. A basic form of this would be the Committee on World Food Security that has been assigned by the World Food Summit to follow the implementation process. The CFS is in charge of monitoring the implementation of the World Food Summit through a reporting mechanism which states delegate to the secretariat. This shows that there is some obligation to the agreement, even if it is low-level. The monitoring mechanism of the CFS depends on the information that states provide and its main mission is to highlight both the best practices and the implementation problems at country level. It does not carry any effective check on state performance; 'the form of the implementation process therefore shows that the right to food is not taken seriously' (Windfuhr, 2002: 7).

This 'delegation' mechanism has a low degree of legalisation in the sense that it cannot require any action from actors that are not meeting the right to food; neither has it a dispute settlement mechanism. Following the adoption of General comment no. 12 by the CESCR, the Commission on Human Rights appointed in 2000 a special rapporteur on the right to food who reports to the Commission and the General Assembly (CFS, 2002c: 2).

In terms of the application of the plan of action at national level, the case of the US is representative of the patterns that have been reproduced so far across the society of states: a new agency, the Interagency Working Group on Food Security (IWG) was formed in 1996 for the implementation of the summit commitments. It is co-chaired by officials from the Department of State, the Department of Agriculture and the Agency for International Development. However, the IWG has proven not to be an effective governance mechanism for achieving the summit hunger reduction goal, since it has no authority to make binding decisions on programme policy or to hold agencies accountable for achieving the World Food Summit goal. Neither a resource plan nor a budget commitment has been put in place for implementing the action plan. Their absence has led to the conclusion that there is a gap between the language the governments use to describe the importance of food security and the actual government response to the problem (Taylor and Tick, 2001: 3, 4).

There is the question whether the summit was an expression of genuine political will or a forum in which public admission of dissent would be difficult. Besides the scepticism provoked by the low level of legalisation of this agreement, 'many people involved in the summit and the development of the action plan believe the process has fostered positive dialogue about food security among government agencies and stakeholders' (Taylor and Tick, 2001: 1).

Poverty-related summits

The agreements on 'poverty' are not as explicit as the hunger-related ones, and they form part of wider agendas such as sustainable development or the 'Millennium goals'. However, it is possible to extract the degree of legalisation within those agreements.

Obligation

These agreements establish a series of commitments at both national and international levels concentrated mainly in the Millennium Development Declaration, which consists of eight goals that comprise 18 targets. By the end of 2004, every developing country will produce at least one report; this is a challenging commitment, since it will mean that many countries will have to build statistical capacity. However, underlying the declarations is the idea that no general solution can be provided to eliminate poverty. These agreements are more an international reaction to a pressing problem than a firm commitment.

Precision

The targets are very clear: 'we agree to halve, by the year 2015, the proportion of the world's people whose income is less than $1 a day' (UN, 2002a: 3). However, the practicalities of this target are not as precise (even if it has been calculated that there are at the moment 1.2 billion people in extreme poverty). The targets defined in the eight goals of the Millennium Declaration are measured through 48 indicators such as the poverty gap ratio, the proportion of population below the minimum level of dietary energy, or average tariffs on agricultural products. Some of the targets are given as quantified, time-bound values for specific indicators. However, for other goals, lack of reliable data limits the ability either to define the target or to monitor progress.

The degree of precision affects also the format of the plan of action, where the statements are relaxed, with room for a great deal of flexibility when interpreting them. For example, the section on poverty (in relation to trade) in the Johannesburg Plan of Implementation states that the aim is to: 'Enhance the capacities of developing countries to benefit from liberalised trade opportunities, through international cooperation and measures aimed at improving productivity, commodity diversification and competitiveness' (UN, 2002a: 31).

Delegation

The UN Department of Economic and Social Affairs is in charge of coordinating the reporting on progress towards the goals of the Millennium Declaration, but there is no mechanism responsible for implementation. There will also be a global report on the Millennium Development goals in 2005 to assess the current progress. The looseness of this agreement in terms of its legally binding dimension has been highlighted by the UN Secretary-General, Kofi Annan, who asked UNDP to be the 'scorekeeper' and 'campaign manager' for the Millennium Development goals, by spreading awareness within the system and across the world (IFAD, 2002: 3).

Another delegation mechanism specifically related to the Summits on Sustainable Development is the Commission on Sustainable Development (CSD). This was created after the Rio Summit in 1992 to monitor and report on the implementation of the agreements. It has no capacity of enforcement. This also suggests that 'poverty' has no centralised accountability mechanism; since it is included in wider agendas (Millennium Declaration and Sustainable Summits), it belongs also to their respective delegation mechanisms.

* * *

The low level of legalisation associated with these agreements raises questions about their purpose. It has been noted, however, that 'legalisation may change the nature of domestic and transnational politics in participating countries ... legalisation could create transnational communities of support for legalised agreements in specific issue-areas' (Goldstein *et al.*, 2000: 399). Even if those commitments are not subject to binding implementation, they can create a certain international consensus and facilitate normative compromise in the areas that need to be tackled to solve the problem of hunger. On this line of argument, 'legalisation' might have a direct effect on the evolution of international norms (ibid.). Certainly that is the case with these agreements; they influence each other and reiterate each other's aims. For example, there are references to hunger in the Millennium Declaration, and requests for reforms in trade are made in both the World Food Summit and the poverty-related declarations. These concerns were also taken into consideration in the WTO Doha ministerial meeting and, even if the result is not binding, there is certainly something happening to the foundations of the WTO in relation to agriculture. In fact, there is now a round of negotiations that deal with concerns expressly regarding agricultural trade. As the WTO's deputy Director General asserted, 'bringing the negotiations on agriculture to a successful conclusion is the key contribution the WTO can make towards achieving global food security' (Mendoza, 2002: 1).

The mechanism of the legalisation process affects also the way in which the elements of the triad hunger–poverty–international trade relate to each other. As already noted, the claims of different thematic summits are interconnected. In addition, there is a tendency in both hunger and poverty declarations to point to international trade as the key issue (of the three) in which institutional reforms must be carried out. The message is that by moving the trade issue forward, the other two will follow, because legalisation is more developed in the WTO than in the other two areas. Non-binding commitments such as the Doha Declaration, even if theoretical to a great extent, can nevertheless influence areas where agreements are more binding.

The counter-argument to this approach to legalisation claims that post-1945 international law consists only of declared goals and ideals and is closer to moral philosophy than to positive law. It is what Dorothy Jones calls the 'declaratory tradition' (Jones, 1992: 42–57) and what Robert Jackson attributes to the phenomenon of 'politicising morality' in today's world politics (Jackson, 2000: 128). According to Jackson, signing declarations means adopting ideals that are laudable on almost any view, but not binding on anyone; therefore, they are not difficult to sign up to and act as good public relations (ibid.: 129).

The review of the three case studies considered in this chapter supports Robert Jackson's view in the sense that the goals regarding hunger, poverty and agricultural trade to which the states committed themselves are not being met, despite receiving apparently overwhelming support. However, aspects of these declarations are moved into areas with higher levels of commitment, such as the new measures in the Generalised System of Preferences, or the fact that the implications of the current structure of international agricultural trade are now at the centre of the WTO's worries. As Jackson himself says at a different stage of his argument: 'There is no doubt but that some international declarations have entered into the international conduct of states and in so doing have significantly affected the character and modus operandi of international ethics and international law' (Jackson, 2000: 125).

4 International trade and the options for eradicating hunger

The previous chapter showed how the connection between international trade and hunger (via poverty) has been widely acknowledged in international society. Several steps, especially in the normative arena, have been taken. However, despite the various commitments, the problem of hunger persists and the way to eradicate it is highly contested. This chapter assesses competing options that have been formulated. It draws on the analysis of hunger provided in Chapter 1 and the actions taken by international society discussed in Chapter 3. The focus is on how the international dimension of poverty is linked to the global trading system generally and to agricultural trade in particular. International trade and poverty are connected by the principles of availability of food for purchase and individual capacity to afford it, both of which have a direct impact on hunger. Within the global market, agricultural trade has a significant impact on economic growth in developing countries, and its dynamics affect the way in which food is produced, distributed and priced.

There are three options available for handling the trading leg of the hunger–poverty–trade triangle: maintain the current liberal trading system, keep the existing system while introducing reforms within it, and bring about a radical change in the system. After analysing them I will identify the one that corresponds best with Vincent's claims for reforms in the economic structure.

Behind the three options stand the main currents of thought on the international political economy. The chapter begins by introducing the liberal theory of international trade. The next three sections spell out the options identified above. Each section is divided into two parts: 'description', which collects the arguments underpinning each option, and 'assessment', which evaluates the viability of each option. This chapter analyses the practical viability of subsistence as a basic right to be supported by international society, and prepares the ground for the overall conclusion on the implications of Vincent's project to introduce basic rights into the society of states.

Theoretical background

This section is organised around economic liberalism, since it represents the nature of the current system. Its historical counterparts – Nationalism, then Marxism, and more recently the Green Movement – will be explained in relation to it.

Economic Liberalism asserts that society should use its resources to maximise wealth and it considers that the market is the most effective means to reach this objective. The price mechanism is the source of mutual gain. Liberal economic theory is committed to a free market and minimal state intervention (laissez-faire, meaning 'leave it alone'), although the optimum relationship between state and market varies substantially within liberal thinking (Gilpin, 1987: 27, 45). However, 'the role of the state became to institute and safeguard the self-regulating market' (Ruggie, 1982: 386). Given the intrinsic value that liberalism ascribes to the individual, the principles of a free market also translate into a political structure that emphasises individual freedoms (Tooze, 1992: 235).

Liberal theory is rooted in Adam Smith's *Wealth of Nations* (1776), extended later in David Ricardo's *Principles of Political Economy and Taxation* (1817). Smith based his theory on the principle of absolute advantage, through which nations should specialise in what they could do best in order to become wealthy by channelling their products into a free trade market. Therefore, economic growth is generated by the division of labour in combination with the market. These principles were expanded later by Ricardo, who created the cornerstone of today's liberal trade doctrine: the law of 'comparative advantage' linked to the benefits of specialisation. He demonstrated that international trade is promoted by the relative cost of goods, which means that countries must specialise in those products that they can produce most cheaply in order to obtain the biggest gains in the market. Therefore, not only is absolute advantage in the production of a good enough reason for a country to enter the international trade system, so too is specialisation in those products with the lowest comparative cost (Gilpin, 1987: 175–8).

The next crucial step in the evolution of liberal theory is the work of the Swedish economists Heckscher and Ohlin (the H-O model, dating from the 1930s). The H-O model asserted that the comparative advantage of a country in international trade comes from the combination of at least three factors of production: land, labour and capital. Comparative advantage is determined by national differences in these 'factor endowments'. The H-O model continues to provide the most accurate account of inter-industry trade (the exchange of manufactured goods for commodities), and the most relevant theory to explain most of the North–South trade in the current economic system, where some countries have advantage in capital, others in land and others in the availability of cheap labour (Kaempfer *et al.*, 1995: 99).

Nationalism claims, by contrast, that economic activity should be governed by the interests of the state, and therefore international trade must accommodate economic protectionism. It emphasises that markets function in a world of competitive states whose national interests can clash. So, economics is a tool of politics, whose primary goal is increasing state power (Jackson and Sorensen, 1999: 178, 179).

Although the roots of nationalism can be traced back to the mercantilist writers of the seventeenth century, the key figure for today's understanding of nationalism is perhaps Alexander Hamilton. In work published in 1791, he argued for a theory of comparative advantage and considered economics to be subordinate to the process of state building, while identifying national power with the development of manufacturing. These ideas, initiated by Hamilton, led to the birth of the German Historical School in the nineteenth century, which criticised classical liberal theories for promoting Britain's position of economic advantage brought about by its technological and industrial development. Members of the German school argued that a true free trade international economy would be possible only when trading partners were equally developed. They advocated the development of the internal infrastructure of the country, together with the establishment of high tariff barriers to protect national industry and the creation of a strong state. This assessment has been adopted today in the critiques of North–South trade relations (Gilpin, 1987: 181–2).

Current supporters of this movement claim that free trade continues to favour the most industrially advanced economies while exposing other economies to the instability of world markets. They argue that free trade undermines national autonomy and weakens state control over the economy. The debate on free trade versus protectionism provides the core of the disputes between liberals and nationalists. Liberals argue that international trade should be conducted by private actors largely free of government control (Moon, 2000: 33). Liberalism privileges consumer welfare and the maximisation of global efficiency creating the chance of benefits for all, under the principle of 'the greater the amount of trade, the greater the economic specialisation and the greater the wealth generated' (Tooze, 1992: 235). However, nationalists see transnational corporations as extensions of state power, playing an important role as foreign policy instruments. They favour protectionism among countries as an end in itself in the internal construction of wealth and power, since economic dependence on other states should be avoided as much as possible. Liberals, despite their theoretical rejection of state intervention, accept protectionism as a temporary measure to protect weak economies before they can jump into the system of free trade.

In historical terms, the liberal international economic system divides into two phases: during the first, from the repeal of the Corn Laws in 1846 until the trade wars of the 1930s, Britain dominated. The second phase, led by the United States, crystallised after the Second World War in reaction to the devastating experience of the high protectionist measures imposed during the interwar years. This phase was defined by the institutionalisation of three pillars of the liberal economic system: the International Monetary Fund, the World Bank and GATT, known as the Bretton Woods system (McKinlay and Little, 1986: 91).

The new system was based on the traditional liberal connection between economic growth and international peace, and it institutionalised the means to regulate international trade and avoid the uncoordinated national policies that could threaten those values. It aimed to avoid the economic mistakes made during the interwar period that had choked international trade (Jackson, J., 2000: 36–7). The theoretical background to the new system is best defined by the H-O model discussed earlier, although with the introduction of an important modification in its concept of comparative advantage, which is now considered a product of corporate competition as well as state policies. This emphasis on the state as an actor is essential in current liberal thinking. 'The state is the primary focus of political economy in a larger state–society complex. The state manages the constraints of the domestic and international domains through domestic policy-making and intergovernmental bargaining, the one being intimately embedded in the other' (Stubbs and Underhill, 2000: 6).

The postwar economic order is defined by Ruggie as 'embedded liberalism', a term which refers to the acceptance in theory of the principle of free trade, while in practice the market counted on high levels of state intervention: 'unlike the economic nationalism of the thirties, it would be multilateral in character; unlike the liberalism of the gold standard and free trade, its multilateralism would be predicated upon domestic interventionism' (Ruggie, 1982: 393).

The biggest step forward in the process of trade liberalisation was made by the Kennedy Round (1962–7), which produced tariff cuts of 35 per cent on 60,000 products followed by negotiations of item-by-item exceptions. However, the round yielded much less progress in the products exported by most poor nations, mainly agricultural and textile goods (Moon, 2000: 95).

The progress of decolonisation in the 1960s brought a change in North–South economic relations, through the expansion of development plans with the US as the biggest lender (Thomas, 1997: 453). The gap between the poor and the rich became more obvious in the 1960s and 1970s and was criticised by dependency theorists who saw it as part of the growth that Western countries were experiencing. This political and economic situation evolved into the developing countries' campaign for a New International Economic Order in the 1970s (discussed in Chapter 2). Behind the demands for an NIEO was an understanding of world order influenced by Marxism.

Marxism presupposes that 'throughout history human beings have acted on the physical world within exploitative class-based societies in which the mass of humanity has been compelled to labour for the enrichment of others' (Linklater, 1996: 123). Marx rejected the liberal view that the economy is a site with benefits for all and saw it as a ground of class exploitation. This corresponds with aspects of the mercantilist view, but applied to relations among classes instead of states. When translated into international political economy, this understanding means that states are driven by ruling-class interests with a bourgeoisie whose members dominate the means of production and, because classes are not confined to a state's borders, class conflict expanding around the world is intrinsic to capitalism (Jackson and Sorensen, 1999: 185).

Since its origins, this doctrine has experienced an intense metamorphosis with three contested traditions stemming from it. First was Marxism-Leninism or Soviet Marxism, which provided the counterpart to liberalism, dividing the world until the late 1980s. Second came Western Marxism or classical Marxism, which grew inside the advanced capitalist states as an oppositional tendency, claiming to be a descendent of Marx via Luxemburg and Gramsci. Third was 'third-worldist neo-Marxism', which is defined by the theories of dependency and world systems (Brown, 1992: 227). It is in the last interpretation that the NIEO took root. Both dependency and world systems theories are based on the older doctrine of imperialism, argued by Lenin, through the law of uneven development, and both deny that capitalism has the developmental impact that Western Marxism attributed to it.

Dependency theory promoted the vision that the international economic structure was divided between a dominant rich core and a dependent periphery, where the mechanisms that facilitate prosperity in the core provoke underdevelopment in the periphery: 'The combined effect of concentration on trade partners and commodity concentration is a dependency of the Periphery on the Centre. Since the Periphery usually has a much smaller GNP, the trade between them is a much higher percentage of the GNP for the Periphery ... [therefore] the Periphery becomes vulnerable to fluctuations in demands and prices' (Galtung, 1991b: 299). Wallerstein's world systems theory adds a third element, the semi-periphery, which is needed 'to make a capitalist world run smoothly' (Wallerstein, 1991: 305). However, the new strength of this layer has led to a 'further weakening of the peripheral areas' (ibid.: 316), while challenging the hegemony of the core.

From the mid-1970s onwards, another current against liberal thinking emerged: the Green Movement. Its political origins are identified with the publication of *Limits to Growth* by the Club of Rome (1972). This report documented how the world was running out of resources to feed people and provide raw material to sustain the dominant industrialised structure. It argued that various facets of the relationship between humans and nature need to be restructured in order to enjoy a secure future. This view has policy implications for the conception of world order, to be outlined later in this section. Although Green Thought in politics can be dated to the

1970s, it did not proliferate until the end of the Cold War (Pettiford and Steans, 2001: 187–90).

The proposal for the implementation of a New International Economic Order failed, but the elements of inequality and criticism that highlighted this debate were transferred into several other agendas. In 1974 the first hunger-related summit (the World Food Conference) took place, and was the start of a series of progressive commitments on the subject that reached their peak in 1996 with the Rome Declaration, as reviewed in Chapter 3. In 1972 the first conference on poverty and the environment was held, and marked the beginning of the Summits on Sustainable Development. In 1971 the GATT provided legal backing for the Special and Differential Treatment (S&D) clause, the system of preferences for developing countries, that has continued its expansion until today's negotiations on agriculture.

The end of the 1970s saw not only the failure of the NIEO, but also other events that hampered the progress of markets: the price of world energy experienced a massive increase and Newly Industrialised Countries (NICs) intensified their competition. The increase in oil prices caused the dollar to rise sharply and competition in energy trade among nations to increase; higher import prices put the developing countries under considerable strain (Thomas, 1997: 454–7). At the same time, rapid technology advances in Japan and other NICs such as South Korea and Brazil produced a large number of manufactures for export, which threatened the economies of other developed countries. As a result, protectionist measures came back strongly into the liberal economic scheme to safeguard the standards of the most advanced economies at a time when there was a relative decline in the competitiveness of the US economy and when the growth of the European Community was based on the protection of its internal market.

After the Second World War and until the 1980s, efforts were concentrated on eliminating tariff barriers that constituted the 'Old Protectionism' associated with the economic collapse of the 1930s. However, other non-tariff protectionist measures (domestic legislation, subsidies, and so on) grew within the economic system, creating the New Protectionism in the 1980s. New Protectionism is based on the economic nationalist ideas outlined above and is in tension with the liberal principles that create the free trade framework; this phenomenon is an aspect of 'embedded liberalism'. This controversial interaction between the two sets of principles has modified liberal thinking in relation to state intervention: 'Liberals are more apt than in the past to stress the role of state policy in the creation of comparative advantage, but they also emphasise its inherent dangers and warn against the overall efficiency losses of economic conflict' (Gilpin, 1987: 223). However, the liberal commitment to free trade remains very different from the idea of economic nationalism, as will be exemplified later with the case of agricultural trade.

The next turning point was the end of the Cold War, with the triumph of liberalism across the world. Soon afterwards, in 1994, the international liberal framework experienced a renewal of free trade values with the substitution of the GATT by the WTO, although two sections of the new agreement, services and agriculture, remained highly protected. They have since then been the subject of critique and reformulation due to their connections with poverty and hunger, as has been documented in Chapter 3 and will be assessed in the remaining parts of this chapter.

* * *

The next three sections of this chapter reflect these tensions through an analysis of the three options regarding international trade in connection with the right to food. Since the focus of this chapter is 'international society', these three options build on the idea that the state is the focus of decision making in the international trade system.

The *first option* chooses to maintain the current system: liberal doctrine mixed with strong levels of protectionism in the dynamics of international trade. This trend claims to evolve in a positive direction in terms of its implications for the number of hungry people in the world; it praises the way the system works and trusts its own dynamics for the improvement of poverty and hunger. This view is portrayed by WTO representatives.

The *second option* favours the current liberal set-up but criticises the protectionist elements that benefit the richest part of the international trade system to the detriment of the poorest. It claims that hunger is a pressing problem and can be solved by the introduction of reforms in international trade mechanisms in combination with temporary aid measures. This option is advocated by several reformist voices within international governmental associations, international agreements and NGOs. These two liberal options also have elements of nationalism. The first option favours New Protectionism, where developed countries determine the norms that protect their markets. The second option advocates the elimination of protectionist elements that unbalance the system by creating a gap between the rich and the poor. At the same time, it feeds on nationalist measures by claiming temporary protection of developing markets, but without abandoning the international liberal structure. Other positions fall within this category, such as 'environmentalism', which accepts the existing political and economic structures of world politics, but pursues changes within them (Paterson, 1996: 252). These are not pursued here, since this section aims only to locate, historically and ideologically, the main tensions that frame the current international trade system and define the three most debated options that can tackle hunger.

The *third option* criticises the overall liberal framework, arguing that it favours only the strong. The main theoretical bodies of thought behind this movement are Nationalism, Marxism and the Greens. The reasons why radical economic nationalists oppose the global market have been outlined above. However, it is important to note that not all forms of nationalism oppose the international market (even if they oppose the free trade message). As indicated above, nationalism can support the idea of an international economy as long as it strengthens national wealth and autonomy. However, this assessment precipitates arguments for both types of nationalists, those who support global expansion and those who want to close their frontiers to the global market, believing that it benefits only highly developed and protected economies to the detriment of weaker economies. The anti-globalisation nationalist movement bases its argument on the latter position, paving the way for a 'food sovereignty' approach.

This alternative also takes elements from the neo-Marxist and Green movements. Marxists see the current trade system in terms of increasing inequality and exploitation that serves the interests of the transnational capitalist class. For Marxists, class struggle and economic exploitation are the main problems of international political economy. What was imperialism and colonisation has been transformed into economic globalisation led by giant transnational corporations. The Greens share these concerns about the dangers of social alienation and the concentration of corporate power at global level; however, they differ from the Marxists in criticising globalisation from a 'cultural' point of view, asserting that the global market creates social dislocation and destroys local community life (Helleiner, 2000: 60–7). Their other major point of divergence is the nature-based approach of Green Thought, which rejects the current development strategies for encouraging economic growth while threatening the survival both of humankind and of the global ecosystem.

In their demands for structural changes, there is no unique Green perspective on world order. One influential strand advocates the decentralisation of power to small-scale communities (Pettiford and Steans, 2001: 188). These Greens support small-scale markets and promote traditional economic activities within a local community context. The other dominant Green alternative goes beyond the community-based order and accepts the role of the state as a negotiator at the global level. These Greens would like to see the existing global economic institutions (WTO, IMF, World Bank) change into bodies that help to shield local vulnerable communities from global markets and transnational corporations (Helleiner, 2000: 60–7). In general, the Greens have played a leading role in organising 'The Other Economic Summit' that has shadowed the annual G-7 Summit over the past decade (TOES, 2002: 2).

Maintaining the current liberal trading system

This option favours the current liberal trade system while making improvements within the limits of its own dynamics. That is, it favours moving towards free trade without distortions, which in turn would improve access to food by the poorest countries as discussed earlier. This option is based on the principle that there is no need for major structural changes within international society. However, the problem with this option is that improvements are eroded by struggles within the system, such as new protectionist measures that inhibit the free trade objective.

Description

What are the effects of international trade on the poverty and hunger levels in developing countries? According to this option, countries benefit from their comparative advantage by 'moving resources from low productivity to high productivity uses' (Stiglitz, 2001: 4). As a consequence, international trade helps poor countries to catch up with rich ones because 'increased trade is a "win–win"; faster growth in poorer countries does not come at the expense of rich countries' (Moore, 2000: 1). Developing countries with liberalised economies (and free of conflicts) grew at a general average of 1.5 per cent a year during the 1990s (statistics given in Chapter 1). This growth is not only in absolute terms for the country as a whole, but also in terms of the poor, who benefit from more opportunities to exploit their productive potential while obtaining higher incomes in the exporting industry (Bread for the World, 1998: 1). However, these growth figures exclude the poorest countries (mainly located in Sub-Saharan Africa), which saw a decline in their exports due to a failure to adapt traditional markets to the new demands of the system. Although international factors have been used to explain why the poorest countries have not been able to increase their exports (discussed in the next section), this option maintains that decline in exports is caused mainly by the internal infrastructure of the state.

Either way, advocates of this option see a correlation between liberalisation and growth (or vice versa: lack of export activity limits growth) and support the idea that international food trade provides food security by making products available at competitive prices and by setting incentives for those countries where a certain product can be produced more efficiently. This view insists that the food security of a country does not lie just in the local production of food but in a multilateral trading system with a diversity of countries supplying food products (Mendoza, 2002: 2). 'Prosperity of developing and least developed countries will mean greater growth in the world as a whole, provided this is accompanied by global market liberalisation ... food trade is vital for ensuring food security. Without trade, countries would have to rely exclusively on their own production, overall incomes would be lower, the choice of goods would be far less. Food trade also has an important role in stabilising supplies and prices. Without trade, domestic fluctuations would have to be borne by adjustments in consumption and stocks' (Cairns Group, 1999: 2).

Advocates of the current system insist that trade has proved to be one of the most effective tools to foster development during the past 40 years.

They stress that the system can provide for preferential treatment to those countries that are disadvantaged. While Article 1 of the GATT prohibits any kind of discrimination, in 1971 a waiver from Article 1 was approved by the member states, creating the legal framework for the Generalised System of Preferences (GSP) under which industrialised countries can grant autonomous trade preferences to developing countries. For example, the European Union has 7,000 products under GSP, of which 3,300 are classified as non-sensitive and 3,700 as sensitive. Non-sensitive products enjoy duty-free access, while sensitive products benefit just from a tariff reduction. In the case of the US, there are 4,600 products under the GSP agreements (Trade and Development, 2002: 1–4). Moreover, both trading giants have created further exemptions in their international trade schemes through the AGOA and EBA plans. In the post-Uruguay Round period, LDC exports to the EU, Canada and Japan that receive high preferences have grown by about 8 per cent yearly on average, outpacing those that face medium or high tariffs (World Bank, 2002b: 54).

This pro-current trade system position feeds on the success of the Doha meeting even if Cancun did not deliver the essential agreements. After the collapse of the Seattle talks, all eyes turned to Doha. The validity of the current international trade system was at stake. Failure to launch new trade talks would have meant that countries were less likely to resist protectionist demands from their domestic lobbies. It would also undermine the efficacy of the WTO as the trade institution (Schott, 2002: 4). Advocates of the current system stress that it is the only proven path out of poverty; it has created opportunities by allowing resources to flow and raising standards of living. Contrary to the criticisms that point the finger at trade for benefiting only the richest, defenders of the system assert that growth of GDP has been accompanied by a general improvement in the population's standard of living. These studies suggest that openness to trade leads to a decline in absolute poverty and they dismiss the idea that it increases inequality (Larson, 2002: 2). An OECD report documents that while 1.2 billion people still live in poverty, the rise in living standards associated with a more liberal trading system has played an important part in lifting about 3 billion people out of poverty after the institutionalisation of the system in 1947 (OECD, 1998: 24). The volume of world trade today is about 16 times what it was in 1950, and the average world GDP level has experienced a constant growth. For example, during the period 1985–96 world GDP rose three times faster than in the preceding decade, and nearly twice as fast as in the 1960s.

In the 1990s world trade registered an annual increase of 6.3 per cent in the volume of global merchandise. Developing countries as a whole increased their presence in world markets, although details behind these headlines reveal divergent trends. For example, among LDCs (mainly dependent on agriculture) trade experienced a sharp contraction, except in those LDCs with oil exports such as Equatorial Guinea, Sudan and Yemen.

For advocates of the current system these figures show a general success, the problem being located in a specific area (Sub-Saharan Africa) and subject to changes during the next decade, since reforming efforts have been started. In fact, advocates claim that the Uruguay Round Agreement on Agriculture (1995) marked an important step and allowed the participation in the international market of products that were traditionally sheltered. In addition, a wide range of non-tariff barriers were abolished (including quantitative import restrictions). However, tariff peaks (percentages in excess of 15 per cent) still exist in most processed products, although they are less common in unprocessed fruits and vegetables and in tropical commodities that the rich countries do not produce. On average, countries that have participated intensely in the international market have grown faster and accelerated poverty reduction (World Bank, 2002b: 44–6).

Defenders of the current system consider a proof of its success to be the fact that 32 countries have joined the WTO since 1986, while the queue wanting to enter continues to grow (OECD, 1998: 19–26).

There are, however, concerns that the current multilateral system erodes sovereignty. In response, this position argues the reverse: 'Trade liberalisation forms part of the overall strategy to maintain and even strengthen a country's capacity to determine its own future by improving its competitiveness and income by making it less vulnerable to external shocks' (OECD, 1998: 14). Therefore, according to this perspective, national governments embrace international rules to enhance their national interests; once this sovereign decision is taken, they are required to abide by such rules. When multilateral rules create restrictions on national government, they are accepted because they further sovereign member countries' mutual interest. Multilateral trade rules impose agreed criteria over specific national rules and countries accept them in exchange for the benefits they bring.

However, the maintenance of the current system depends on establishing a balance among the tensions created by its own internal problems. A review by the World Bank of the experience to date on the implementation of the Uruguay Round Agreement on Agriculture (URAA) indicates that further trade liberalisation has been difficult to achieve due to a series of obstacles in both developed and developing countries. Ingco (2002: 3) identifies the following obstacles:

- Significant trade and domestic policy distortions remain in national, regional and global trade. High agricultural protectionism continues to restrict world agricultural trade even after the URAA. The average tariff on agricultural products is 45 per cent in OECD countries and 20 per cent in developing countries, while for non-agricultural products the average is 5 per cent.
- High tariff barriers and tariff escalation remain in many countries: this level of protection varies among countries and across commodities.

- Levels of domestic support and protection have increased in recent years: although these levels declined when the URAA was first implemented, domestic support has increased in some countries as a response to low world prices since 1998. A recent example is the new US farm bill. The EU, even if it introduces the EBA programme, spends US$114.5 billion for producer support.
- High levels of export subsidies continue to distort world markets for key commodities: although the URAA places limits on export subsidies for individual commodities, it also allows some flexibility. It is of that flexibility that countries take advantage.

To keep the momentum of the present system, it is necessary to juggle the agreements for further trade liberalisation with internal protectionist measures. A balance must be struck to ensure that domestic production survives the expansion of trade. In terms of the problem of hunger, the current structure celebrates its contribution to the reduction in the number of hungry people by 20 million during the 1990s; this is considered a success bearing in mind the population growth. However, estimates suggest that on existing levels of reduction (2.5 million a year), it will take over a century to achieve the WFS target to bring down the number of undernourished to about 400 million.

Assessment

This option suggests that the existing economic structures will slowly solve the problem of hunger, but that the targets in the international agreements will be met much later than the time frame set by the states. This long-term strategy will work, however, only if the system survives the internal tensions between the protectionist and liberal elements. This is reflected, for example, in the rhetoric of the Doha Declaration and the growing protectionism in agriculture.

The EU agreed at Doha to reduce its direct support to farmers, although it later insisted that its commitment was subject to its trading partners applying similar measures. Hence, the US farm bill was a setback in this process, as was the lack of commitment from the European Union to cut subsidies, even after the reform of redistribution of the Common Agricultural Policy (CAP) approved in 2003. The CAP affects developing countries in two ways: it undermines producers by dumping subsidised goods on their local markets and it reduces the potential for developing countries to export farm products to European markets (Green, 2002: 3).

The US farm bill, signed into law by President Bush on 13 May 2002, introduced a contradiction between that country's demands for trade liberalisation abroad and its own national politics (Murphy, 2002: 2). The impact of the bill on the economies of developing countries has been criticised by both governmental and non-governmental sources. The member countries of the South American trade group, Mercosur, as well as the EU and Australia, have openly challenged the legality of this agreement in relation to WTO rules. They unanimously considered it a 'big step backward', and the World Bank called 13 May 2002 'a sad day for world farmers' (ICTSD, 2002: 1–4).

These measures cause a great deal of damage to the world's poor. Even if their global economic repercussions for poor countries have not yet been calculated, they have a clear impact on the production of developing countries, whose foodstuffs cannot compete with those of highly subsidised countries. For example, initial predictions forecast that Argentina and Brazil will suffer combined losses of some US$3.9 billion per year resulting from a drop in their exports of commodities such as soya beans, cotton and cereals (ICTSD, 2002: 1). These two protectionist mechanisms also have repercussions for the conditions of the international market which is flooded by those products through the dumping mechanism. This makes it more difficult for Third World countries to reduce their tariffs as part of their own process of liberalisation.

The tensions between the EU and the US, together with the high protectionist elements of other countries such as Japan, have a considerable degree of influence on the way in which the international system works. Sometimes it is the decision of an influential country or group of countries (international community) that freezes the wider process of liberalisation or determines its depth according to their interests. As the FAO's Director General has put it, 'national governments have an important role to play in reducing the severe distortions in global agricultural markets and establishing a more equitable international system for agriculture' (Diouf, 2001a: 1). Furthermore, a study carried out by the OECD has concluded that: 'the reluctance of some industrialised countries to support calls for further trade and investment liberalisation often forms part of a broader reaction and resistance to the far reaching changes in technology, firm conduct, work patterns, employment prospects, income distribution, intensified competitive conditions or role of the government, that are commonly attributed to the process of globalisation' (OECD, 1998: 16).

Developed countries' tariffs and subsidies reduce potential economic growth in developing countries. The losses amount to US$20 billion, equivalent to 40 per cent of aid in 1998 (CI, 2000a: 2). At the same time, these protectionist measures impose high costs on citizens in developed countries through taxes and price increases in the products they purchase. The cost to consumers in OECD countries has been estimated to be as much as US$300 billion per annum (OECD, 1998: 11). For example, the EU's CAP has been calculated to cost an average family of four an indirect amount of around US$1,500 a year in artificially higher prices; moreover, subsidies paid directly to farmers cost the taxpayer US$100 per head (ibid.: 93). In addition to this, implementing WTO obligations carries a cost that was not properly addressed at the time of the Uruguay Round. For example, the cost of implementing three Uruguay Round agreements is US$150 million, an amount that exceeds the annual budget for development of several least developed countries (CI, 2000a: 2).

In terms of the global growth in the standard of living, critics of the current system argue that while GDP growth statistics might mean a good deal to economists or to the elites of developing countries, they do not say much about self-sufficient villages. In fact, the majority of the research on the effects of trade liberalisation so far concentrates on aggregate national export levels and GDP, rather than on its impact on the lives of poor people. This is the case of the small farmers that the second option will consider.

Sustainability of hunger reduction under the current structure is dependent on the impact of a series of decisions on the internal dynamics of the system. Given the recent tensions between liberalisation and protectionism, continued reduction is not guaranteed. These intrinsic weaknesses of the system question the sustainability of the liberal mechanism, with concerns about instability and inequality. Instability comes from the management of the increasing liberalisation of the world economy and inequality arises from the disadvantaged position of most Third World states. Underlying these features is the tension between vulnerability and efficiency that runs through the liberal set-up (Buzan *et al.*, 1998: 97, 99). The combination of fears stemming from this account suggests the possibility of the system falling into crisis because of structural instability, increasing protectionist reactions or the heightening of existing inequalities among other possibilities (ibid., 1998: 98). This argument is supported by historical examples such as the Great Depression, the international debt crisis in the early 1980s, and the financial collapse in Asia during the late 1990s.

The case study analysed here reflects these internal problems of the system: the disputes around agricultural trade liberalisation are a central cause of instability, which has already provoked the collapse of the Seattle ministerial meeting in 1999 and, as Vincent pointed out, threaten the legitimacy of the international trade structure. Further controversies have gained increasing importance during the different phases of the agricultural negotiation process, and the recent farm bill has fuelled the international debate. As remarked above, it is still too early to assess the overall consequences of these measures, which intensify the degree of uncertainty surrounding them. Therefore, these elements suggest that the current system might not be able to maintain the status quo because of backsliding, but also because of the risk of a crash precipitated by internal contradictions.

* * *

Despite these criticisms, advocates of the current system assert the positive role played globally by international trade in reducing poverty and hunger, considering also the growth of population in absolute numbers. As documented in Chapter 1, the absolute numbers of undernourished have fallen over the past two decades, despite an increase in population of 1,600 million people which has taken place mostly in developing countries, precisely where the problem of hunger is mainly located. However, taking 1980, 1990, 1995 and 1999 as benchmarks in looking at population growth, the trend is declining, although still within the expectation of a strong increase (from the current 6 billion to 9 billion in 2030). However, it is too early to establish whether this pattern will be maintained in the next few years and how it will affect the proportional figures for hunger reduction. Although increases in population are a factor in defining a country's performance, they are not totally determining, as some of the examples given in Chapter 1 reveal, in cases where countries with high population growth have been able to reduce the number of undernourished.

The net reduction in the number of people defined as hungry (by 20 million in the 1990s) does not meet the heads of states' commitment to halve the numbers by 2015, nor does it satisfy Vincent's concerns about basic rights.

Maintaining the existing system while introducing reforms

While not abandoning existing economic structures, this option presses for a number of specific reforms aimed at accelerating the solution to the hunger problem. These reforms extend beyond the internal vulnerabilities of the current system addressed in the previous section. They offer alternative strategies for managing tensions within the liberalisation process in order to redress the inequality of developing countries. These reforms build on the strengths of the system and aim to overcome its weaknesses, without precipitating a major crisis or even a crash.

Description

The reforms have been proposed on several fronts: trade policies, creation of a Development Box, reform of the Marrakesh Decision and sub-global arrangements.

Equitable trade policies

This approach calls for a global reform of agricultural trade complemented by the construction of sustainable agricultural systems in developing countries, to include the elimination of market-distorting export subsidies, export credits and direct payments and tariffs in developed countries. It criticises the current trade structure embodied by the WTO.

From this perspective, the position of poor countries within the WTO differs from that of richer ones, placing them at a disadvantage within the world trade system. Factors seen by the WTO as strengths – free trade, equitable access to rule-based trading systems, democratic principles and benefits of the WTO for the world's poor – have all provoked fierce criticism.

The WTO may claim to support free trade, but its critics offer a scenario where rich countries and corporations tend to protect their markets rather than liberalising them. As a result, 'the winners are those who can create monopoly price situations, maintain comparative advantage and deflect competitive pressures' (Smith and Patrick, 2000: 3). When translated into the policies that the WTO embodies, this means richer countries have liberalised those sectors in their interest, while sectors crucial for the development of poor countries, such as agriculture, remain highly protected.

Patents are also included in the principle of free trade. However, the Trade Related Intellectual Property Rights Agreement (TRIPs) does not recognise the rights of local communities to patent their indigenous knowledge, allowing it to be absorbed by foreign companies.

Similarly, the WTO claims to promote *equitable access to a rule-based trading system,* but critics attack both the rules of the system and the Dispute Settlement process. They point to rules that clearly benefit the richest countries to the detriment of the poorest. In sectors such as agriculture, developing countries are prohibited from establishing subsidies, while this is a practice dominant across the developed countries. Only 25 of the current WTO members are entitled to use export subsidies (Cairns Group, 1999: 1).

Regarding the Dispute Settlement mechanism, WTO provisions are 'binding on governments, and states that fail to bring their national laws into compliance with those WTO provisions face a wide range of trade sanctions' (Smith and Patrick, 2000: 4). The disputes are assigned to a panel of corporate bureaucrats and corporate lawyers, and access to their evidence is strictly limited. Given the costs that a selection of legal advisors required to defend the case would imply, poor countries usually do not pursue illegal measures which could potentially be illegal within the WTO framework. In fact, of the 117 cases brought before the WTO by 1999, the United States alone initiated more than 50 (ibid.: 4–5).

Critics also attack the claim that the *WTO is democratic.* In fact, the WTO allows each member country a single vote in order to guarantee a democratic approach to decision making. Nevertheless, developing countries' leaders in Seattle complained about the lack of democracy in the organisation, and this contributed to the breakdown of the negotiations. The G-15 also emphasises this need for the developing world to have a voice in the process of reforming the international system. It is a group of (now) 17 developing countries from Asia, Africa and Latin America that was set up to foster cooperation and provide input for other international groups, such as the World Trade Organisation and the Group of 7 rich industrialised nations (G15, 2002: 1–4). In April 2000, the G-77 (now 133 countries) held the South Summit in Havana. They focused on the concern that the South is 'collectively endangered' by the global economic system that has been constructed by the rich countries. The message of the summit was essentially that the forces of globalisation are enriching the West while sentencing the South to more misery. The summit asked for the establishment of international economic relations based on justice and equity and called for a reform of the international economic governance that makes it more democratic, more transparent and better attuned to solving the problems of development (Chomsky, 2000: 1–7). Essentially, this is the message that the G-20 brought to Cancun (as explained in Chapter 1) and resulting disputes with the established agenda caused the talks to collapse.

Critics blamed the richest members of the group (the Quad countries – the US, Canada, Japan and the EU) for this breakdown on the grounds that they reached agreements in secret meetings and used their political and economic strength to create consensus in favour of these agreements (Smith and Patrick, 2000: 5). The politics of agricultural subsidies illustrates this tactic; while the Agreement on Agriculture calls for the reduction of subsidies by between 20 per cent and 36 per cent, countries protect themselves using alternative measures. The United States and the European Union, for example, have created the 'Green Box' where certain support policies are excluded from any reduction agreement; this gives them the opportunity to maintain or even increase subsidies (CETIM, 1999: 3).

Finally, critics attack the WTO insistence that it *aims to benefit the world's poor*, both at the international level by improving the economic standards of poor countries and at the national level by raising their incomes. Critics focus on the gap in economic growth between rich and poor nations, and express a high degree of scepticism about the link between import liberalisation and economic performance. They dismiss the WTO's idea of 'openness' as the key to growth: 'The idea is not merely to be integrated into global commodity chains; it is to extract profit from your particular location in them ... to presume that these relationships [liberalisation and growth] hold universally represents a giant leap of faith in the face of mounting evidence to the contrary' (Smith and Patrick, 2000: 7).

A study produced by the international agencies IFAD, FAO and WFP, *Reducing Poverty and Hunger* (Rome, 2002) looks at the gap between the international agreements to eliminate hunger and poverty, and the specific action that has been taken both nationally and internationally. This report insists that the eradication of poverty and hunger is achievable, but it requires a series of measures that are not being translated into practice. The programme presupposes that the 2015 target can be reached within a sustainable development framework (CFS, 2003a: 1). As stated in Chapter 1, three-quarters of the poor in developing countries live in rural areas and the increasing numbers of the urban poor are affected by the crisis in the agricultural sector. Therefore, there is a general agreement that the agricultural sector has priority in developing countries to determine the future of both hunger and poverty.

As explained in Chapter 1, the relationship between hunger and poverty forms a vicious circle where extreme poverty is the root of hunger and simultaneously hunger causes poverty by creating a trap of low productivity; hunger reduces the capacity for physical activity and the ability to develop physically and mentally. Only well-nourished people can make use of their labour capacity to contribute to growth and development (FAO, 9/4/00n: 2). Fighting hunger is not simply a moral imperative from a basic rights perspective, but also a large economic benefit. It has been calculated that by meeting the WFS 2015 deadline, the value of those extra years of healthy life would amount US$120 billion per year. These earnings would come from agricultural development (both in production and in market infrastructure) that would expand the demand for goods and services, both domestically and internationally. Parallel calculations have been done by the World Health Organisation, which claims that hundreds of billions of dollars per year would be saved if the improvement of health and nutrition was met (FAO, 2002a: 3). The same logic would apply to the resources destined for international aid.

This view is based on the idea that while poverty reduction takes time, the hungry need immediate relief. The 'Reducing Poverty and Hunger' report (FAO, 18/4/02: 4) develops a twin-track strategy for the rapid reduction in poverty and hunger: on the one hand, the introduction of direct measures to provide food to those in extreme hunger in order for them to be able to lead an active life. On the other hand, the establishment of a consistent agricultural and development plan that includes the opening of local markets in return for earning and employment opportunities for the poor. These measures operate at the national level (for example, in an equitable distribution of land) and in the international arena where international trade is a key element. This section concentrates on international trade issues.

The main concern is the lack of any substantial progress in the liberalisation of trade in farm products. One of the most controversial elements in the process of liberalisation is the removal of OECD subsidies, which would benefit not only developing countries but consumers and taxpayers in developed countries.

Developing countries, however, would benefit, in particular, by the removal of trade barriers for commodities in which they have comparative advantage (sugar, fruit and vegetables); the reduction of tariffs for processed tropical commodities (coffee, cocoa); a more preferential access for the poorest of the least developed countries; and fair safety levels that allow developing countries to compete more efficiently in markets abroad (FAO, 18/4/02: 23). Even if the 48 least developed countries benefit from some kind of preferential market access in all Quad countries, a number of factors erode their effectiveness, and these include non-tariff measures and graduation mechanisms (in which a specific threshold is set on per capita income). Non-tariff measures include anti-dumping, safeguards and rules of origin (World Bank, 2002b: 54).

In terms of direct action against hunger, the FAO has calculated a figure of US$5 billion a year for global nutrition intervention programmes. With regard to the complementary long-term strategy, the FAO estimates that an investment in the agricultural sector of US$24 billion would be required to achieve the target of halving the number of hungry people by 2015. This amount (at 2002 prices) includes US$5 billion destined to providing the undernourished with food, plus US$19 billion required for eliminating hunger and rural poverty through agricultural growth (FAO, 2002a: 16). To finance this proposal would require a combination of domestic and external funding according to the following pattern.

The ratio for agricultural development is usually 65:35 between domestic and external funding respectively. If the Millennium Development goals were to be met, a breakdown of 50:50 would be required between external flows in the shape of Official Development Assistance (ODA) and domestic contributions. Even if 50:50 is the starting average across developing countries, this re-partition would have to be flexible according to the levels of undernourishment and poverty of the specific country. For example, in the case of Sub-Saharan Africa, where the prevalence of hunger is very high, the ratio between ODA and domestic resources would be 60:40; the same mechanism would apply to those regions where the number of undernourished is not as high. Traditionally the distribution of official resource flows has not been allocated on the basis of the proportion of hunger in the world.

To achieve the 50:50 average, these adjustments will require an average increase in the national budgets of developing countries of 20 per cent of the total expenditures on agriculture (FAO, 2002a: 17–19). As for ODA, it would have to be doubled from US$8 billion in 1999 to US$16 billion per year, although in the most recent years for which figures are available (the 1990s) it has gone in the opposite direction. In 1999, the official global development assistance for agricultural development amounted to US$8.1 billion, which represented a decline of 31 per cent from 1990. In that decade, while the international community strengthened its commitment (through several declarations and agreements) to attack poverty, the actual official development assistance diminished. Donors identified their fiscal deficits as the main cause of the cuts. But even after deficits declined from 4.3 per cent of GDP in 1993 to 1.3 per cent in 1997, official development assistance continued to decrease. According to the *World Development Report*, this decline has occurred because aid flows are determined more by political and strategic interests than by poverty reduction goals (World Bank, 2001: 190).

The potential success of these structural reforms is connected with the progress of liberalisation in the international agricultural markets.

According to advocates of this option, further liberalisation of international agricultural trade would help to finance the programme to create a more balanced international economic system. Resources would come from the reduction of the internal protectionist measures of the agricultural sector. Total expenditure in support of agriculture in OECD countries in 2000 came to more than US$327 billion a year, a figure that exceeded the combined GDP of all the developing countries of Sub-Saharan Africa. This amount will increase when the new farm legislation in the US comes into effect (Diouf, 2001b: 3). It is generally accepted that the removal of subsidies in the US and the EU would not cause a moral problem in relation to the poor of the rich countries, since the money is directed mainly to the owners of large farms. For example, in the US, 25 per cent of farms (the largest ones) receive 89 per cent of all support, and the remaining 1.6 million farms are given very little. A similar pattern occurs in the EU where 25 per cent of farms receive 70 per cent of support and produce 73 per cent of farm output (World Bank, 2003: 108).

However, while such protectionist measures are intensified in the richer countries, as has happened with the US farm bill, it becomes very difficult for developing countries to reduce their protection if the most fierce supporters of free trade are breaking the rules (Bhagwati, 2002: 28).

* * *

Liberalising agriculture in rich countries would benefit their own citizens, since it is heavily subsidised by them through taxes. The current levels of agricultural protection are a major factor influencing world production, distorting trade and depressing world prices of agricultural products (Ingco, 2002: 2). According to a study carried out by the World Bank, if all trade barriers in agriculture were removed globally, an extra US$191 billion in global welfare would be accumulated. This figure appears in a case study that the World Bank has made in its global economic report published in 2003 where it expands on the idea that trade regulations have a direct impact on poverty levels because poverty can be attacked directly through reforms in trade. The report creates a scenario in which international trade works in favour of the poor. It is the assessment parallel to what the FAO has done in direct relation to hunger (as examined above), and intensifies the relationship between trade and hunger via poverty. The study analyses the case in which rich countries would be subject to a maximum tariff in agriculture of 10 per cent and an average tariff of 5 per cent. These numbers for developing countries would be 15 per cent and 10 per cent respectively. This would mean that, for example, the relatively self-sufficient EU would become dependent on imports for two-thirds of its grain and oilseeds (World Bank, 2003: 48). If this scenario was implemented, it would generate global gains of US$291 billion, of which US$193 billion would come from liberalisation of agriculture. Reform of agriculture, specifically in rich countries, would provide an additional US$20 billion for developing countries by 2015 (World Bank, 2003: 50). Overall, the putative reforms would lift 144 million people out of poverty by 2015, with the greatest reduction coming in Sub-Saharan Africa.

This proposal makes sense in terms of economic liberalism, making better use of taxpayers' money and reducing the price of the products that consumers buy. However, at the moment it is hard to conceive of countries renowned for their protection of agriculture (such as the US, most EU members and Japan) agreeing to a reduction, for example of two-thirds, of their wheat production, given that such decisions cost votes.

* * *

Advocates of these reforms see a pattern in the current structure that, in its international dimension, needs to be broken both by external assistance and by further liberalisation of the markets. Aid in itself, without the removal of trade barriers, will not – even in the long term – eradicate hunger and poverty. By the same token, trade liberalisation without a proportional redistribution of resources in the short term will not be enough in itself, given the lack of infrastructure in developing countries to compete under the international standards set by the WTO. The areas of the agricultural sector in developing countries that need urgent action are: installation of adequate food production and processing technologies; education and training in areas such as quality control; development of infrastructure for distribution, irrigation and communication; and institution building in the form of research centres and regulatory bodies (WEF, 2002: 2).

The alternative offered by this option builds on the current system but it requires extensive reforms that lead to further liberalisation while tackling the problem of hunger rapidly and directly through aid. It is the idea of 'aid to expand trade' rather than 'aid versus trade' (FAO, 18/4/02: 28). This option of tackling hunger without delay by introducing firm reforms in the current system is seen, not as a favour to developing countries, but as a way to make the system more efficient in the long run: 'We firmly believe that it is fundamentally wrong to consider assistance to the poor and hungry an act of charity. Eradicating extreme poverty and hunger is a moral imperative, but it also makes great economic sense' (ibid.: 6).

However, the success of these measures requires a degree of commitment across the national and international spectrum: 'Formal responsibility for eliminating hunger rests with the governments of both developing and developed countries working in partnership with each other ... success will depend on the full engagement of the international community and civil society in all its dimensions' (FAO, 2002a: 21). The FAO has suggested the creation of an International Alliance against Hunger to coordinate the efforts discussed above to achieve the 2015 deadline.

Further ideas on how to modify the current international trade system in favour of a more equitable distribution have been put on the table. These include the creation of a 'Development Box', reform of the Marrakesh

Decision and the strengthening of the regional level, together with the improvement of market access and the promotion of sustainable agriculture.

Creation of a Development Box

This measure would be the developing world's equivalent of the exemptions enjoyed by developed countries under measures such as the Green Box. The Development Box would provide a series of exemptions for developing countries that are not meeting their basic food security and would focus on those crops that constitute the main means of livelihood for the poor. This mechanism would allow poor countries to benefit from the international market while protecting their own agricultural sector and markets by creating the pressure to comply with WTO minimum standards. They would promote a greater domestic support while developing a stable level of food security. This box would also protect the country against cheap imports that compete with domestic agricultural production (UK Food Group, 2002: 3). This would require the prohibition of agricultural dumping.

Dumping has been defined as export sales at a price below the normal price in the domestic market (Suppan, 2002: 17). This practice does not consider all the elements involved in the production cost, where subsidies and tax incentives play a key role. Advocates of reform in this sector claim that an official measure to calculate the full cost of a product should be established in order to avoid uncontrolled dumping that has damaging side effects in the domestic markets of developing countries. The proposed 'full cost' calculation would include: the price paid by the farmer to produce the commodity, the subsidy paid by the government, the cost of transport, the costs of marketing and a reasonable profit (ibid.: 17, 18). Applying this measure would help to put the products from countries where agriculture is protected by high subsidies on a level similar to those where government help to the agricultural sector is almost non-existent. Developing countries cannot compete with the incentives that OECD countries offer to the agricultural sector, which, as of June 2002, pays US$1 billion a day to their farmers in agricultural subsidies. That amount is more than six times the development assistance destined for poor nations (Mendoza, 2002: 3). Dumping not only affects the potential of a country to compete in the export market, but also damages the domestic market by destroying local systems of production, such as small family farms.

The Development Box has been proposed both by developing countries and by NGOs concerned with fair trade issues. In November 2001 in Qatar, WTO member governments refused to include the Development Box on their agenda. In the same way, Development Box supporters asked the Doha ministerial board to discuss an agreement for the application of binding Special and Differential (S&D) provisions, which was also rejected.

This proposal was built on the idea that S&D provisions should not be charitable or temporary exemptions from trade rules, but necessary tools in the development of a multilateral trade system (Suppan, 2002: 19).

Reform of the Marrakesh Decision

The Marrakesh Decision in 1994 promised financial support to net food-importing developing countries and least developed countries to assist them during their integration into the international economy. This support was destined for the improvement of their agricultural structure and it ensured the provision of food aid to compensate for the fluctuations of the international market prices until the time when these countries were strong enough to stand by themselves in the global economy. This commitment has not been translated into practice (see Chapter 1) despite considerable fluctuations in international prices. Research carried out by the FAO showed that about 14 per cent of a US$10 billion jump in the total food import bill of LDCs and NFIDCs (Net Food-Importing Developing Countries) in 1995 was due to the measures established in the Uruguay Round. However, another study published simultaneously by the International Monetary Fund stated that the rise in food prices seen in the international market was unrelated to the round, concluding, therefore, that the implementation of the Marrakesh Decision was not necessary. The international financial institution had its own reasons to favour that version, since it would be responsible for compensating developing countries for sharp increases in their food import bills. The WTO Committee on Agriculture, however, accepted the IMF position and the Marrakesh Decision was not implemented (Suppan, 2002: 14).

Advocates of the reforms required by the Marrakesh Decision want several modifications: the establishment of a fund based on contributions from the major agricultural exporters to provide NFIDCs with imports at concessional prices at times of high international prices; commitments for the provision of technical assistance to facilitate agricultural development and avoidance of long-term dependency; finally, this assistance should become subject to regular WTO notification (UK Food Group, 2002: 4).

The FAO recommended to Agreement on Agriculture (AoA) negotiators that, given the magnitude of the food security problem in poorer WTO members, support for agriculture in these countries is required for production growth. 'However, proponents of agriculture trade liberalisation are extremely reluctant to acknowledge any negative effects resulting from the AoA' (Suppan, 2002: 6).

Sub-global arrangements

This option, compatible with the previous measures, consists of strengthening the regional level while forming part of the global economy.

It would encourage trade among developing countries with similar economic conditions without detaching themselves from the current (and hopefully reformed) international framework. It would still be based on further liberalisation measures to foster commercial activities among themselves. This is the claim that the Delegation of Rural Organisations of Africa pressed for at their 2002 meeting by calling for a reinforcement of agricultural economic cooperation among African states to ensure the protection of their foods in the context of competing imported products (Rural Organisations, 2002: 4).

Rich countries' blockage is not the only problem that developing countries face; they also encounter high trade barriers in other developing countries (Ingco, 2002: 3). However, the role of trade and liberalisation among Third World countries is not the focus of this book, despite its importance. The focus here is the more controversial issue of international trade that takes place between developed and developing countries, where issues of equality, responsibility and legitimacy are at stake.

Assessment

Although the FAO's programme has suggested how this option can be achieved practically, the cost of the project is highly contested. It requires getting rid of protectionist measures in developed countries while increasing them in developing countries on those products that come from the highly subsidised markets in richer countries. This measure is compatible with developing countries liberalising their markets with other developing countries.

For the advocates of this option, there is a substantial benefit to be obtained across the trading structure. According to OECD figures, liberalisation from the Uruguay Round has delivered a global tax cut of more than US$200 billion per annum (OECD, 1998: 9). However, critics of further liberalisation point out that this figure ignores a vast number of people, mainly the poor, who have experienced a negative impact, especially in the area of agriculture. Agriculture is also linked to non-trade concerns, mainly in the richer core of countries, even if in these countries the agricultural output represents only 3 per cent of the GDP (World Bank, 2003: 53). Although this option considers these factors, it is difficult to establish the exact balance, since it involves further liberalisation and weaker groups might still be put at risk.

The case study developed by the World Bank on how further liberalisation would benefit both sides of the equation does not concern itself with this possible negative impact. The report accommodates the possible damage that low-income countries can suffer through the opening of markets and the increase in world prices as a result of the removal of subsidies. By way of response, it argues that the changes would occur over a period of 10 years, making it possible for the system to absorb the necessary adjustments. It recommends the creation of a programme of development assistance through which food-importing countries would take advantage of new trading opportunities within a more liberalised market. By the same token, food-exporting countries would benefit from the higher world prices, especially for products crucial for development, such as sugar, cotton, wheat and groundnuts (World Bank, 2003: 138).

Advocates of protectionist measures insist that developing countries be allowed to increase their import tariffs as a temporary measure until they are ready to face international competition. Since these poor countries cannot match the subsidies that richer countries offer to their domestic producers, tariffs are thought to be an adequate way to protect their market until their infrastructure is strong enough to compete with incoming products. However, this measure can provoke counter-productive outcomes, given the possibility of protected markets becoming dependent on those safeguarding measures and not developing the capacity to compete.

Therefore, the problem of sovereignty is a factor in this option for both developed and developing countries: international trade regulations and aid measures can affect states' sovereign decisions on trade and non-trade concerns (protection of the countryside, farm culture, and so on). On the trade side, the richest core of international society may not be willing to adopt the series of necessary reforms, and an attempt to do so could be undermined by a powerful country's policies. For non-trade reasons, developed countries also have considerable reservations about opening their markets further. In parts of these countries, agriculture supports rural communities, rural employment, cultural heritage, recreation and tourism, biological diversity, landscape, food quality and safety, and the welfare of animals. These different elements would be affected by opening the frontiers to more liberalising measures (IGC, 2002: 1, 2).

Reforms in the international structure need to be accompanied by the implementation of measures at the national level in developing countries, such as the correct use of agricultural development aid. A question about the potential for success of these measures hangs over the majority of LDCs, since they often possess very weak state structures: the so-called quasi-states, which 'are still far from complete, so to speak, and empirical statehood in large measure still remains to be built ... they lack established institutions capable of constraining and outlasting the individuals who occupy their offices' (Jackson, 1990: 21). It follows that 'not only economies or societies but also governments are underdeveloped' (ibid.: 136). Along these lines, Vincent also took into consideration the political weakness and economic underdevelopment of these countries by suggesting the implementation of a mechanism to monitor the performance of the financial aid from the North (Vincent, 1986a: 146).

The problem of weak or failed states in connection with hunger is manifested in some of the causes outlined in Chapter 1, such as corruption or internal wars. Although there are no precise estimates, corruption costs the developing world billions of dollars each year and affects societies that need every single dollar for development (Deen, 2002: 1, 2). Several international programmes have been introduced to achieve a greater degree of transparency, which is crucial for encouraging larger amounts of aid (Annan, 15/1/02: 1, 2).

State weakness is perhaps most widespread in Sub-Saharan Africa: 'The African State has been for the most part weak both as a state (i.e. low levels of socio-political cohesion) and as a power (i.e. commanding small economic, political and military resources)' (Buzan and Waever, 2003: 278). A combination of national and international elements forms the nature of these states and no single cause can be isolated. On the national side of the equation, aspects such as kin-based entities, military leaders, insurgent movements and corruption can be found. On the international side, colonisation and later decolonisation were responsible for creating artificial borders without considering traditional political boundaries. Within this framework, the international economic structure has also been seen to contribute to weak and failed states. The background to this interpretation is the work of dependency theory highlighted above together with other more recent reactions against the current system (covered in the next section on anti-globalisation movements). These understandings posit that in the current system the economic advantage of the core exists at the expense of developing countries, which as a consequence do not have the material means to build strong states. It is this imbalance in the current system that advocates of the second option address, trying to find solutions to the inequalities that the core provokes through its position of advantage. This does not eliminate, however, the part of responsibility that hinges on the domestic level, which becomes especially prominent in the case of failed states.

Failed states are those 'which cannot or will not safeguard minimal civil conditions for their populations: domestic peace, law and order, and good governance ... such states have an international legal existence but very little domestic political existence' (Jackson, R., 2000: 296). Clapham gives a more precise twist to the term and considers 'failed states' to be those 'limited number of cases in which any recognised form of government has collapsed altogether ... and [those states] have to be saved' (Clapham, 1998: 156). Both Jackson's and Clapham's definitions imply a status quo of armed anarchy and political chaos. How international society should respond to these cases is a widely debated question along the lines of responsibility, sovereignty and individual security.

Most failed states confront starvation as the specific result of a total political breakdown that creates a state of civil war (15 hunger emergencies in the world caused by man-made disasters as of October 2002). Although specific hunger crises fall outside the parameters of this research, structures that provoke these failures create a permanent problem running across the system, and are therefore connected with hunger as a 'resident emergency'. Part of this phenomenon relates to the operational inequalities of the system: 'juridical sovereignty created by decolonisation has not worked to promote either economic or political development in Africa' (Buzan and Waever, 2003: 289). In terms of economic development, this pattern is accentuated by the inequalities of the current system that representatives of the second option campaign to change.

Together with specific trade reforms, this option requires the transfer of aid from rich to poor countries to improve their agriculture infrastructure in order to generate international trade on equal terms. In many cases, the best way to increase food security is by strengthening the agricultural sector (FAO, 14/1/02c and FAO, 14/1/02d). These resources would come from the reduction of the protectionist measures themselves. However, the trajectory of agricultural aid in the past decade does not support the viability of such an increase. Official aid to agriculture in the developing countries rose from US$11 billion a year in the early 1980s to US$14 billion in 1988, but decreased to US$8 billion as of 1999 (FAO, 18/4/02: 21). In recent years, the developed world has paid less attention to helping developing countries in their agricultural sector. In fact, the Marrakesh Decision regarding agricultural development that followed the Uruguay Round has not even been implemented.

Consequently, the figures on agricultural aid need, first of all, to change in a positive direction. Even if this amount of aid were to be given, the question about its administration in the recipient countries would still remain because of national corruption, control of population growth and domestic discrimination against certain groups.

Finally, further liberalisation is not enough to pull countries out of poverty and hunger. In the words of the FAO's Director General, 'Trade globalisation will not end hunger and poverty but it has a critical role to play. If developing countries are given an equal opportunity with the wealthier countries to develop agriculture and export farm goods, all will gain' (Diouf, 2000a: 2). However, that does not excuse the role played by international trade, which is the message of this option besides its cause–effect risks: 'It is the moral responsibility of the international community to ensure that globalisation does not lead to an ever widening gap between the poor majority and the wealthy few' (ibid.: 3). In the terms investigated in this research, food security is dependent on national production, access to international markets and availability of foreign exchange to buy imports (WEF, 2002: 2).

Before evaluating this section in relation to Vincent's argument, I will analyse the other possible set of reforms in the next section. Once the wider picture is drawn, I assess which practical dimension best matches Vincent's position.

Radical change in the system

The liberal economic system has been seriously challenged before and after the end of the Cold War from two very different sources that wished to see it overturned. During the Cold War criticism came from the Non-Aligned Movement and led to demands for a New International Economic Order, reviewed in Chapter 3. The background to that line of thought was the communist Soviet-led economic approach. Although the end of the Cold War seemed to vindicate liberal thinking, the ideological confrontation persisted and evolved into the anti-globalisation movement, which had a very different mandate from the Soviet one, especially regarding the role of the state. This perspective has led to a loss of public confidence in the liberal system represented by the WTO. Concerns linked to the pursuit of free trade have grown as attention has focused on development, environment, food security and public health.

Description

The main alternative to the liberal system in the twentieth century was the option followed by the Soviet Union based on a 'centrally planned economy' instead of a 'market economy'. The Soviet Union turned away from the market system with the 'revolution from above' launched by Stalin in 1927 and based on rapid industrialisation and collectivisation of agriculture. His plan was to establish collective mechanised farms, leaving more people available to work in the industrial sector. This measure, central to the elimination of capitalism, encountered strong resistance among the farmers. As a result about five million people were deported and never heard from again. Forced collectivisation resulted in a catastrophic famine in 1932–3, since it caused a disruption of agricultural productivity. By 1940, 97 per cent of all peasant households were collectivised and state-owned; people in collective farms worked for subsistence wages and agricultural production continued at very low levels. More than a decade after the break-up of the Soviet Union, most agricultural land is still owned by the state (as much as 90 per cent according to the US Department of Agriculture) and the infrastructure is not ready to compete in the international market. Russian agriculture is still heavily protected and subsidised by the government, with tariffs of about 40 per cent on agricultural imports. Economic experts claim that the solution is for Russia to develop a system of private ownership, transferring property rights and opening the economy to a better investment climate (Kothari, 2001: 1–3; Tully, 2000: 2, 3).

China was another example of the commune-based farming system; however, its failure to realise China's agricultural potential led policy makers to introduce reforms in 1978. Initially the changes focused on providing farmers with income incentives, but they were quickly followed by a complete restructuring of the agricultural sector. In less than five years, the government dismantled the control of production from a collective farming system to a household-based farming structure (World Bank, 2001: 61–64). Since the reforms, China brought down the number of its people living in poverty from 60 per cent in 1978 to 17 per cent in 1994 (OECD, 1998: 25).

The New International Economic Order, which was inspired by liberal/anti-liberal Cold War tension, led to a campaign for an alternative economic structure that proved unsuccessful by the beginning of the 1980s. The demands for change have moved into the North–South dialogue within the WTO framework, where Third World countries now ask only for their position in the current system to be improved, and not for the elimination of the system itself.

Since the Cold War, reaction against the existing system has been associated with the anti-globalisation movements. Their most public expression came in 1999 with the Seattle protests when the WTO was holding its third ministerial conference: some 30,000 anti-free-trade demonstrators closed down the meetings for a day and the mayor of the city declared martial law for a week (Latif, 2001: 2). Similar expressions of opposition were repeated at the World Bank meeting in Washington in April 2000 and, on a lesser scale, in every subsequent gathering linked to the international economic system. Their origins can be traced to reactions to IMF programmes 25 years ago. These protests are just the tip of a current wave of discontent that extends across the international landscape: 'for each protester willing to travel hundreds or thousands of miles to express his/her disaffection with the way things are, there are thousands of sympathisers back home' (Stiglitz, 2001: 1). They form the so-called 'global democracy' movement advanced by a commitment to community, equity and planetary life. 'Although it has no identifiable organisational and institutional form, it is taking on a striking sense of coherence and acquiring the power to at least make corporate elites very nervous' (Korten, 2000: 2).

In terms of agricultural trade, protesters complain about the economic activity of transnational corporations oriented to maximise profits at the expense of social equity and environmental protection. They also react to the gap between the rich and the poor and against the lack of accountability of the dominant corporations (McLaughlin, 2000: 2). The critics view the trade regime as a form of exploitation of the poorest countries and claim that free trade benefits the rich at the expense of the poor. They argue that even the percentages of growth registered in the poorest countries favour only the elites and not the population in general.

They define the WTO as 'a selective protection of developed countries' special interests coupled with radical and quick opening of developing economies to global markets' (Smith and Patrick, 2000: 8). After Seattle, the idea has grown that 'globalisation is not irreversible'. This wave of thought insists that free trade is an illusion and further liberalisation will be harmful, due to the unequal conditions of production across the international market. Therefore, keeping these countries in direct competition will lead to the destruction of the poorest ones, since they have the weakest economies (CETIM, 1999: 2). The alternative concentrates on the national level through self-reliance and sustainable structures. Advocates of this anti-liberalisation option consider that participation in the world economy is the root of the problems faced by developing states. They assert that the international economic system is ruled by corrupted governments and greedy multinational corporations. The policy implications of this option are to cut off links with the world or reduce them as much as possible through protectionist measures (Diaz-Bonilla, 2001: 1).

In terms of agriculture and access to food, this current reaction against the system claims that the implementation of international trade principles in developing countries cancels out their ability to protect low-income producers from overwhelming competition; as a result, these practices undermine their livelihood and food security (WEF, 2002: 2). Small farmers can be driven out of business by larger producers, both domestic and international, dedicated to exporting their produce. Even if small businesses survive the competition of the larger ones, they will still be exposed to further erosion from volatile price fluctuations in the market. In the same way, the global economy can raise the salaries of those involved in the export production chain, but it can also destroy traditional means of subsistence in the local economy and disadvantage the disenfranchised people, increasing their vulnerability and inequality (Bread for the World, 1998: 3–4). International markets have created a global race for 'who will work for less', setting countries against each other, resulting, in many cases, in a lack of adequate healthcare provision or unacceptable environmental standards (Food First, 1998: 2).

According to the critics, the internationalisation of markets benefits both the transnational corporations and the elites of the developing countries that concentrate the ownership of resources and land. Those who control resources channel production into more lucrative markets abroad, while the majority of people are too poor to buy the food grown in their own country. At the same time, large corporations sustain strategies of deforestation and crop production that satisfies the international demand for tropical or out-of-season products in developed countries (Food First, 1998: 2). Moreover, the corporate sector has seen in recent years an increasing number of mergers that have strengthened its power.

In the light of these factors, opponents of free trade claim that trade reform has been accompanied by growing land alienation, weakening of food entitlements, an increase in the number of hungry people, greater intensive farming and damage to agricultural biodiversity (UK Food Group, 2002: 1). The international food trade responds to the demands of populations already well nourished and does not ensure adequate nutrition globally (CETIM, 1999: 5). The experience of small farmers, therefore, is a negative one because they lose control of their own food production and distribution. In the meantime, the control of the world food system has fallen into the powerful hands of agribusiness. Traditional agriculture is excluded from the economic landscape because it lacks the technology to defend itself.

Critics consider the international agricultural system 'unfair, inappropriate and disloyal'. 'Unfair' because it expands at the expense of local economies while enriching only the transnational and national elites; 'inappropriate' because international free trade does not correspond to any real need but serves only the profits of the elites; 'disloyal' because agriculture is heavily subsidised in developed countries and because small-scale producers are discouraged by inequitable fiscal burdens (CETIM, 1999: 4).

The alternative solution has been called *'food sovereignty'*: 'Food sovereignty is the right of a people and its nation to define their own agricultural and food policy, which take precedence over macro economic policies. It is the right of each nation to maintain and develop its capacity to produce its basic food for a balanced diet, respecting cultural and productive diversity' (Peasant Meeting, 2001: 3).

This understanding of food distribution was the theme of the World Forum on Food Sovereignty held in Havana, Cuba, in September 2001 with the participation of 400 delegates from peasant and indigenous organisations, fishing organisations, social agencies, and academics and researchers from 60 different countries. They produced a declaration stating that food security is not viable in the trade system promoted by the WTO and international financial institutions. They claimed that the exclusion of millions of people from access to food is 'a consequence of determined economic, agricultural and trade policies on a global, regional and national scale that have been imposed by the powers of the developed countries and their corporations for the purpose of maintaining and increasing their political, economic, cultural and military hegemony' (WFFS, 2001: 2).

Their main objections to the current system are:

1 Food is not just another merchandise; therefore, it cannot be treated according to market logic.
2 Liberalisation of international agricultural trade does not guarantee people's right to food.
3 The liberal concept of comparative advantage disrupts national food systems. Basic commodities from wealthy countries, imported cheaply, destroy domestic production. This precipitates an internal restructuring of the production mechanism in favour of the export market. For example, the WTO requires each member to provide a 4 to 5 per cent

minimum import access regardless of need; in the case of developing countries, this measure can have disastrous consequences for the internal markets in basic domestic foods (IATP, 2002: 8).

4 The food model promoted by transnational corporations creates a kind of food imperialism by establishing itself as the right way forward and threatening the diversity of people's food cultures and their cultural and ethnic identities.

5 The expansion of the system represented by the WTO weakens the developing states, since it promotes practices that disregard the rural population in the design and adoption of public policies.

In the light of these objections, the Food Sovereignty Declaration opposes any interference by the WTO in agriculture, using the slogan 'Keep the WTO out of food'. Instead, representatives of this approach foster the implementation of a radical agrarian reform, adapted to the conditions of each country, to provide their populations with an equitable access to productive resources. This idea underpins several movements, some of which favour a community approach detached from international markets, while others support international trade but advocate a framework different from the existing WTO one. In total, more than 1,200 groups and organisations from more than 85 countries back the anti-WTO campaign (Chossudovsky, 1999: 6).

The community-based approach focuses on the development of food production at the local level by small producers. Its followers reject the 'green revolution', which develops an infrastructure concentrating on land oriented to cash crop production for export. Instead, they promote a farmer-based low input agriculture to meet the needs of a domestic population. They advocate the creation of a self-arranging market economy composed of local enterprises with each individual having the ownership of the assets on which his or her livelihood depends (Korten, 2000: 15).

At the other end of the spectrum, the proposals of two significant organisations, Via Campesina and the World Parliamentary Forum, supported by other non-governmental organisations, reflect the demand for a restructured approach to international trade. This approach wants to promote international trade mainly through regional integration schemes among producer organisations, very different from WTO liberal parameters (WFFS, 2001: 7, 6). They have formed an international coalition of NGOs and movements from the North and the South called the People's Food Sovereignty movement, which produced the 'Food and Agriculture Statement' (June, 2002). Their main message is to remove agriculture and food from the WTO's agenda and establish an alternative international trade framework for food. This new international framework, already mentioned in the Food Sovereignty Declaration, would require:

- an International Convention replacing the Agreement on Agriculture and other relevant WTO regulations. This convention would promote food sovereignty;
- an international, legally binding Treaty that defines the rights of peasants and small producers;
- a reformed United Nations with a new forum to negotiate rules for sustainable production and fair trade;
- an independent dispute settlement mechanism that deals with problems such as dumping;
- a World Commission that defines the rights of peasants and small producers.

The emphasis given to these innovations varies among the different organisations. For example, Via Campesina calls for the abolition of the WTO while the World Parliamentary Forum wants to diminish its power. Via Campesina is radical in its statement: 'The WTO is a totally inappropriate institution for democratic decision-making and policy formulation on important issues such as food sovereignty, health and environment legislation, management of genetic resources, water, forestry and land, and the organisation of agricultural markets' (NFFC, 2002: 3). It campaigns for an alternative democratic institution where every country has the right to define its own agricultural policies, which would include the right to prohibit imports in order to protect domestic production. The democratic basis of this organisation would be extended to include greater representation for individuals and communities. Via Campesina suggests that this alternative institution could be established under the United Nations (ibid.: 3–5).

On a similar line, the World Parliamentary Forum calls for the creation of a new international framework under the control of the UN. Although it does not ask for the abolition of the WTO, it does call for the exclusion of certain areas (including agriculture) from the organisation. It believes that these areas should be the responsibility of other multilateral organisations focused on social, environmental and human rights topics (WPF, 2002: 4).

Supporters of the anti-liberalisation movements agree that the WTO's promotion of trade as the only viable solution to poverty is misleading, since its interest lies in benefiting the richest core of the international trade system. The defenders of locally based production stress that 'all efforts to destroy the rights and agricultures of peasants and small farmers must be recognised as violations of their human rights and condemned as agricultural genocide' (Committee WSSD, 2002: 4). As a particular example of this, the Declaration of Rural Organisations of Africa (2002) claims that the WTO agreements have made domestic markets vulnerable by imposing policies that affect the amount of resources to be shared at the community level. The problems created by the inclusion of domestic markets in the international dynamics of export and import have precipitated negative repercussions in a region where 95 per cent of the food production is carried out by small farmers. This movement wants recognition of the fact that small family farms are at the heart of Africa's food sovereignty (Rural Organisations, 2002: 2).

In support of these alternative approaches, 'The Other Economic Summit (TOES)' was created in 1984. Since 1988 it has held an annual meeting to coincide with the summit of the leading industrial countries (i.e. the G-7: the US, Canada, Britain, France, Germany, Italy and Japan). TOES opposes the current international trade system and promotes economics that incorporate the sustainable use of natural resources and the engagement of all people in the development process. Its main focus for action is the local community (TOES, 2002: 1–2).

According to this perspective, a solution for the problem of hunger cannot be found without addressing the need for a strong family economy and a balance between rural and urban populations. Globalisation has destabilised family farming all over the world. Cheap imports of food produced in the North with heavy subsidies have harmed local production in many cases. Even if city dwellers initially are the beneficiaries of these cheap imports, in the long term they are victims of it: the disappearance of the local market causes the elimination of the local structure of production and, as a consequence, small farmers seek refuge in the cities which then become overcrowded. Food aid can also be problematic, especially when it is used as an outlet for Northern surpluses, since it has an impact on local economies (Weid, 2002: 5, 6). An empirical study made by John Madeley on the impact of trade liberalisation in 39 countries showed how 'cheap' imports are putting farmers in developing countries out of business, while in another 16 developing countries the Agreement on Agriculture has led to a surge of food imports but no increase in food exports (Madeley, 2000: 1–10). It is important to note here that the WTO has not made impact studies of the Agreement on Agriculture itself and refuses to assess the consequences for developing countries of new measures of trade before negotiating them. This refusal has been seen by critics to be a self-protection measure that the WTO uses in order to continue the negotiation process regardless of demonstrable negative impacts of the present agreements on developing countries (Suppan, 2002: 10).

Assessment

The communist states represent one alternative to the liberal system that has been tested in practice and found not to work. From Eastern Europe to Central Asia, governments are now reforming their agricultural systems, transforming farms from centrally controlled government collectives to market-driven privately owned businesses. China adapted itself to the liberal system relatively quickly, but Russia is still operating under the effects of the previous regime while trying to incorporate itself into the liberal system. So, the liberal system (in combination with a lower or higher degree of protectionist measures) seems to be the way forward for economies that have experienced other alternatives. This reality test eliminates centrally planned economies from the option of a radical reshaping of the current system considered in this section.

This option is left, therefore, with only the proposals along the lines of the anti-globalisation movements. It assumes that globalisation is reversible and dismisses the costs it would have for those who now benefit – developing countries included. As Keohane has put it, 'reversing this process would be catastrophic for investment, economic growth and electoral success' (Keohane, 1995: 177). There are too many uncertainties around this option: it does not offer a clear alternative that has proved to be successful. If the alternative to the liberal framework does not work, the implications could be very costly, as the examples of the former Soviet Union and China have shown.

On the international front, representatives of this option do not offer a consistent well-developed project. There are calls for the creation of an institution that substitutes for or complements the WTO, but they lack a firm plan that addresses both the details of implementation and the risks involved. In this sense, the question over the future of this option is comparable to the uncertainties of the current liberal system portrayed in the first option. The fact that the existing structure is undermined by a high degree of vulnerability supports the advocates of this position, who do not see a sustainable future in the present patterns of inequality. Therefore, their proposition is an alternative to a system that runs the risk of crashing anyway.

The extreme exponents of this option seem to idealise the local community-based approach without offering an account of the costs that would be generated by reverting to the subsistence patterns of a self-sufficient mode of production. For example, the poorest countries in the world are the Sub-Saharan countries, which, in many areas, sustain only a low level of self-sufficient agriculture, due to adverse weather conditions and lack of technology to work in such a climate.

Other developing countries have very populous cities whose nutritional requirements would not be supplied by subsistence production. Advocates of this position argue that the reason why cities are so densely populated is because small farmers have been put out of business by external competition. As John Madeley asks, 'how much longer will the devastation of Third World agriculture go on, and how far will the trek of people from countryside to town have to stretch, before trade liberalisation is tempered so that it does not ruin the livelihoods of some of the world's poorest peoples?' (Madeley, 2002: 1). However, even if this has been corroborated by particular case-studies, it is not correct to blame the external market alone for poverty and hunger. In many countries, even if the excess of city dwellers were to move to the countryside on the basis of a more self-sufficient approach, they would find that a large amount of land is in the hands of the elites of the country, as is the case in Brazil (mentioned in Chapter 1) where 4.5 million peasant families have no land at all. Linked to the earlier discussion on weak states, Kaplan warns how '95 per cent of this population increase will be in the poorest regions of the world, where governments now show little ability to function, let alone to implement even marginal improvements' (Kaplan, 1994: 59).

This position, as a consequence, encounters the problem of how to feed the growing population, because its adherents have ignored the phenomenon of overpopulation, or the excess in 'the numbers of people in an area relative to its resources and the capacity of the environment to sustain human activities; that is, the area's carrying capacity' (Ehrlich and Ehrlich, 2002: 3). The current trade structure, at its most elemental level (and without considering politico-economic strategies), presupposes that a state's demand for goods equals the volume of goods that it produces in insufficient quantities or not at all; this pattern is applicable to both the developed and developing worlds. From a Malthusian perspective, the community-based alternative could have devastating effects for the net food-importing developing countries. This perspective is reflected in current work of the Worldwatch Institute, which shares the concern that food supplies cannot match population increase. In this sense, 'the decrease in capital availability of food is inevitable, until eventually a point is reached at which starvation, or some other disaster, drastically reduces the human population to a level which can be sustainable by the available food supply' (Thomas, 1997: 462). This third option seems to assume that excessive population will be depleted by starvation, which seriously undermines the individual-centred approach of this movement.

This assessment of population growth is also a problem for the first option in the sense that it retards hunger reduction: the numbers of people coming out of poverty and hunger are quickly replaced by new people born into poverty. Population growth is not a major obstacle, however, for the second option where food is seen to be a problem mainly in terms of distribution both nationally (within poor countries) and internationally (between rich and poor countries). Data set out in Chapter 1 show that food availability has grown in recent years above the required daily amount of calories and that the Earth has the capacity to feed 12 billion people provided there is effective regional and international trade.

Returning to the alternative analysed in this section, the anti-liberal voices are represented by different variants, from the radical positions just criticised, whose adherents advocate a local community-based approach, to the voices that campaign for the eradication of the current liberal WTO-based system in favour of an alternative framework for international food trade based on the rights of peasants, small producers and poor countries. It is not clear, however, why this alternative system would work since it has to measure the impact of overthrowing the current structure with no guarantees of being a consistent well-developed alternative. Another essential point that questions its viability is the fact that it is driven mainly by voices of the non-state element; states that are disadvantaged within the existing international trade system want to reform the system rather than withdraw from it or see it collapse. With few exceptions, developing nations support trade liberalisation, even if they strongly object to those mechanisms of the WTO that benefit rich countries and burden poor ones. Nevertheless, elements of this radical option have been channelled into the other two options, as will be discussed in the next chapter on international society and world society.

Anticipating Vincent's position

The three options analysed in this chapter reflect the fundamentally contested nature of the trade question where there is no consensus about how to solve the hunger–poverty problem. Assessing the impact of liberalisation on small farmers in developing countries, for example, varies across the spectrum. All three options accept that agricultural liberalisation has reduced purchasing power for some of the small farmers. The interpretation of this fact, however, varies across the three positions of the spectrum. For the first option, the reductions fail to outweigh the benefits generated by the current system. For the second option, the reductions must be taken into consideration and a series of compensatory protection and aid measures should be applied. For the third option, however, the reductions are only one of many factors that justify the need for a radical restructuring of the present system.

   In the next chapter, I argue that Vincent's position on reform corresponds to the second option. As seen in Chapter 2, Vincent envisages the elimination of hunger in international society as a project similar in scope to the elimination of the slave trade, requiring a combination of aid and reform of the existing structural arrangements, but not the elimination of the system. This would not mean a radical uncertain reshaping of the current system in favour of something unknown (the third option), but a series of normative and practical reforms along the lines of the second option. Vincent certainly opposed the first option, leaving things as they are. At the current rate of reduction, it will take over three centuries to rid the world of hunger. Given this trajectory, the case for keeping the current system as it is becomes unsustainable.

   By contrast, the second option aims to tackle hunger through a combination of direct action in the form of aid with structural reforms of the existing system's infrastructure. The reforms would promote further liberalisation but protect the weaker, least developed markets. The next chapter will use Vincent's guidelines to evaluate this option further.

5 Can international society eliminate hunger?

Having examined the right to food and its connection with international trade, this chapter returns to the theoretical framework introduced in Chapter 2. The analysis of trade and hunger is used to reassess and expand on Vincent's take on world society and international society, and on pluralism and solidarism. The expansion helps to expose the potential for international society to eliminate hunger. Following Vincent's distinction (and connection) between 'policy' and 'practice', I differentiate between normative and practical realms.

The normative dimension draws on a positive law approach, where international agreements, if only at the level of soft law, provide a rights framework to the access to food (as analysed in Chapters 2 and 3). 'Normative' refers here to 'standards of behaviour, obligations, responsibilities, rights and duties as they pertain to individuals, states and the international state system; it ranges over all aspects of the subject area, including international law and international political economy' (Evans and Newham, 1997: 382).

The practical dimension has been examined in previous chapters and reflects the current state of food insecurity alongside the measures implemented in international society to overcome it.

This overall assessment is carried out within the theoretical framework used in the book: it draws on the pluralist–solidarist debate on international society and clarifies the role of world society, which underpins Vincent's project of basic rights.

The chapter is divided into three sections. The first summarises the main elements of the argument developed so far. The second discusses Vincent's four voices of world society in relation to the normative and practical elements involved in the previous chapters. Section 3 relates the four voices to the pluralist–solidarist debate.

Summary of the key points in the argument so far

The section of Vincent's work analysed in this book belongs to the last part of his career when he became an advocate of solidarism calling for a cross-cultural consensus on basic rights in order to strengthen sovereignty. Vincent's theory on basic rights, anchored in a universalist perspective, investigated whether it is possible, at a very basic level, to talk about a global understanding (a common floor) of rights that cuts across the cultures of the world. He wanted to build a practical agenda to realise human rights in international society. By concentrating on the right to subsistence, Vincent drew attention away from humanitarian intervention, normally oriented towards crises created by the breakdown of the state, and focused on the 'routine practices' of international society that have crucial repercussions for the number of deaths by starvation.

Vincent's proposal is not about overthrowing the current system but about introducing a project of basic rights that adds to its legitimacy. He compares it to the elimination of the slave trade, and as Robert Jackson has noted, projects such as the elimination of slavery or decolonisation did not involve a repudiation of the system but the institutionalisation of these ideals to correct major anomalies and injustices (Jackson, 2000: 126).

Vincent looks at what international society can do to overcome the problem of hunger without undermining the principle of sovereignty. He channels his argument along the lines of permanent structural reforms that promote the equality of the 'submerged 40 per cent'. His position accounts for this book's focus on international trade. The analysis in the previous chapters updates and extends Vincent's underdeveloped discussion of the right to food. Chapter 1 assesses the dimensions of the problem of hunger and Chapter 3 provides an account of what international society is doing about it. On the basis of this evidence, Chapter 4 then examines the three main options that have been put forward to eliminate hunger in international society in the context of the international trade–poverty–hunger triad. Chapter 4 concludes that Vincent's approval aligns best with the second option. This option entails costs and risks, because it requires international efforts and country specific programmes, as well as the establishment of structural reforms in the trade system that will be difficult to bring about.

The approach used in this book presupposes an integral link between hunger, trade and poverty. The connections are made clear by the different international agreements outlined in Chapter 3. At the World Food Summit, governments agreed that the eradication of poverty (Commitments 1 and 2) is essential to improve access to food and emphasised that trade is a key element in achieving food security (Commitment 4). By the same token, in the Millennium Declaration, which renewed the commitments of the 1995 World Summit for Social Development, governments reiterated the connections between poverty and hunger. Later on, at the UN Conference on Least Developed Countries, in the WTO Doha Declaration, at the Johannesburg Summit and at the Cancun Summit, the government representatives insisted on the link between trade and poverty.

The nature of the relationship between international trade and poverty, however, is contested. For advocates of the liberal system, international trade has been crucial for reducing poverty and they back up their argument with GDP growth statistics. For the anti-liberal end of the spectrum the connection between international trade (as represented by the WTO) and poverty is a negative one. International trade is seen to have increased the number of poor people by throwing small producers out of business. The middle option emphasises the relationship between international trade and poverty by seeking to enhance the elements of international trade that affect the world's poor positively and reduce to a minimum the negative effects it can have on certain sectors of the population.

The generally accepted way (in both public discourse and academic analysis) to break the vicious circle between poverty and hunger is to tackle poverty in order to reduce hunger. The right to food depends on the amount of food available and the income to purchase it. Both availability and affordability are related to many other factors. Chapter 1 highlights the local, national and international elements that can cause hunger, although subsequently this book deals only with international trade links between developed and developing countries.

Given that agriculture employs more than 70 per cent of the population in low-income countries, there is a very close relationship between agricultural trade and access to food. Whether people get enough food depends on whether food is available and whether it is affordable; agricultural liberalisation affects this pattern in terms of range, quality and prices of consumer goods, and in terms of purchasing power. However, the relationship is very complex in the case of small farmers, who form the majority of the population in developing countries. Their purchasing power is determined by whether they can compete in the international market; whether dumped imports of highly subsidised products from developed countries are flooding their market and sending them out of business; whether the price at which they can sell their products covers the price of the agricultural inputs (seeds, fertilisers, and so on); and, in the case of the landless rural poor, whether paid work is available. The cities also experience the consequences of the negative effects of trade liberalisation on the businesses of small farmers, given the increase of migration from the countryside. The degree to which agricultural trade liberalisation affects different countries depends on many factors, such as the proportion of trade in the GDP, the diversity of a country's agricultural exports or other indirect factors such as political or economic instability in the country (CI, 2001: 11, 12).

The three competing options reflect in very different ways how trade liberalisation (in particular that of agricultural trade) is one of the factors that determine availability and affordability of food, positively for the first option, positively and negatively for the second option and negatively for the third option. Having documented and evaluated the three options, I have argued in the previous chapter that Vincent's claims for reforms in the name of basic rights correspond to the second option. This chapter analyses the normative and practical viability of the second option.

World society

While international society refers to the society of states, and its dimensions have been widely debated across the literature of the English school, world society has not received the same degree of conceptual development. The ambiguity surrounding the term 'world society' and its boundaries with international society are a problem across the literature. Because of this lack of clarity it is important to present the different contexts in which world society appears in Vincent before drawing conclusions at the end of this section. Vincent does not conceptualise world society explicitly but simply applies the term in his discussion of human rights. World society, however, acquires four different connotations in his writings: as challenge or complementary feature to international society, as an extension to international society, as opponent of international society and as a philosophical position on universality.

There is a significant common denominator here: the analytical differentiation between the realm of the state (international society) and the non-state (world society). Building on that crucial distinction, the four connotations of world society do not necessarily compete with each other, but represent four voices that highlight the distinction between state and non-state actors. They provide insights into the different sides of world society and how their relationship with international society can be complementary or in tension. These four voices of world society present in Vincent enrich the study of the international political economy from an English school angle. I examine now the four sides of world society and their links with international trade, which serves both to structure the contested issues in international trade and to widen the scope for understanding where the problems lie regarding its relationship with poverty and hunger.

As complementary feature or challenge to international society

In this account, world society forms a realm of non-state subjects separable from the international society of states. It is the dominant interpretation of world society across the literature of the English school. However, the nature of the relationship between the societies (challenging or complementary) remains a subject of controversy.

Vincent did not take a clear position, although he certainly acknowledged the distinction: 'The argument for non-intervention chooses the framework of the society of states, while the case for humanitarian intervention, asserting human rights that states have a duty to observe, derives from the framework of the individual' (Vincent, 1978: 44). Sometimes, world society disrupts his argument, because transnational forces can corrode international society. He usually saw world society as contradicting the principles of international society to which he had himself adhered.

This interpretation of world society also encompasses other non-state subjects besides the individual. For Vincent, 'the transnational idea of world society accommodating a host of different actors and institutions' consisted of 'groups other than states such as multinational corporations and liberation organisations' (Vincent, 1992a: 262, 253).

However, as his thinking evolves and enters human rights territory, the concept of world society becomes pressing although still not clarified. He suggests that world society is a product of the international development of human rights which opposes international society. In this sense, international society is for him a hindrance to the expansion of such a world society. This suggests a confrontational relationship where one dominates the other: 'when the argument for equality is pressed on behalf of individuals, it is one that must abandon altogether the society of states and come to grips with the hierarchical account of world society, which seeks individuals or classes as the analytical referent object' (Vincent, 1978: 44).

Vincent strongly identifies world society with the expansion of human rights at the international level after 1945. In the same vein he writes, 'Human rights have arrived in international society ... but international society still predominates and it is a gatekeeper in the way of the progress of world society' (Vincent, 1986b: 264). However, he points out that: 'the world society which exists in virtue of the arrival of human rights on the international agenda is uneven and sometimes scarcely visible' (Vincent, 1986a: 105).

Even if world society conflicts with the principles of international society, there may still be a dialectical relationship with international society. As already quoted, 'we might extend a cautious welcome to both the penetration of the state and to its strengthening itself in response' (Vincent, 1986a: 150–2). In order for sovereignty to move forward, principles of international society and world society need to be mutually supportive. Instead of this implied interconnection, Vincent separates world society from any such interaction with international society: 'The ramparts of international society are being defended against the invasion of world community' (Vincent, 1986b: 261).[1]

The view that international society and world society are necessarily antagonistic contradicts Vincent's own assessment of international law: 'The perspective of international society ... is confronted by the emergence of a global cosmopolitan culture which is stretched across all cultures, and of which the international law of human rights is an expression' (Vincent, 1986b: 2). International law, according to English school writings, is an institution within the society of states; its focus is on relations among states. At the same time, international law protects individuals, as its evolution after 1945 shows. Vincent observes how the provisions under the 1950 European Convention on Human Rights and the ECOSOC (Economic and social Council) Resolution 1503 allow individuals to appeal directly to international institutions over their own state (Vincent, 1986a: 95). International law seems to underpin both international society and world society respectively.

In other parts of his writings, Vincent implies that a connection exists between the two types of society. In his discussion of basic rights he recognises a counter-theme of 'human rights consolidating the state rather than transcending it' (Vincent, 1986a: 150–2). Elements of world society seem to be in dialogue with international society, rather than in the antagonistic relationship he embraced in previous discussions. In this sense, the strengthening of world society can also strengthen international society (Neumann, 1997: 59).

In this interpretation, it is clear that world society takes non-state actors as its subject. However, Vincent left open the question of how international society and world society relate to each other. Although his statements about the tension between international society and world society relate to human rights, the understanding parallels the first option, where the state and non-state are also differentiated. As in Vincent's interpretation, there is a confrontational as well as a constructive relationship. State and non-state actors are complementary in the sense that the state defines its economic power and growth in relation to the development of trade carried out by non-state actors. They are in tension, when policies of stronger countries adversely affect individuals in less powerful states. However, it is clear that in the first option the state dominates, setting the political and legal frame for the trade activities carried out at world society level (i.e. the state establishes the international rules associated with the WTO).

As extension of international society

This understanding of world society is exemplified in the following statement: 'International society might admit institutions other than states as bearers of rights and duties in it, recognising to that extent their equality and welcoming them into what would then have become a world society' (Vincent, 1978: 37). He develops the idea of world society as a more complete international society, 'the society of states however prominent is only one strand of the great society of humankind' (Vincent, 1990a: 241). This world society is the ultimate stage in the evolution of international society and takes states, individuals and the transnational as its subject. The joining force of these elements would be the ability to prioritise individual rights, as he explains in his article 'Grotius, Human Rights and Intervention' (ibid.: 242).

Vincent's understanding of world society as a more inclusive phenomenon than international society is also present in 'The Idea of Rights in International Ethics' (1992). This article constitutes an attempt to develop the significance of rights. Under the heading 'Rights in a cross-section of world society' he includes the levels of the individual, the state and groups 'other than states' such as multinational corporations and liberalisation organisations (Vincent, 1992a: 253–61).

He observes how institutional arrangements can protect human rights through international law and asserts that 'while states still constitute the membership of international society, they have taken a revolutionary purpose, adding the needs and interests of individuals and groups other than states to their traditional preoccupation with peace and security among themselves' (Vincent, 1986a: 93). It is in this sense that he sees international society dissolving itself into a world society. However, his analysis of human rights machinery reveals the lack of commitment to human rights in practice and the ongoing tension between the universal and regional understandings of human rights. These two factors lead to the conclusion that 'the world society that might be said to exist in virtue of the acknowledgement of and commitment to universal human rights is then uneven and in several places barely visible. But it does not mean that it does not exist at all' (ibid.: 105). He maintains that world society 'has not yet taken a form concrete enough to uphold it in practice' (Vincent, 1978: 31).

This understanding of world society is linked to two key ideas in Vincent: equality and universality. Equality is the idea of 'groups and individuals having equal standing with states' (Vincent, 1986a: 93). At the same time, this world society is universal in the sense that it 'is more inclusive than the society of states, extending its rules to individuals and groups across the globe' (ibid.: 105).

At this juncture, Vincent takes a different route to the previous understanding of world society, with human rights adding legitimacy to the system of sovereign states rather than posing a challenge (Vincent, 1986a: 151). But despite viewing world society as a more developed international society, he continues to define justice in terms of the state structure: 'It may or may not be true to say that the factual basis for a society of states is being eroded, but this society remains normatively relevant so long as the justice constituency which exists in virtue of a sense of community is more visible within state frontiers than across them' (Vincent, 1978: 45).

Given his commitment to the normative capability of the state, a world society made up of states, individuals and transnational entities does not seem different from his solidarist understanding of international society where there is consensus on values (basic rights), order (sovereignty) and issues of humanitarian intervention. The statements used to define a more inclusive world society are also seen to promote a solidarist international society, hence the possibility of the state being strengthened by the expansion of human rights. The common denominator is the complementary legal relationship that exists between state and non-state actors (which is a feature of solidarist liberal international society). Moreover, even when Vincent introduces the idea of an inclusive world society, he does not abandon the state structure. On the contrary, he hints at the possibility of the state becoming more robust as a consequence of the homogenisation provided by basic rights; the consolidation of this world society is linked to the viability of basic rights. Again, this is a feature of a solidarist international society based on human rights. In this sense world society is constructed on the principles of his human rights argument: an inter-cultural dialogue is required, where common understandings are selected and promoted through a process of agreement or consensus.

This understanding of world society takes states and individuals as its subject.[2] The three elements stand in a relationship of equality that is parallel to the claims embodied in the second option.

The second option, as expanded in Chapter 4, tries to protect the weak from the economically powerful through changes in both the practical and normative sides of the current system. It aims to establish a multilateral trading system that opens the interests of the most powerful to competition, but also promotes conditions that assist both small and large countries (subsidies, development box, tariffs, and so on). On the normative side, this option demands further reform of the procedures to ensure that all countries benefit, and it assists the integration of states, individuals and the transnational on the route to that goal.

Half of the least developed members of the WTO have no representation in Geneva and those that are represented have only a single representative; when a government is not present it cannot influence a final decision. By contrast, developed countries have substantial and permanent representation and they also hire experts to deal with technical subjects.

Demands have been made for poor countries to have a greater voice in WTO forums in order to ensure that international priorities, agreements and standards, as in trade and intellectual property rights, reflect their needs and interests (UNDP, 2001: 9–11). These claims assume the existence of a functioning state. But campaigning for developing countries to have a greater voice in international forums in some cases can be a very complicated matter since the government recognised internationally does not necessarily represent the whole of a country. A feature of failed states, and often of weak states too, is that the government does not exercise control over all its territory, with certain areas being controlled by insurgent movements. Sometimes these movements are involved in international transactions, usually regarded as the domain of the state, and obtain recognition not only from some transnational corporations, which have no reservations about negotiating with them for economic gains, but also from other governments.

Another central topic is the improvement of accountability, which includes giving to the general public greater access to information about the WTO, such as who is accountable for decisions taken by the organisation. On this line, the WTO is asked to develop a mechanism of national consultation with civil society to ensure that the negotiations take into account the issues that worry people, not just the state and the firm's interest (CI, 2000a: 1–5).

This second option also asks for the WTO to allow international NGOs to observe the meetings and, when appropriate, to contribute to the discussions. Intergovernmental bodies, except for the WTO, usually admit NGOs. However, in recent years the trade organisation has improved access to its documents (CI, 2000a: 4). This integration of the non-state element is at a more advanced stage in the cases of the World Food Summit and the poverty-related summits. The World Food Summit, an event centred on states, included the attendance of 25 United Nations agencies, 55 other IGOs, and representatives from nearly 500 NGOs. Their participation started during the preparatory process of the summit at national, regional and international levels through different consultations by governments. In terms of the plan of action, the Rome Declaration on Food Security was clear about the simultaneous involvement of all parties, even if states are responsible for the signed commitments: 'Within the global framework, governments should cooperate actively with one another and with the United Nations organisations, financial institutions, intergovernmental and non-governmental organisations, and public and private sectors, on programmes directed toward the achievement of food security for all' (FAO, 1996e: 2). The plan of action insists on this relationship; and each objective of the plan starts with the following statement: 'Governments, *in partnership* with all actors of civil society, as appropriate, will ... [description of the objective]' (ibid.: 3–27).

The poverty-related summits have also involved the contribution of several spheres across the state and non-state level. For example, the Copenhagen Declaration on Social Development also embraces the format of 'governments working in partnership with civil society'. The Brussels Conference on LDCs was attended by more than 6,500 participants from governments, specialised agencies, NGOs and individuals. In preparing the UN Conference on LDCs in 2001, UNCTAD tried a new approach, keeping the intergovernmental mainstream while creating a side dialogue among different sized companies, women and young entrepreneurs to address current topics of interest (UNCTAD, 2001: 1, 2).

These developments link with Vincent's view of integrating the state and non-state into a new world society. However, this world society is not different from his solidarist understanding of international society (as explained above), where the distinction between the state and non-state persists even when the level of integration is high.

As hostile opposition to international society

Vincent's third view of world society, like the first, separates international society and world society, but in this case, world society is hostile to international society: 'I use the term world society to describe the framework of morality that encompasses groups of this kind whose claims, not being accommodated by the society of states, are voiced in a tone which is hostile to it' (Vincent, 1978: 28).

The first account of world society expresses a tension between world society and international society because of the possibility that a new global order based on human rights could undermine the society of states. In this third account, however, the tension is provoked by the hostility of non-state actors that feel excluded from international society. Here, world society refers to 'the individual and certain actors and institutions in world politics whose concerns have been regarded conventionally as falling outside the domain of diplomacy and international relations' (ibid.: 20). Vincent himself provides examples of the kind of subjects that this world society could have: 'The claim of a tribe or a cultural group in some sense to survive the depredations of its host state recognised if nowhere else by the class of professional anthropologists; the claim of a multinational corporation to penetrate the domain of the sovereign state recognised by those who assert the autonomy of the economic order; or the claim to recompense an exploited class now voiced by the Third World under the title of the New International Economic Order' (ibid.: 29). This understanding can be extended to the anti-globalisation movements that have proliferated over the past decade.

The analysis of the third option shows that it is driven mainly by voices of the non-state sector who oppose the current liberal structure and feel excluded from it. The protests at Seattle clearly reveal this level of opposition. As noted earlier, disadvantaged states within the international trade system try to channel their criticisms in a different way by asking for improvements in the system, but not for their exclusion from it or for the eradication of the system itself.

This third option represents a sector of non-state actors (individuals, NGOs, media, and so on), which is different from those non-state actors in the second option who criticise the current structure, but do not campaign for its elimination; rather, they suggest that the system can be reformed and ask for greater involvement in it. By contrast, the voices favouring the third option do not aspire to a place for their ideas in the current system but demand its dissolution in favour of a wholly different economic set-up. Nevertheless, Vincent believes that they can have some impact on the current structure because '[they] assist in the building of a transnational justice constituency which might civilise state behaviour' (Vincent, 1978: 44).

For example, activists were able to stop the WTO Ministerial Round in Seattle (1999) and the violence surrounding the events precipitated a degree of reflection and concern behind the WTO closed doors, which resulted in a series of publications from the WTO explaining its objectives with greater transparency than ever before. The WTO is now more self-conscious about its approach and areas of controversy.

Some elements of the campaigns confronted by these groups across world society have been filtered into the current system. They have created awareness of the need for further discussions and, in some cases, they have effectively pushed international society to adopt reforms, such as the internal changes in the WTO just mentioned.

Another example is the concept of 'food sovereignty', which was developed in the Havana Declaration (September 2001). It was produced by delegates from peasant and indigenous organisations, fishing organisations, social agencies, academics and researchers from 60 different countries. No states were involved; however, the concept of 'food sovereignty' has entered the language of international society and there is a growing concern about its compatibility with the rules of international trade. Even though the concept is at its very early stages of development, it has already had some impact on current debates about improving the liberal system, such as the appeal to avoid negative consequences of international trade on small farmers in developing countries. 'Food sovereignty' is no stranger in public discourse although often expressed in different terms. For example, President George W. Bush said in a speech to US farmers: 'It is important for our nation to grow foodstuffs to feed our people. Can you imagine a country that was unable to grow enough food to feed the people? It would be a nation subject to international pressure. It would be a nation at risk. And so, when we are talking about American agriculture, we are talking about a national security issue' (Bush, 2001: 1). This quotation exemplifies why it is so difficult for developed countries to introduce change. Agriculture is not just an economic matter; it also raises political issues on a par with national security.

As empirical side of Vincent's philosophical position on universality

Finally, world society is for Vincent a philosophical concept that presents humankind as individuals joined across political frontiers. This approach establishes human rights as a universal value and takes the individual as its subject. World society embodies the philosophical idea of cosmopolitan universality and exists 'in virtue of the arrival of human rights on the international agenda' (Vincent, 1986a: 105). For Vincent, world society emerged in 1945 with the expansion of human rights to the international level. Just as international society has European roots, so this philosophical conception of world society shares the same origins.

This approach asks whether the conception of world society is associated with the expansion of principles cultivated originally in European international society or is associated with elements inherent in individuals throughout the world. In other words, is world society the product of ideological imperialism, natural law or an interchange among cultures? Moving away from the natural law tradition, Vincent opts for a cross-border dialogue in line with the negotiations represented in international human rights law. When drawing up a theory of universal human rights, 'we should start, not with the several societies of which world society is composed, but with the society formed among those societies' (Vincent, 1992b: 281).

Vincent detaches himself from the natural law tradition and roots his theory in a 'pragmatist epistemology', where values are agreed through a dialogue of competing conceptions among cultures (Dunne, 1998: 169). He talks about cultural interchange as the shaper of moral principles that affect the individual in the process of interstate relations. He observes the nature of the debates in the General Assembly on the content of human rights and sees that 'one might find more evidence for competing conceptions of what world society should consist of than a solidarist conception of what world society now is' (Vincent, 1986a: 101). In the same way that Vincent talks about the existence of several world societies, he warns about the dangers of cultural relativism by insisting that 'it simply serves as an excuse for the despotism of custom' (Neumann, 1997: 56).

According to this approach, world society represents a cultural convergence that runs in parallel with international society. Here the problem is to delimit the scope of world society, to analyse the potential for dominance of one culture and to investigate whether the world consists of a limited number of cultures each with its own indestructible core or whether they develop and change over time (Hurrell, 1998: 23). To quote Vincent, 'we have considered the question of human rights in world politics from ... the point of view of the reception of a common conception of human rights in world society as a whole' (Vincent, 1992b: 286).

Vincent's philosophical commitment to universality produces, in practice, a sum of distinct world societies that calls into question the 'global' element itself. If world society is global, then the possibility arises of a dominant culture extending its values through 'imperialistic' measures. If world society is not global, then clashes among different world societies cannot be avoided and world society is culturally determined rather than based on a universal human society. This could also affect the idea of world society where individuals are the referent objects, since culture, rather than individuals, could be the analytical referent. For example, the Cold War division of West–East–Third World (where the subjects of the same rights are the individual, the state or the group respectively) indicates how volatile the elements of world society can be when trying to define the nature of its scope, global or not.

Vincent resolves these potential contradictions by aspiring to a world society that possesses basic rights to establish 'a floor under the societies of the world' (Vincent, 1986a: 148). The theory guiding his investigations of basic rights is that 'the ties which bind individuals to the great society of humankind are deeper than the traditions and institutions that separate them' (Dunne, 1998: 169). The final chapter will examine this position and assess it in the context of the right to food.

The theoretical and normative grounds for establishing a theory of basic rights in international society connect with Vincent's understanding of world society as a philosophical concept that depicts humankind as individuals joined across frontiers. This understanding also lies behind the universal agreement on the principle of the right to food. There is now a consensus expressed in positive international law about the universal right to be free from hunger that embraces all the cultures of the world. Moving away from the natural law tradition, Vincent associated this philosophical position with an evolving inter-cultural conversation that has prompted the developments in international law traced in Chapter 3. General comment no. 12 (achieved in 1999) is currently the most advanced legal document available concerning the right to food.

* * *

Although the three options disagree about how to end hunger, they all accept, without question, the basic right to be free of hunger, and thus share Vincent's implicit conception of world society.

Conclusion: world society

Vincent's writings do not conceptualise world society explicitly. But we can extrapolate from his work range that for him, world society is structured around human rights, and can both complement (voices 1, 2 and 4) and undermine (voices 1 and 3) international society. An overall assessment of these voices of world society in the context of international trade suggests, however, that the differentiation between state and non-state arenas can help to simplify the concept of world society and its relation to international society. Instead of having four competing interpretations, we can identify two analytical spheres (state and non-state) where the relationship between international society and world society is 'variable' or 'negotiable'. The three options used to approach international trade here, therefore, can be seen to negotiate the relationship between international society and world society in distinctively different ways.

I base that differentiation between the realm of the state and the non-state in both Vincent and a certain English school consensus that sees the two societies as two different realities: 'world society is seen to operate on a different but no less significant level of analysis' (Little, 1998: 75). I also support that distinction not only according to English school discussions, but taking into consideration the practical–normative discourse, especially in the area of human rights–basic rights. This literature distinguishes between the realm of states (international society in the terminology of the English school) and the global understanding of the individual (world society). I therefore adopt here the traditional point of reference that uses states as the subject of international society and individuals and the transnational as the subject of world society. According to the understanding embraced here, world society has two elements: the *individual*, whose identity comes from belonging to the human race (global) and gives way to movements such as human rights, and the *transnational* level. When these two dimensions interact with the state, we obtain an arena delimited by international law: science, technology, market, environment, humanitarian ideals, social welfare (that is where the features of international solidarist society are anchored).

This distinction is the theoretical background for the conclusions of the book regarding the basic right to food in international society, since it helps to demark what exactly belongs to the state (the chosen subject of this research). This final analysis will be made through the assessment of the pluralist–solidarist debate.

International society: solidarism–pluralism

Although Vincent did not confront the pluralist–solidarist debate, he was the first advocate of the solidarist current of thought that has proliferated since then in the English school. In thinking about human rights in the context of international society, Vincent established the solidarist foundations on which a group of English school writers have subsequently built.

Like Vincent, their main concern is human rights, and 'for a solidarist model to be realised in practice, states need to act as guardians of basic rights everywhere' (Dunne, 1998: 175). Dunne is specifically concerned with the role of individuals in the society of states, and Knudsen (1999) and Wheeler (2000) have examined the solidarist grounds for humanitarian intervention. Mayall defines solidarism in terms of degree of homogeneity and in opposition to pluralism. For Mayall, given that states have differing interests and values, pluralism is the view that international society is limited to ensuring that states coexist in relative harmony by creating a framework where conflicting values can be accommodated (Mayall, 2000: 14). By contrast, solidarism is 'the view that humanity is one, and that the task of diplomacy is to translate this latent or immanent solidarity of interests and values into reality' (ibid.: 6). It follows that 'solidarism involves an idea in which the interest of the whole forms the central focus rather than the independence of states in which it is made up' (Alderson and Hurrell, 2000: 9).

Buzan (2004) has criticised the tendency in the English school to identify solidarism so closely with the human rights project and, to a lesser degree, with collective security. He argues that these are not the only two possibilities and he defines international solidarist societies as those 'where the focus is not only on ordering coexistence and competition, but also on cooperation over a wide range of issues, whether in pursuit of joint gains (e.g. trade) or realisation of shared values (e.g. human rights)' (Buzan, 2004: 49).

These different dimensions of solidarism are implicit in Vincent's approach, which presupposes that basic rights, and in particular the right to food, reflect the existence of 'shared values'. According to these values, the individual is the subject of the right to food, although this individual right has been translated into international law where states acknowledged a universal responsibility to protect it through agreements, in particular on poverty and trade. There is, therefore, an established framework of 'common rules', even if their capacity to bind states may be very low (this point is discussed further below). The practical assessment of Vincent's project also demonstrates that cooperation exists in the area of shared values (right to food) and in the pursuit of joint gains (international trade). These areas, moreover, are interconnected.

While Bull tried to insert his concerns about morality into the relation between order and justice, Vincent defended the state's moral responsibility on the grounds of justice. In the tensions between interstate order and justice, Vincent privileged humankind by claiming that the ties that bind individuals, like the right to life, are stronger than those that separate them (Wheeler, 1992: 479–480).

By contrast, Bull was sceptical that international society could ever reach agreement on the universal criteria needed to protect individuals beyond a state's frontiers. However, both Bull and Vincent, as the respective representatives of pluralism and solidarism, move into each other's territory when trying to distinguish their own positions.

Vincent privileges humankind when insisting that states must protect individuals beyond their borders, but at the same time he bases his argument on the principle of sovereignty in international society and admits that only the state has normative capacity to protect moral claims. Here appears a strong pluralist tendency within Vincent's work: states are heralds and shapers of sovereignty and non-intervention, together with their solidarist moral responsibilities in international society. He refers to the possibility of basic rights being, not a challenge to the system of sovereign states, but something that has added to its legitimacy on the basis of the common floor established by cosmopolitan consensus (Vincent, 1986a: 151).

By the same token, Bull was reluctant to accept the implications of rejecting agreements on justice in international relations. Attracted to the argument that order might best be preserved by strengthening justice in international relations, Bull tried to argue that order and justice are interdependent (Wheeler, 1992: 470–4). Coming from different angles, both Bull and Vincent were concerned with the principle of sovereignty in international society and with the role of morality (expressed through justice, human rights and ethical concerns).

The comparison between Bull (especially in his Hagey Lectures) and Vincent demonstrates that viewing international society from a pluralist or a solidarist point of view is counter-productive because neither is sufficient in itself to describe contemporary international relations. Vincent's work in particular shows that a solidarist international society, while moving away from the pluralist perspective, still retains elements of it, including state sovereignty and a degree of particularity. Several authors have made this point, but the most explicit contribution comes from Buzan (2004) who identifies solidarism and pluralism as ends of a spectrum so that elements of solidarism can build on pluralism without either necessarily cancelling the other out.

The attempts by international society to deal with hunger, discussed in earlier chapters, support this approach to the pluralist–solidarist debate. International trade, and in particular agricultural trade, presents protectionist measures within a liberal framework. The resulting tension has precipitated an array of disputes such as the US–EU controversy on subsidies or the ongoing disputes between developing and developed countries. There is without doubt a solidarist framework where states have institutionalised a system of cooperation in order to obtain joint gains. But this framework also embraces pluralist elements such as the protection of internal markets, reflecting the specific interests of a country or group of countries.

The second option, which aims to introduce reforms in the current system, moves away from the elements of pluralism and towards a higher degree of solidarism. Yet, elements of pluralism would be present, with protectionist measures still being used as a temporary solution to safeguard weak economies in developing countries from the effects of opening their markets to stronger, well-established, economic actors. Since these are temporary measures, the result in the long term would be a higher degree of solidarism. But this option also favours purely solidarist measures, with transitional aid being distributed to poor countries while they integrate into the system.

The current international economic system is global in rhetoric, but not in practice. As earlier chapters demonstrate, the core is highly solidarist in its understanding of the rules of the game and their influence on global regulations of trade under the WTO. At the same time, this core of states operates on a more solidarist basis among themselves than with the other parts of international society, where higher levels of pluralism apply. So, the current international trade system combines, in its global approach, strong practical elements of pluralism alongside much more solidarist rhetoric.

These solidarist features cohabit with the pluralist ones, sometimes building on them (such as in the mutual recognition of sovereignty as the basis of the agreements) and at other times in tension with them (an example being the conflict between higher and lower levels of integration and competing national interests).

There is, therefore, a split between solidarism at the normative level and a more pluralist practice. In fact, the more pluralist regulations of international trade oriented to preserve national interests are binding, while the more solidarist ones such as commitments to 'the reduction, with a view to phasing out, of all forms of export subsidies' are not. The level of solidarism and pluralism built into agreements varies. There is more solidarism in relation to certain WTO agreements and to the trade of some products (for example, manufactures), while pluralism prevails in the agricultural sector. What defines the degree of solidarism that operates in the economic sector? This question underpins the constant criticisms of inequality that persist in the system. In the analysis carried out here, it seems that the core of rich states still determines whether solidarism or pluralism prevails in a specific sector, and the overall solidarist–pluralist ratio in trade.

Although Vincent did not directly discuss the pluralist–solidarist debate, he did use its language to develop his argument about basic rights. He called for higher degrees of solidarism, but built on the foundational principles of pluralism. As he observed, '[basic rights] might require a radical shift in the patterns of political power in order that resources can reach the submerged 40 per cent in developing societies' (Vincent, 1986a: 145). This 'political restructuring' requires an increase in the number of shared values on the economic and basic rights fronts, and a higher degree of legalisation to support collective action focused on resolving the 'pressing problem of starvation'.

The international agreements analysed in this book belong to the realm of soft law and hence are not binding in the strict sense. They display a consistent degree of solidarism, with states agreeing on general principles and objectives. However, pluralism is also present because these agreements are not tied down in the areas of 'obligation', 'description' and 'delegation'. Such flexibility gives states the opportunity to interpret the agreements in accordance with their national circumstances. In the context of the right to food, it seems that solidarism is found first in the international soft law environment, accompanied by pluralist practice. But there is potential for a more solidarist practice to follow later.

International law is ahead of practice in the normative realm by setting goals accepted by states across international society. This explains the value of these agreements. The fact that the objectives laid down in these agreements are not met does not mean that they are irrelevant, as some pluralists, such as Jackson, suggest. International law (soft law in this case) can identify a problem and shape the solution (even if initially only as an ideal), demonstrating the need for progress in the practice of international society to reduce the number of hungry people.

Vincent's 'political restructuring' is strongly connected to the dilemmas of sovereignty. At solidarist levels, 'the terms in which sovereignty is understood are always open to negotiation' (Buzan, 2004: 49). Vincent's own ideas evolved from an absolute concept of sovereignty in line with a pluralist understanding, to one where sovereignty is subject to legitimising principles. Even when he backs up the possibility of human rights strengthening the state, the tension between the two types of sovereignty can be appreciated across his writings.

Samuel Barkin has worked further on this topic of sovereignty and human rights, and (without referring specifically to Vincent) overcomes the tension by documenting how sovereignty is a system of recognition among states based on a constitutional structure that changes over time. According to this position, human rights are now becoming part of the legitimisation of a new understanding of sovereignty, rather than a constraint upon it (Barkin, 1998: 231). In terms of public discourse, 'in addition to its classic functions in the area of law enforcement, health, education and foreign policy, the State must now meet increasing demands for more equity, more justice, a sound environment, and a greater respect for human rights ... furthermore, the state must also be well equipped so that, in negotiating the rules within which globalisation is to take place, national interests are preserved' (UN, 8/1/01: 4).

Current tensions in the economic system reflect this negotiated dimension of sovereignty, where countries try to find a balance between the terms that they want to control of their internal markets and international trade agreements. For example, Keohane understands sovereignty as 'less a territorially defined barrier than a bargaining resource for a politics characterised by complex transnational networks' (Keohane, 1995: 177). He attributes this shift in the understanding of sovereignty to an increased interdependence, which simultaneously provokes elements of discord given the growth in bargaining channels (ibid.).

Critics of the WTO are well aware of this development. They observe the WTO invading sovereignty in countries with developing economies, but more particularly in the area of agricultural trade, which affects food security and non-trade concerns (protection of the countryside or the maintenance of an agricultural culture that seems to be essential for certain countries). The OECD insists that international trade regulations do not undermine sovereignty since states choose to abide by the rules.

This debate poses a central obstacle to progress in the second option: 'Attention should be drawn to the role of the state as the focus of decision-making in a system of competitive states that is, in turn, interdependent with a transnational market economy ... how, and in whose interest, the "national interest" is determined is precisely the problem' (Stubbs and Underhill, 2000: 7). Keohane argues that 'the institution of sovereign statehood is being modified, although not superseded, in response to the interests of participants in a rapidly internationalising political economy' (Keohane, 1995: 177). On the one hand, countries want to preserve their national interest while pursuing joint gains. On the other hand, the system is criticised for serving only the interests of the richer few while losing potential growth in poor countries because of the way in which it operates. Critics ask for a more balanced approach with a bigger commitment from the strongest section of international society.

Vincent was radical about the need for change and asked that whoever has the power to do something to eliminate the problem of hunger should do so through a combination of aid and structural reforms. He failed, however, to specify that aid donors must take care not to violate a recipient's sovereignty, since aid can distort the local economy and therefore undermine basic rights. Nevertheless, Vincent's approach does require that aid is linked to reform. Aid by itself is insufficient.

Vincent also overlooked the fact that Third World countries have duties or responsibilities as well as rights. Corruption and inadequate social policies must be addressed at the national level, but developing states must also open their markets to other developing countries that share similar characteristics (even if as a temporary measure they still protect themselves in relation to richer exporters which enjoy subsidy-related advantages).

Vincent concentrated on a universalist approach and ignored the national and regional dimensions, which is crucial for the applicability of basic rights. Even if the right to food is accepted as a universal basic right across cultures, its implementation takes place at the national level. By the same token, reforms in international trade require modifications in the global framework represented by the WTO, but they must take into account the sub-systemic differences between rich and poor states.

* * *

Finally, and to recapitulate, we are talking here about two kinds of interconnected liberal solidarism: one based on human rights and particularly basic rights where there is a high degree of consensus in terms of values but little application when translating the consensus into action, and a solidarism based in the market, explained here through the features of international trade. The bases are now in place for the final assessment of the viability of the basic right to food in international society.

6 Conclusion

Assessment of Vincent's basic rights project

This chapter threads together the arguments of the book in order to draw conclusions about Vincent's basic rights project. The first section reassesses the relevance of Vincent's approach for analysing the basic right to food in international society. The focus is not on the philosophical merits of basic rights but on how viable basic rights are as a project across the society of states. In the second section, I highlight and assess the neglected role of international political economy in Vincent's analysis.

The viability of the basic right to food

The existence of a universal basic right to food has now been accepted across international society. The normative, as well as the philosophic-political, grounds for such a right are well established in positive law (on international soft law grounds), giving this right an advantage with respect to the rest of the human rights discourse. There is even an agreement in international law about what constitutes freedom from hunger with a specific caloric measure. This normative consensus vindicates Vincent's desire to build a common floor of basic rights for the societies of the world through an inter-cultural dialogue. The normative consensus indicates that states from opposite corners of the world have come together on the grounds of positive law and have signed international agreements that recognise the right to food regardless of their cultural, political or social background.

However, on the *practical* front, the scenario changes when examined from the perspectives of solidarism and pluralism. By concentrating on the right to subsistence, and particularly on freedom from starvation, Vincent attempted to exclude ideological obligations from human rights discourse. For Vincent (1986a: 126), the right to subsistence makes provisions for both 'unity and diversity' and does not favour any particular culture. He did not identify what these 'ideological obstacles' were, but after exploring his project in detail it is clear that there were many ideological hurdles both outside the English school (controversies surrounding the human rights debate included North–South and East–West divisions) and within it (pluralism–solidarism).

Although there is greater consensus on the right to subsistence than on other aspects of the human rights dialogue, Vincent's attempt to exclude all ideological disputes through his focus on basic rights, and on the right to food in particular, still encounters controversy and practical difficulties. For example, the most significant international agreement so far regarding the elimination of hunger is the World Food Summit 1996. The first objective, within the first commitment of the declaration, is symptomatic of these difficulties: '[Governments commit themselves] to prevent and resolve conflicts peacefully and create a stable political environment, through respect of all human rights and fundamental freedoms ... transparent and accountable governance and administration in all public and private national and international institutions, and effective and equal participation of all people, at all levels, in decisions and actions that affect their food security' (FAO, 1996c: 6). This objective shows that the 'basic right to food' has clear ideologically contested connotations. For example, all of the terms 'create a stable political environment', 'respect of all human rights and fundamental freedoms' and 'effective and equal participation of all people' are open to wide and heated debate.

In terms of pluralism–solidarism, Vincent tried to avoid the controversy precipitated by humanitarian intervention. He treated the right to food as a minimum cross-cultural floor. By establishing universal agreement on this basic right, measures to reduce hunger should thereby circumvent the humanitarian intervention problematic linked to the other components of basic rights (the right to life via the right to security). There is a remarkable consensus on this right across both international society and world society. None of the three options designed to deal with the problem of hunger generates tension between international society and world society. The basic right to food and the urgent need to eradicate hunger are universally accepted in international and world society.

Although the right to food is an adopted common value across international society on theoretical-positive law grounds, it is not shared to the same degree on the practical level. The number of hungry people amounts to nearly 800 million and yet agreement on international policies (not to mention national ones) for the implementation of the right to food is far less well developed than the consensus on normative grounds. It is in the application of the measures to solve the problem that the clashes between international society and world society occur (most accentuated in the case of the third option).

The practical application of the right to food turns out to be different, but just as problematic as ensuring the right to security. While Vincent's focus on the international economic structure in relation to hunger helps to avoid the problem of humanitarian intervention, it confronts new problems associated with the different approaches to the international economic structure. It also raises one of the key issues found in the humanitarian intervention debate: Why does one set of countries have to pursue policies that assist other countries? Why should citizens of one country help citizens of another?

The answers to these questions take different ideological forms that relate to the issue of responsibility at the individual, state and transnational levels. The analysis in this book suggests that there are two ways of approaching the question. First, in the global framework embodied in the WTO, where all partners look for joint gains; the conspicuous benefits gained by one group at the expense of another create a tension within the current system. The WTO structure, therefore, requires an element of solidarism achieved by states 'coordinating their policies, undertaking collective action, creating appropriate norms, rules and organisations and revising the institutions of interstate society' (Buzan, 2004: 147).

Second, richer countries can gain economic benefits by cutting down their protectionist measures. The reductions are translated into savings in the budget that come from lower taxes and in cheaper food for the consumers of wealthy countries, who pay higher prices for their highly subsidised food. These two solutions favour both parties in the long term. Vincent, however, wanted those with power to take more radical steps through aid and structural reforms. Both these steps require more participation and a greater sense of responsibility.

Opening the international market to more Third World products raises trade and non-trade concerns. Reducing subsidies also confronts obstacles, such as the failure to drive the agricultural trade negotiations forward at the Cancun Summit and the discord surrounding the reforms of the CAP.[1] Progress requires not only a state-to-state resolution of problems but the commitment by the citizens of one country to balance the system in order to benefit the citizens of another. As Wheeler insists, 'feelings of sympathy for the suffering of others ... might mean a willingness to bear the costs of a long-term strategy of forcible humanitarian intervention, but it most certainly requires liberal societies to take practical steps that would reduce the number of slow deaths through poverty and malnutrition' (Wheeler, 1997: 22).

To reiterate Vincent's view, 'in regard to the failure to provide subsistence rights, it is not this or that government whose legitimacy is in question but the whole international economic system in which we are all implicated' (Vincent, 1986a: 127). For Vincent, the reforms in the system are not just an option for helping out other countries, but an element that determines the legitimacy of the system itself. The ultimate goal for this kind of international legitimacy is the reform of all the international structural elements that have repercussions for hunger. Thus, it would be an internal application of the 'power to do something about starvation' (structural reforms) and not just implementing external measures (aid, development policies).

The basic right to food, however, has wider implications for international society than trade alone, and these implications infringe on issues related to humanitarian intervention. The link can be established via Vincent's argument that 'the failure of a government of a state to provide for its citizens' basic rights might now be taken as a reason for considering it illegitimate' (Vincent, 1986a: 127). Although Vincent did not develop this argument any further in relation to the right to subsistence, it suggests that his solution to national violations of the right to food (such as the case of Zimbabwe mentioned in Chapter 1) would be humanitarian intervention on a par with the right to security. However, that is beyond the scope of this book, which focuses only on hunger caused by the routine practices of the international economic system.

The international agreements analysed in Chapter 3 stress that poverty and hunger cannot be eradicated through anti-hunger programmes alone but require permanent changes in economic structures. Some progress in this area has been made, such as the EBA and AGOA projects, the reform of the distribution of the CAP and the EU–US agreement achieved in August 2003. Although not significant enough to make dramatic changes, these steps indicate that the problem is acknowledged and that leaving things as they are is not an acceptable position. Statistics on hunger in the mid-2000s revise previous figures and show that without more radical changes, the aim of halving the number of undernourished will not be achieved until well beyond the target date of 2015. To reach that goal, the reduction in the number of hungry people would have to be accelerated to 26 million a year, more than 10 times the current pace (FAO, 2003: 6).

The comfortable position maintained in the 1990s resting on the belief that hunger was being reduced is no longer justifiable, because the reduction in the number of hungry people is lower than the initial 6 million per year originally calculated (FAO, 17/10/02: 8). No substantial progress can be reported yet. The pace of reduction is too slow to meet the existing commitments, and hunger persists as a very pressing problem. This poor record strengthens the second option, which acknowledges the need for major reforms both at the level of policy making and of action if the campaign against hunger is to remain a serious objective.

There are, unfortunately, strong reasons for pessimism (arising from failure to meet the summits' deadlines and from severe delays in the agricultural negotiations), but nevertheless Vincent's project remains viable in theory and practice. The discussion of the pluralist–solidarist dichotomy supports this view. Although pluralist practice acts as a brake on a growing solidarist normative consensus, nevertheless it is possible that the solidarist consensus will be followed slowly by more solidarist actions. The analysis of the right to food reveals growing efforts to narrow the gap between theory and practice through diverse series of proposals. International efforts to eliminate hunger have intensified in the past 10 years, in line with the rejection of the option of leaving the numbers as they are. Hunger is still a pressing problem (a 'resident emergency' in Vincent's words). However, the developments that took place in the 1990s (after Vincent's death) show some movement in the direction that he initially suggested, even if the lack of practical progress is subject to the criticism of being hollow rhetoric.

The fact that a great deal of work remains to be done (comprising a higher degree of legalisation matched by practical plans at national and international levels) does not mean that the elimination of hunger is not possible within the existing system. However, this potential does not guarantee practical action. The biggest test that international society faces in the run-up to the 2015 goals is to overcome the stagnation of the past decade (despite the progress on paper) and deliver changes that match the new levels of consensus. The 1990s have defined the problem of hunger with unprecedented precision and have brought about a series of international commitments. We are now in a second stage, the decade that must deliver solid changes in line with the commitments, if the intention of fighting hunger is to continue being taken seriously. 'A fair trading system, coherent international and national policies and targeted investment are all required if the world is to feed all its people. Trade reform that furthers this goal is both possible and of the utmost priority' (WEF, 2002: 2). The plans put forward by FAO (on hunger reduction) and by the World Bank (on poverty reduction) have provided the figures that set out how this can be achieved. Despite the potential economic gains incorporated in the plan, cutting down the subsidies and opening the markets further raise non-trade concerns with serious political consequences. How wealthy countries answer the challenge of balancing their domestic agendas with their international commitments will be the biggest test in the next few years. One thing is clear: continuing with the existing policy can no longer be taken as an adequate response.

Vincent's contribution to the English school

This final section assesses whether Vincent's underdeveloped contribution on the right to subsistence should become part of the mainstream of English school thinking. This section is divided into the elements of his conceptual framework used in this book to analyse the right to subsistence: international society, world society, international political economy and human rights.

Vincent made a substantial contribution to the English school concept of *international society* through his project on basic rights. By examining the moral concerns that had worried his predecessors, he also helped to clarify the pluralist–solidarist dichotomy set out by Bull. He does not explicitly analyse solidarism, but draws on the concept in an attempt to bridge the pluralist elements of international society with the idea of a cosmopolitan world society. His focus is on the role of basic rights in international society and he sees the basic right to subsistence as the first step to realising a human rights agenda. Solidarism is viewed as a product of this development.

This approach to subsistence is a crucial innovation that has been overlooked by the English school: solidarism can be (and is) upheld in the normative structure of international society regarding the right to food. As explained in the previous chapter, the background to such a degree of solidarism is an understanding of international society where elements of pluralism and solidarism cohabit in the context of the international economic system. Vincent, however, failed to recognise the force of his own arguments. The potential of his contribution has also been largely bypassed in English school thinking, although Dunne and Wheeler have manifested their concern with the problem of starvation, which they call 'silent genocide'.[2]

Essential to Vincent's understanding of a solidarist international society is *world society*. As with international society, Vincent does not formally conceptualise world society. Its meaning has to be extracted from several usages registered in his writings. Four connotations, termed 'voices' here, can be identified, although they all differentiate between state and non-state actors. Once Vincent's implicit concept of world society has been clarified, however, it proves to be a useful tool to study elements of international political economy (IPE) through the lenses of the English school.

Vincent placed the *international economy* at the centre of his theory of basic rights, an area of international relations that has traditionally been neglected in English school discourse. Although Vincent's argument is built around human rights, his statements cross into the territory of IPE by questioning the legitimacy of the structure of the international economy. The international economic system is held responsible for the routine violations of human rights. By contrast, humanitarian intervention questions the legitimacy of a particular government as an exceptional feature in international society. Vincent did not pursue the implications of his new perspective for the English school dialogue. An investigation of his writings, however, corroborates that the economic sector occupies a key position in his attempt to think about international society and world society, and makes a substantial contribution to the ongoing solidarist–pluralist debate.

Pointing to the English school, Buzan and Little (2001b) have suggested how its trilogy of key concepts (international system, international society, world society) can play a fruitful role in the analysis of IPE especially with regard to the concept of globalisation (2001b: 38). In Chapter 4, I argue that 'classical theories' cannot by themselves explain the current international economic system. In the present system a liberal framework may dominate, but it combines elements from nationalism (protectionist measures) and neo-Marxism (the economic expansion led by transnational corporations). The English school goes beyond classical divisions and offers new frontiers of thought with the international society framework. This framework needs to be applied to IPE, where the pluralism–solidarism debate can facilitate the conversation. The neglect of IPE leaves a gap in the English school's understanding of international relations.

Claims have been made for the introduction of the market as an institution of international society. As Buzan notes (2002b: 28), 'the most obvious candidate for elevation to the status of constitutive institution would be the market … it is a principle of organisation and legitimisation that affects … how states define and constitute themselves, what kind of other actors they give standing to and how they interpret sovereignty and territoriality' (ibid.). International trade is a feature of this institution and combines with regulations surrounding it such as the international order provided by the WTO.

Viewing the market as an international institution creates a source of order and reinforces the connection established earlier between international trade and hunger. This strengthens Vincent's project of basic rights, which was part of his theoretical attempt to distance himself from Bull's idea that human rights law would be subversive of the principles of international society. States agree on a theoretical defence of the right to food; they have also linked it in part to international trade. By making this connection, attempts to reduce hunger are channelled through the market as an institution (a provider of order) and, as a consequence, basic rights should not be subversive of international order.

Finally, Vincent made a substantial contribution to *human rights discourse*. He identified a minimum consensus as the essential guide to policy: 'The human rights placed at the center of policy should be basic rights in the sense of rights that everyone ought to enjoy regardless of political circumstances' (Vincent, 1986c: 39). Vincent argued in favour of the ideological neutrality of basic rights, even if their practical application is contested due to the clash of economic interests.

Apart from the work of Henry Shue, little has been written on basic rights. Shue drew on basic rights as a way to cut through the controversial debate on establishing priorities among human rights. Vincent accepted Shue's reconciliation between civil-political and economic-social rights and tightened it further by defining the foundations of basic rights. He identified the 'basics of basic rights' and introduced them as a normative-practical project in international society. Vincent advanced the idea of promoting a global culture that could help international society to work more smoothly. The various food summits held throughout the 1990s are a first step in this direction.

* * *

To recapitulate, Vincent's legacy has opened a line of enquiry in the English school on the role of human rights in international society and it has inspired English school thinkers who work, in particular, on the issue of humanitarian intervention. However, I have explored another aspect of

Vincent's work: the right to subsistence and the routine violation of this right in international society. Neither he nor his fellow writers working in this area have looked at the implications of this issue. After documenting the practical dimensions of hunger and starvation, his statement that 'starvation is a resident emergency in the society of states' is beyond dispute. The latest statistics present an even more urgent global situation than that suggested by previous estimates. However, the way to tackle the problem is highly contested and multidimensional. I have looked here only at the part played by international trade in the structural problem of hunger. More work remains to be done on the other national, regional and international elements involved.

Vincent's project on the basic right to subsistence points to an avenue of research in the English school that is worth exploring in greater detail, which extends the existing work on human rights that focuses on the right to security. The emphasis on the basic right to food has identified the existence of a unanimous normative consensus. This consensus provides a more solid base on which to build the human rights agenda within an emerging solidarist international society. The normative consensus is an asset for the solidarists, which the right to security has, as yet, failed to supply. The English school has so far focused its solidarist project on individual security issues, where achieving normative consensus is much more difficult than in the case of routine hunger. Although the right to food has yet to be put fully into practice, its developments at the level of international law in the 1990s are a useful solidarist tool. At the risk of stating the obvious, having a normative consensus is already a step in favour of a solidarist project in international society. This advantage of the normative achievements rests on the pattern established earlier of solidarist progress at the normative level marching ahead of pluralist practice. Solidarist practice can follow solidarist normative consensus. An example of this evolution is the code of conduct on the international distribution of pesticides. Initially established by the FAO in 1985 and supported later by the UNEP, the code involved low obligation, high precision and moderate delegation. After a series of consultations over the years, the member states of both organisations increased their level of obligation and it became an internationally binding treaty (Abbott and Snidal, 2000: 444). Other examples of this dynamic can be found in the analysis presented earlier in this book: the WTO today, for example, is a stronger institution than the GATT of 50 years ago and this is the result of continuous efforts to expand trade rules over the years. The latest development is the new ongoing agricultural negotiations. Other instances of practical steps being made in solidarist soft-law commitments are the AGOA and EBA plans, although it is premature to assess their impact.

There is a range of IPE structural problems that complicate the task of implementing the right to subsistence. As a consequence, the English school must make room for IPE in its conceptual framework. But these problems are not a reason to neglect this right; the way forward requires higher levels of legalisation to support the reforms in the second option.

Vincent anticipated the way to produce a viable normative consensus across the cultures of the world. In doing so, he identified a new resource for those working in the solidarist arena. Building on this normative consensus, the next challenge for advocates of a solidarist agenda is to explore ways in which to turn theory into practice. This task is of interest to the English school and parallels the extensive work being carried out in individual security.

My conclusion is that neither of these research agendas should be given priority over the other; both need to be developed. Although they point to different problems in international society, there are also areas of common concern, such as establishing the basis for a minimum cross-cultural floor from which to start building an international political consensus. Vincent opened a line of thinking about human rights that can substantially enrich the internal English school dialogue by bringing IPE into play. To do this, however, further work is required on the relationship between pluralism and solidarism, which I have started to address in this book.

It is clear that international society has acknowledged that hunger is a violation of basic human rights. The task of theorists and practitioners is to ensure that this normative consensus is turned into a reality. To finish with Vincent's own words, 'while some human rights violations are "supervisible", others elsewhere remain "invisible"' (Vincent, 1986a: 100). Deaths by hunger are 'invisible', not only in the practice of international relations but also in the English school discourse on human rights.

Notes

1 The problem of hunger

1   The Global Poverty Report was written by a consortium of multilateral finance organisations including the World Bank, the IMF, the African Development Bank, the European Bank for Reconstruction and Development and the Inter-American Development bank.
2   The Cairns Group is a coalition of countries united by their wish for freer and fairer agricultural trade. Its members are: Argentina, Australia, Bolivia, Brazil, Canada, Chile, Colombia, Costa Rica, Fiji, Guatemala, Indonesia, Malaysia, New Zealand, Paraguay, the Philippines, South Africa, Thailand and Uruguay.
3   Since 1971, the United Nations has denominated as 'Least Developed Countries' a group of states (currently 49) that have deep structural problems and need the highest amount of support in their development efforts. They are: Afghanistan, Angola, Bangladesh, Benin, Bhutan, Burkina Faso, Burundi, Cambodia, Cape Verde, Central African Republic, Chad, Comoros, Democratic Republic of the Congo, Djibouti, Equatorial Guinea, Eritrea, Ethiopia, Gambia, Guinea, Guinea-Bissau, Haiti, Kiribati, Lao People's Democratic Republic, Lesotho, Liberia, Madagascar, Malawi, Maldives, Mali, Mauritania, Mozambique, Myanmar, Nepal, Niger, Rwanda, Samoa, Sao Tome and Principe, Senegal, Sierra Leone, Solomon Islands, Somalia, Sudan, Togo, Tuvalu, Uganda, United Republic of Tanzania, Vanuatu, Yemen and Zambia.

2 Basic human rights

1   This list does not belong to a specific source; it is the result of a personal observance of how the term is used in the public discourse across several writings and speeches.
2   Originally published in 1980, I have used here the second edition, which was published in 1996, where a chapter on US policy has been altered in relation to the first edition. However, the rest of the argument (which Vincent followed) is the same.
3   These opening paragraphs already hint at the theoretical complexity captured in the international society tradition as discussed by the English school. Before advancing any further into the conceptual ground, it should be noted that the brief account of names listed here does not intend to marginalize other members of the English school who have made substantial contributions to the movement. This account is only a highlight of the evolution of the School necessary to contextualise 'international society' as a particular trajectory of thought.

3 Basic rights in international society

1   In the public discourse, as well as in the academic, international community does not have a fixed meaning; the majority of times it refers to 'the West'. However, in the extract just quoted it means intergovernmental organisations.

5 Can international society eliminate hunger?

1   Vincent uses 'world community' and 'world civil society' as synonyms of world society.
2   When using 'transnational' in this book I follow Vincent's definition of the term: 'groups of states, such as multinational corporations and liberalization organizations'.

6 Conclusion: assessment of Vincent's basic rights project

1   The reforms and their controversies have been explained in Chapter 4.
2   This term is used by Wheeler in his 1997 piece, although in an email conversation he acknowledged Dunne's contribution in creating it.

Bibliography

Note: Internet references follow two types of format: the websites that contain non-modifiable documents such as declarations, press releases, articles and conference papers are referenced just by the year in which they were published – e.g. FAO (1996) *Rome Declaration on World Food Security*. The websites where the content is subject to variations and new inputs are referenced by the exact date when the information used in the book was extracted. When several documents have been downloaded on the same day, they have been organised in alphabetical order and distinguished in the text by a letter next to the date – e.g. FAO (9/4/00e) 'Food and Population, FAO Looks Ahead' and the date is given in the order day, month, year. Some of the authors included here (FAO, UN, WTO) have both types of documents. In that case, the references by year are listed first – e.g. FAO (1998b) – and the fully dated documents follow straight afterwards – e.g. FAO (14/1/02b).

Abbott, Kenneth, Robert Keohane, Andrew Moravesik, Anne-Marie Slaughter and Duncan Snidal (2000) 'The Concept of Legalization', *International Organization*, 54: 3, 401–419.

Abbott, Kenneth and Duncan Snidal (2000) 'Hard Law and Soft Law in International Governance', *International Organization*, 54: 3, 420–456.

ACP (2001) 'ACP Group's Position Ahead of the WTO Conference', ACP Press Release, Brussels, 7 November.

Action Against Hunger (2001) *The Geopolitics of Hunger, 2000–2001: Hunger and Power*, Boulder, CO, Lynne Rienner Publishers.

ADB (2000) *Global Poverty Report* http://www.adb.org/Documents/Reports/Global_Poverty/default.asp

ADB (2001) *Global Poverty Report* http://www.adb.org/Documents/Reports/Global_Poverty/default.asp

Adler, E.M. Barnett (1998) *Security Communities*, Cambridge, Cambridge University Press.

AGOA (2000) 'African Growth and Opportunity Act: Background' http://www.agoa.gov

AGOA (2002) 'President Approves Tariff Preferences' http://www.whitehouse.gov/news/releases/2002/01/20020102-4.html

Agritrade (2002) 'The WTO Position on the WTO Agreement on Agriculture', Technical Centre for Agricultural and Rural Cooperation, March.

Ajami, Fouad (1982) 'Human Rights and World Order Politics' in Richard Falk, Samuel Kim and Saul Mendlovitz (eds) *Toward a Just World Order*, Boulder, CO, Westview Press.

Akaha, Tsuneo and Kendall Stiles (eds) (1991) *International Political Economy: A Reader*, New York, HarperCollins.

Alderson, Kai and Andrew Hurrell (2000) *Hedley Bull on International Society*, London, Macmillan.

Alston, Philip (1979) *Human Rights and the Basic Needs Strategy for Development*, London, Anti-Slavery Society.

Alston, Philip (1984) 'International Law and the Human Right to Food' in Philip Alston and Katarina Tomasevski (eds) *The Right to Food*, Dordrecht, Martinus Nijhoff Publishers.

Alston, Philip and Henry Steiner (1996) *International Human Rights in Context: Law, Politics, Morals*, Oxford, Oxford University Press.

Alston, Philip and Katarina Tomasevski (eds) (1984) *The Right to Food*, Dordrecht, Martinus Nijhoff Publishers.

Amin, Samir (1988) *Eurocentrism*, Ipswich, Biddles.

Annan, Kofi (2002) 'From Doha to Johannesburg by Way of Monterrey', Conference paper, LSE, London.

Annan, Kofi (15/1/02) 'Annan Urges Third World to Fight Corruption to Attract More Aid' www.globalpolicy.org/socecon/un/2002/0115annan.htm

Archibugi, Daniele, David Held, and Martin Köhler (eds) (1998) *Re-imagining Political Community*, Cambridge, Polity Press.

Armstrong, David (1999) 'Law, Justice and the Idea of a World Society', *International Affairs*, 75: 3, 547–559.

Aspen Institute (1975) *The Planetary Bargain: Proposals for a New International Economic Order to Meet Human Needs*, Princeton, NJ, Princeton University Press.

Associated Press (2000) 'UN to Discuss Poverty at Summit' http://www.geocities.com/SoHo/Exhibit/9095/

Baehr, Peter R. (1996) *The Role of Human Rights in Foreign Policy*, 2nd edn, London, Macmillan.

Bage, Lennart (2002) 'International Conference on Financing for Development', conference statement, Mexico, March.

Barkin, Samuel (1998) 'The Evolution of the Constitution of Sovereignty and the Emergence of Human Rights Norms', *Millennium*, 27: 2, 229–252.

Baylis, J. and S. Smith (eds) (1997) *The Globalization of World Politics*, Oxford, Oxford University Press.

Becker, Elizabeth (2003) 'Delegates from Poorer Nations Walk out of World Trade Talks', *New York Times*, 15 September.

Bedau, Hugo Adam (1979) 'Human Rights and Foreign Assistance Programs' in Peter Brown and Douglas MacLean (eds) *Human Rights and US Foreign Policy: Principles and Applications*, Lexington, KY, Lexington Books.

Beetham, David (ed.) (1995) *Politics and Human Rights*, Oxford, Blackwell.

Beetham, David (1999) *Democracy and Human Rights*, Cambridge, Polity Press.

Bernal, Luisa (2003) 'Developing Country Proposals on Modalities for Further Reform in Agriculture', Trade Observatory, February. www.tradeobservatory. org/library/uploadedfiles/Developing_Country_Proposals

Berntsen, Donald (2000) 'The Malthus Syndrome' http://www.kalama.com/~dgberntsen/MaltSynSum.htm

Berthelot, Yves (2001) 'The International Financial Architecture: Plans for Reform', *International Social Science Journal*, 170, 586-596.

Beshoff, Pamela and Christopher Hill (1994) *Two Worlds of International Relations: Academics, Practitioners and the Trade in Ideas*, London, Routledge.

Bhagwati, Jagdish (2002) 'The Poor's Best Hope', *The Economist*, 22 June, pp. 25–28.

Blaikie, Piers, John Cameron and David Seddon (1983) 'The Logic of a Basic Needs Strategy: With or Against the Tide?', Discussion Paper number 79, School of Development Studies, University of East Anglia, Norwich.

Booth, Ken, Marysia Zalewski and Steve Smith (eds) (1996) *International Theory: Positivism and Beyond*, Cambridge, Cambridge University Press.

Braun, Joachim (2002) 'Conclusion of the Berlin Workshop on the Code of Conduct on the Right to Food', Federal Ministry of Consumer Protection, Food and Agriculture, Centre for Development Research, Bonn.

Bread for the World (1998) 'Hunger in a Global Economy: Hunger Report' www.bread.org

Bridges (2003) 'Agreement on EU CAP Reform Expected by End-June', *Bridges Weekly Trade News Digest*, Vol. 7, number 22, 18 June.

Brown, Chris (1992) 'Marxism and International Ethics' in T. Nardin and D. Mapel (eds) *Traditions of International Ethics*, Cambridge, Cambridge University Press, 225–244.

Brown, Chris (1995) 'International Theory and International Society: The Viability of the Middle Way', *Review of International Studies*, 21: 2, 183–196.

Brown, Seymon (1996) *International Relations in a Changing Global System*, Boulder, CO, and Oxford, Westview Press.

Brownlie, Ian (ed.) (1999) *Basic Documents on Human Rights*, 3rd edn, Oxford, Clarendon Press.

Bull, Hedley (1966) 'The Grotian Conception of International Society' in Herbert Butterfield and Martin Wight (eds) *Diplomatic Investigations: Essays in the Theory of International Politics*, London, Allen & Unwin, 51–74.

Bull, Hedley (1977) *The Anarchical Society. A Study of Order in World Politics*, London, Macmillan.

Bull, Hedley (1984) *Justice in International Relations*, Hagey Lectures, University of Waterloo, Ontario.

Bull, Hedley, Benedict Kingsbury and Adam Roberts (eds) (1990) *Hugo Grotius and International Relations*, Oxford, Clarendon Press.

Bull, Hedley and Adam Watson (eds) (1984) *The Expansion of International Society*, Oxford, Oxford University Press.

Burchill, Scott and Andrew Linklater (1996) *Theories of International Relations*, London, Macmillan.

Bush, George W. (2001) 'Remarks to the Future Farmers of America', July 27, Washington DC. http://grassley.senate.gov/album/ffa.htm

Butterfield, Herbert and Martin Wight (eds) (1966) *Diplomatic Investigations: Essays in the Theory of International Politics*, London, Allen & Unwin.

Buzan, Barry (1991) *People, States and Fear*, Brighton, Harvester Wheatsheaf.

Buzan, Barry (1993) 'From International System to International Society: Structural Realism and Regime Theory Meet the English School', *International Organization*, 47: 3, 327–352.

Buzan, Barry (1999) 'English School as a Research Programme', Conference paper, BISA, Manchester.

Buzan, Barry (2001) 'World Society: An Approach Through English School Theory', discussion paper, University of Bristol, 7–8 June.

Buzan, Barry (2002) 'Rethinking the Solidarist–Pluralist Debate in the English School Theory', Conference paper, ISA, New Orleans.

Buzan, Barry (2004) *From International to World Society?*, Cambridge, Cambridge University Press.

Buzan, Barry and Richard Little (1994) 'The Idea of International System: Theory Meets History', *International Political Science Review*, 15: 3, 231–256.

Buzan, Barry and Richard Little (2000) *International Systems in World History: Remaking the Study of International Relations*, Oxford, Oxford University Press.

Buzan, Barry and Richard Little (2001a) 'The "English Patient" Strikes Back: A Response to Hall's Mis-diagnosis', *International Affairs*, 77: 4, 943–946.

Buzan, Barry and Richard Little (2001b) 'Why International Relations Has Failed as an Intellectual Project and What to Do About It', *Millennium: Journal of International Studies*, 30: 1, 19–39.

Buzan, Barry and Ole Waever (2003) *Regions and Powers: The Structure of International Security*, Cambridge, Cambridge University Press.

Buzan, Barry, Ole Waever and Jaap de Wilde (1998) *Security: A New Framework for Analysis*, London, Lynne Rienner Publishers.

CA (2000) 'European Communities Proposal: Export Competition', WTO, Special Session, 18 September.

Cairns Group (1999) 'Developing Countries and Agricultural Trade Liberalisation' www.cairnsgroup.org/papers/paper_trade_liberalisation.html

Cairns Group (2002) 'The WTO Agricultural Negotiations: Cairns Group Aspirations' http://www.dfat.gov.au/media/speeches

Calvert, Susan and Peter Calvert (1996) *Politics and Society in the Third World*, Hertfordshire, Prentice Hall Europe.

Cammack, Paul (1997) *Capitalism and Democracy in the Third World: The Doctrine for Political Development*, Edinburgh, Leicester University Press.

Cammack, Paul, David Pool and William Tordoff (1993) *Third World Politics*, 2nd edn, Baltimore, MD, and London, Johns Hopkins University Press.

Carr, E.H. (1946) *The Twenty Year's Crisis 1919–1939: An Introduction to the Study of International Relations*. London, Macmillan.

Castells, Manuel (2000a) *End of Millennium*, 2nd edn, Oxford, Blackwell.

Castells, Manuel (2000b) *The Rise of the Network Society*, 2nd edn, Oxford, Blackwell.

CETIM (1999) 'Agricultural Free Trade Imposed on the South through WTO Agreements and Its Consequences', Human Rights Sub-Commission: E/CN.4/Sub.2.

CFS (2002a) 'Assessment of the World Food Security Situation', Rome, June. http://www.fao.org/DOCREP/MEETING/004/Y6441e/Y6441e00.HTM

CFS (2002b) 'Follow-Up to the WFS Plan of Action: Progress in the Implementation of Commitments III, IV, VI', Rome, June. http://www.fao.org

CFS (2002c) 'Progress in the Implementation of the Right to Food', Rome, June. http://www.fao.org/DOCREP/MEETING/004/Y6761e.HTM

CFS (2002d) 'Report on the Follow-up of the World Food Summit Plan of Action: Canada', *World Food Summit Plan of Action*, CD-Rom.

CFS (2002e) 'Report on the Follow-up of the World Food Summit Plan of Action: EU', *World Food Summit Plan of Action*, CD-Rom.

CFS (2002f) 'Report on the Follow-up of the World Food Summit Plan of Action: Japan', *World Food Summit Plan of Action*, CD-Rom.

CFS (2002g) 'Report on the Follow-up of the World Food Summit Plan of Action: USA', *World Food Summit Plan of Action*, CD-Rom.

CFS (2003a) 'Anti-Hunger Programme', Rome, May. http://www.fao.org/DOCREP/MEETING/006/Y8908e.HTM

CFS (2003b) 'Assessment of the World Food Security Situation', Rome, May. http://www.fao.org/DOCREP/MEETING/006/Y8827e/Y8827e00.HTM

CFS (2003c) 'Membership of Committee on World Food Security', Rome, May. http://www.fao.org/DOCREP/MEETING/006/Y9227e.HTM

CFS (2003d) 'Recent FAO Initiatives in the Fight Against Hunger', Rome, May. http://www.fao.org/DOCREP/MEETING/006/Y8937e.HTM

CFS (2003e) 'Report on the First Session of the Intergovernmental Working group for the Elaboration of a Set of Voluntary Guidelines to Support the Progressive Realisation of the Right to Adequate Food in the Context of National Security', Rome, May. http://www.fao.org/DOCREP/MEETING/006/Y9025e.HTM

Chomsky, Noam (2000) 'Summits', Znet Commentary www.globalpolicy.org/msummit/millenni/chomsky.htm

Chossudovsky, Michel (1999) 'WTO: An Illegal Organisation that Violates the Universal Declaration of Human Rights', *Derechos* www.derechos.org/nizkor/doc/articulos/chossudovskye.html

Chowdhuri, Satyabrata (1999) 'Hunger in the Third World', *Third World Network*, March.

CI (2000a) 'The Way Forward for the Multilateral Trading System', Trade and Economics Briefing Paper, number 1.

CI (2000b) 'The Agreement on Agriculture, Post-Seatle', Trade and Economics Briefing Paper, number 2.

CI (2001) 'The Agreement on Agriculture: An Impact Assessment', Consumers International.

Clapham, Christopher (1998) 'Degrees of Statehood', *Review of International Studies*, 24, 143–157.

Clark, Ian and Iver Neumann (eds) (1996) *Classical Theories of International Relations*, London, Macmillan.

Clay, Edward and Olav Stokke (2000) *Food Aid and Human Security*, London, Frank Cass.

Cole, John (1976) *The Poor of the Earth*, London, Macmillan.

Committee for the WSSD (2002) 'Sustainable Development is Not Possible Unless the Rights of Peasants and Small Farmers Are Guaranteed' www.peoplesfoodsovereignty.org/news/statements/workshopstate.htm

Cox, Robert (1981) 'Ideologies and the New International Economic Order: Reflections on Some Recent Literature' in Richard Little, Michael Shackleton and Michael Smith (eds) *Perspectives on World Politics*, London, Open University Press.

Cronin, Bruce (1999) *Community Under Anarchy: Transnational Identity and the Evolution of Cooperation*, New York, Columbia University Press.

Cronin, Bruce (2001) 'Defining the Limits of Sovereignty: Multilateral Intervention and the International Community', manuscript, later published in Richard H. Ullman and Michael Keren (eds) *Dilemmas of Intervention: Sovereignty versus Responsibility*, London, Frank Cass.

Cronin, Bruce (2002) 'Peacekeeping, Human Rights and the Tension Between Transnationalism and Intergovernmentalism in the United Nations', *Global Governance*, 8: 1, 53–72.

CTA (2002a) 'Developing Countries Launch Special and Differential Treatment Paper', *Trends and Prospects: The Run up to Doha*, Technical Centre for Agricultural and Rural Cooperation.

CTA (2002b) 'When the Elephants Fight', *Trends and Prospects: The Run up to Doha*, Technical Centre for Agricultural and Rural Cooperation.

Cutler, Claire A. (1991) 'The "Grotian Tradition" in International Relations', *Review of International Studies*, 17: 1, 41–65.

De Haen, Hartwig (2002) 'What the New Figures on Hunger Mean' www.fao.org/english/newsroom/news/2002/9703-en.html

Deen, Thalif (2002) 'Development: UNDP Helps Fight Corruption in Third World', *One World* www.oneworld.org/ips2/sept98/17_11_085.html

Denny, Charlotte and Larry Elliot (4/9/02) 'Shaping up for Seattle at the Beach', Finance, *The Guardian*, p. 24.

Diaz-Bonilla, Eugenio (2001) 'Agricultural Trade and World Trade Organisation', Conference paper, A World Bank Development Forum Electronic Conference, 18 June–18 July.

Diouf, Jacques (2000a) 'Global Trade Alone Will Not End World Hunger', *International Herald Tribune*, 18 February.

Diouf, Jacques (2000b) 'Call on Parliamentarians to Promote a Fairer World Trade System and Advocate National Targets for Reducing Hunger', FAO Press Release, Berlin, 16 November.

Diouf, Jacques (2001a) 'States Have an Obligation to Ensure that Nobody Dies of Hunger', FAO Press Release, 17 September.

Diouf, Jacques (2001b) 'The Tragedy of Hunger in a World of Abundance', FAO Press Release, Rome, 3 November.

Donelan, Michael (1991) 'States, Food and the World Common Interest' in Cornelia Navari (ed.) *The Condition of States*, Milton Keynes, Open University Press.

Donnelly, Jack (1989) *Universal Human Rights in Theory and Practice*, Ithaca, NY, Cornell University Press.

Donnelly, Jack (1998) *International Human Rights. Dilemmas in World Politics*, Boulder, CO, Westview Press.

Dreze, Jean, Amartya Sen and Athar Hussain (eds) (1995) *The Political Economy of Hunger*, Oxford, Clarendon Press.

Dunne, Tim (1998) *Inventing International Society: A History of the English School*, Basingstoke, Macmillan.

Dunne, Tim (2000) 'Sociological Investigations: Instrumental, Legitimist and Coercive Interpretations of International Society', *Millennium*, 30: 1, 67–91.

Dunne, Tim and Nicholas Wheeler (1996) 'Hedley Bull's Pluralism of the Intellect and Solidarism of the Will', *International Affairs*, 72: 1, 91–107.

Dunne, Tim and Nicholas Wheeler (eds) (1999) *Human Rights in Global Politics*, Cambridge, Cambridge University Press.

EC (2002) 'EU and Developing Countries: Facts and Figures', Directorate General Trade, Brussels.

Economist (11/5/02) 'Trade Disputes: Dangerous Activities', *The Economist*, pp. 91–93.

Economist (15/6/02) 'Hunger Always with Us', *The Economist*, p. 88.

Economist (13/7/02) 'Will These Modest Proposals Provoke Mayhem Down on the Farm?', *The Economist*, pp. 35–36.

Economist (17/7/02) 'Cleansing the Augean Stables', *The Economist*, p. 14.

Edkins, Jenny (2000) *Whose Hunger? Concepts of Famine, Practices of Aid*, Minneapolis, University of Minnesota Press.

Ehrlich, Anne and Paul Ehrlich (2002) 'The Population Explosion' http://www.2think.org/tpe.shtml

Elliot, Larry (2002) 'Stop Recycling Peanuts to Africa', Finance: *Guardian Weekly*, 1–7 August.

Elkins, David (1995) *Beyond Sovereignty: Territory and Political Economy in the Twenty-First Century*, Toronto, University of Toronto Press.

Esipiu, Manoah (2002) 'Dear Africa: Eat GMO Food or Starve', Reuters, 28 July. www.mindfully.org/GE/GE4/Eat-GMOs-Or-STARVE-Africa28jul02.htm

EU (2000a) 'Agriculture's Contribution to Environmentally and Culturally Related Non-Trade Concerns', Discussion Paper Four, International Conference on Non-Trade Concerns in Agriculture, Ullensvang, Norway, 2–4 July.

EU (2000b) 'Agriculture's Contribution to Rural Development', Discussion Paper Two, International Conference on Non-Trade Concerns in Agriculture, Ullensvang, Norway, 2–4 July.

EU (2000c) 'Food Quality, Improvement of Market Access Opportunities', European Communities Proposal, World Trade Organization, Committee on Agriculture, Special Session, 28 June.

EU (2000d) 'WTO Negotiations on Agriculture – EC Comprehensive Negotiating Proposal', Conclusions of the Agriculture Council on 20–21 November.

EU (2001a) 'EU Approves "Everything But Arms" Trade Access for Least Developed Countries', Press Release, Brussels, 26 February.

EU (2001b) 'Outcome of WTO Ministerial Conference in Doha' http://trade-info.cec.eu.int/europa/2001newround/index_en.php

EU (10/12/01a) 'EU Agriculture and the WTO' http://trade-info.cec.eu.int/europa/2001newround/index_en.php

EU (10/12/01b) 'Europe's Position in the WTO Farm Trade Talks' http://europa.eu.int/comm/agriculture/external/wto/index_en.htm

EU (16/7/02a) 'Dialogue with NGOs on WTO Negotiations and Agricultural Aspects' http://europa.eu.int/comm/agriculture/external/wto/dialogue/index_en.htm

EU (16/7/02b) EC Position Papers http://europa.eu.int/comm/agriculture/external/wto/officdoc/index_en.htm

Evans, Graham and Jeffrey Newham (1997) *Dictionary of International Relations*, London, Penguin Books.

FAO (1996a) 'Complementary Perspectives on Nutrition', *World Food Summit* http://www.fao.org/docrep/003/w2612e/w2612e05a.htm

FAO (1996b) 'Food, Agriculture and Food Security', *World Food Summit* http://www.fao.org/docrep/003/w2612e/w2612e01.htm

FAO (1996c) 'Food Requirements and Population Growth', *World Food Summit* http://www.fao.org/docrep/003/w2612e/w2612e4a.htm

FAO (1996d) 'Investment in Agriculture: Evolution and Prospects', *World Food Summit* http://www.fao.org/docrep/003/w2612e/w2612e10b.htm

FAO (1996e) 'Rome Declaration on World Food Security and Plan of Action', *World Food Summit* http://www.fao.org/docrep/003/w3613e/w3613e00.htm

FAO (1996f) 'Success Stories in Food Security', *World Food Summit* www.fao.org/docrep/003/w2612e/w2612e02.htm

FAO (1996g) 'Technical Background Documents', *World Food Summit* http://www.fao.org/docrep/003/w2612e/w2612e00.htm

FAO (1997) *The Sixth World Food Survey* http://www.fao.org/WAICENT/FAOINFO/ECONOMIC/ESS/wfs.htm

FAO (1998a) 'Report of the Development of FIVIMS', *Committee on World Food Security*, 24th Session, Rome, 2–5 June. http://www.fao.org/docrep/meeting/W8497e.htm

FAO (1998b) 'Guidelines for National Food Insecurity and Vulnerability Information and Mapping Systems', *Committee on World Food Security*, 24th session, Rome, 2–5 June. http://www.fao.org/docrep/meeting/W8500e.htm

FAO (1999a) 'World Food Summit and its Follow-up' http://www.fao.org/docrep/x2051e/x2051e00.htm

FAO (1999b) *The State of Food Insecurity in the World* http://www.fao.org/docrep/

FAO (2000a) *Committee on World Food Security*, 26th session, Rome, 18–21 September. http://www.fao.org/docrep/meeting/x7468e.htm

FAO (2000b) 'Nutritional Status and Vulnerability', *The State of Food Insecurity in the World* http://www.fao.org/docrep/x8200e/x8200e00.htm

FAO (2000c) *The State of Food Insecurity in the World* http://www.fao.org/docrep/x8200e/x8200e00.htm

FAO (2000d) 'Extracts Related to the Follow-up to the World Food Summit from the Reports of the FAO Regional Conferences', *Committee on World Food Security*, 26th session, Rome, 18–21 September. http://www.fao.org/docrep/meeting/x7468e.htm

FAO (2000e) 'Report on the Development of Food Insecurity and Vulnerability Information Systems', *Committee on World Food Security*, 26th session, Rome, 18–21 September 2000. http://www.fao.org/docrep/meeting/x7468e.htm

FAO (2001a) 'Further Slowdown in Hunger Reduction', FAO Press Release, Stockholm, October.

FAO (2001b) *The State of Food Insecurity in the World* http://www.fao.org/docrep/003/y1500e/y1500e00.htm

FAO (2001c) 'Too Little Progress in Fighting Hunger since 1996: Call for New Political Commitment', FAO Press Release, Rome, 18 April.

FAO (2001d) 'Undernourishment', *The State of Food Insecurity in the World* http://www.fao.org/docrep/003/y1500e/y1500e00.htm

FAO (2002a) 'Anti-Hunger Programme: Reducing Hunger through Agricultural and Rural Development and Wider Access to Food', Conference paper, International Conference for Development, Monterrey, Mexico, 18 March.

FAO (2002b) 'Declaration of the World Food Summit: Five Years Later' http://www.fao.org

FAO (2002c) 'Private Sector: Agricultural Trade Task Force', World Food Summit: Five Years Later, Rome, June. http://www.fao.org

FAO (2002d) 'World Food Summit' http://fao.org/wfs/main_en.htm

FAO (2002e) 'World Food Summit and its Follow-up' http://fao.org/docrep/X2051e/X2051e00.htm

FAO (2003) 'The State of Food Insecurity in the World 2003'. http://www.fao.org/docrep/006/j0083e/j0083e00.htm

FAO (9/4/00a) 'A Note on Methodology; How the Numbers Are Calculated' http://www.fao.org/FOCUS/E/SOFI/glo-e.htm

FAO (9/4/00b) 'Counting and Locating Hungry People' http://www.fao.org/FOCUS/E/SOFI/Count-e.htm

FAO (9/4/00c) 'Factors That Bring about Change' http://www.fao.org/FOCUS/E/SOFI/change-e.htm

FAO (9/4/00d) 'Food and Nutrition Division' http://www.fao.org/WAICENT/FAOINFO/ECONOMIC/DEPT/es960003.htm

FAO (9/4/00e) 'Food and Population, FAO Looks Ahead' http://www.fao.org/NEWS/2000/000704-e.htm

FAO (9/4/00f) 'Food Insecurity and Vulnerability Information and Mapping Systems' http://www.fao.org/FOCUS/E/SOFI/fiv-e.htm

FAO (9/4/00g) 'Global Perspectives' http://www.fao.org/WAICENT/FAOINFO/ECONOMIC/ESD/gstudies.htm

FAO (9/4/00h) 'Incidence of Malnutrition in Vulnerable Areas' http://www.fao.org/FOCUS/E/SOFI/mal-e.htm

FAO (9/4/00i) 'Meeting the Challenge' http://www.fao.org/FOCUS/E/SOFI/way-e.htm

FAO (9/4/00j) 'Progress and Setbacks in Developing Countries' http://www.fao.org/FOCUS/E/SOFI/dev-e.htm

FAO (9/4/00k) 'Towards the World Food Summit Target' http://www.fao.org/FOCUS/E/SOFI/

FAO (9/4/00l) 'Undernourishment around the World' http://www.fao.org/FOCUS/E/SOFI/

FAO (9/4/00m) 'Vulnerable People, Who and Why' http://www.fao.org/FOCUS/E/SOFI/vul-e.htm

FAO (9/4/00n) 'Well-being of Young Children' http://www.fao.org/FOCUS/E/SOFI/child-e.htm

FAO (9/4/00o) 'What is a National FIVIMS?' http://www.fivims.net/nat1.htm

FAO (14/1/02a) 'A Question of Commitment' http://www.fao.org/FOCUS/E/SpeclPr/ Spro10-e.htm

FAO (14/1/02b) 'Critical Role of Agriculture' http://www.fao.org/FOCUS/E/SpeclPr/Spro04-e.htm

FAO (14/1/02c) 'Depth of Hunger: How Hungry Are the Hungry' http://www.fao.org/FOCUS/E/SOFI00/sofi002-e.htm

FAO (14/1/02d) 'Estimating Prevalence and Depth of Hunger-Methodology' http://www.fao.org/FOCUS/E/SOFI00/sofi004a-e.htm

FAO (14/1/02e) 'Ethics in Food and Agriculture' http://www.fao.org/ethics/index_en.htm

FAO (14/1/02f) 'Extracts from Legal Documents' http://www.fao.org/FOCUS/E/rightfood/right6.htm

FAO (14/1/02g) 'Factfile' http://www.fao.org/NEWS/FACTFILE/FF9605-e.htm

FAO (14/1/02h) 'Food, Agriculture and Food Security, Developments since the World Food Conference and Prospects' http://www.fao.org/docrep/003/w2612e/w2612e01.htm

FAO (14/1/02i) 'Food, a Fundamental Human Right' http://www.fao.org/FOCUS/E/rightfood/right1.htm

FAO (14/1/02j) 'Food Security and the Coming Millennium' http://www.fao.org/FOCUS/E/WFDay/WFFig-e.htm

FAO (14/1/02k) 'Hunger Spans Three Millenniums' http://www.fao.org/FOCUS/E/WFDay/WFHun-e.htm

FAO (14/1/02l) 'Identifying the Hungry' http://www.fao.org/FOCUS/E/rightfood/right3.htm

FAO (14/1/02m) 'People at Grave Risk from Hunger' http://www.fao.org/FOCUS/E/WFDay/WFGra-e.htm

FAO (14/1/02n) 'Report of the Panel of Eminent Experts on Ethics in Food and Agriculture' http://www.fao.org/DOCREP/003/X9600E/X9600E00.htm

FAO (14/1/02o) 'Role of Research in Global Food Security and Agricultural Development' http://www.fao.org/docrep/003/w2612e/w2612e09a.htm

FAO (14/1/02p) 'Special Programme for Food Security' http://www.fao.org/FOCUS/E/rightfood/right4.htm

FAO (14/1/02q) 'Special Programme for Food Security' http://www.fao.org/FOCUS/E/SpeclPr/SproHm-e.htm

FAO (14/1/02r) 'World Food Security, Monitoring and Information' http://www.fao.org/WAICENT/FAOINFO/ECONOMIC/ESA/fsecurit.htm

FAO (21/1/02) 'Recent Shocks to Food Security' http://www.fao.org/docrep/003/y1500e/y1500e04.htm

FAO (18/4/02) 'Reducing Poverty and Hunger' http://www.fao.org/DOCREP/004/Y6684E/Y6684E00.htm

FAO (4/6/02) 'Fostering the Political Will to Fight Hunger' http://www.fao.org/docrep/meeting/003/Y0024E.htm

FAO (1/9/02) 'WTO Multilateral Trade Negotiations' http://www.fao.org/trade/wto.asp

FAO (2/9/02) 'The Way Ahead' www.fao.org/docrep/003/y1500e/y1500e06.htm

FAO (17/10/02) 'The State of Food Insecurity in the World 2002' http://www.fao.org/DOCREP/005/Y7352E/Y7352E00.HTM

FAS (2001) 'World Food Summit: Interpretative Statements by the Government of the United States of America' www.fas.usda.gov/icd/summit/interpre.html

Fawn, Rick and Jeremy Larkins (eds) (1996) *International Society after the Cold War*, London, Macmillan.

Ferguson, Yale H. (1998) 'Hedley Bull's *The Anarchical Society* Revisited: States or Polities in Global Politics?' in B.A. Roberson (ed.) *International Society and the Development of International Relations Theory*, London, Pinter, 184–209.

Finger, Michael and Philip Schuler (2002) 'Implementation of WTO Commitments', *Making Global Trade a Tool for Development*, World Bank Group.

Fischler, Franz (2001) 'EU Ready to Walk the Farm Liberalisation Walk', EU Institutions Press Releases, 26 September.

Food Fighters (2003) 'The World Trade Organisation's Agreement on Agriculture: A Fair Deal?' www.aseed.net/agrocadabra/wto-brochure/wto-brochure-en.htm

Food First (1997) 'International Code of Conduct on the Human Right to Adequate Food', Institute for Food and Development. www.foodfirst.org/progs/humanrts/conduct.html

Food First (1998) '12 Myths about Hunger', Institute for Food and Development. www.foodfirst.org/pubs/backgrdrs/1998/s98v5n3.html

Forbes, Ian and Mark Hoffman (eds) (1993) *Political Theory, International Relations and the Ethics of Intervention*, London, Macmillan.

Forks, Grand (2003) 'WTO: Great Expectations', Trade Observatory, 15 September. http://www.tradeobservatory.org/News/index.cfm?ID=4793

Frieden, Jeffry and David Lake (eds) (2000) *International Political Economy: Perspectives on Global Power and Wealth*, London, Routledge.

G15 (2002) 'The Group of 15 Summit' http://www.photius.com/g15/g15.html

Galtung, Johan (1991a) 'A Structural Theory of Imperialism' in Richard Little and Michael Smith (eds) (1991) *Perspectives on World Politics*, 2nd ed., Routledge, London, 292–304.

Galtung, Johan (1991b) 'The New International Economic Order and the Basic Needs Approach' in Tsuneo Akaha and Kendall Stiles (eds) *International Political Economy: A Reader*, New York, HarperCollins, 287–307.

Galtung, Johan (1994) *Human Rights in Another Key*, Cambridge, Polity Press.

Geneva Working Group (2003) 'Towards Food Sovereignty: Constructing an Alternative to the World Trade Organization's Agreement on Agriculture', Geneva, 19–21 February.

Ghosh, Pradip K. (ed.) (1984) *Third World Development: A Basic Needs Approach*, London, Greenwood Press.

Gilpin, Robert (1987) *The Political Economy of International Relations*, Brighton, Princeton University Press.

Gilpin, Robert (1991) 'Three Ideologies of Political Economy' in Tsuneo Akaha and Kendall Stiles (eds), *International Political Economy: A Reader*, New York, HarperCollins, 3–25.

Goldstein, Judith, Miles Kahler, Robert Keohane and Anne-Marie Slaughter (2000) 'Introduction: Legalization and World Politics', *International Organization*, 54: 3, 385–399.

Goldstein, Judith and Lisa Martin (2000) 'Legalization, Trade Liberalization and Domestic Politics: A Cautionary Note', *International Organization*, 54: 3, 603–632.

Green, D. (2002) 'The Rough Guide to the CAP' www.cafod.org.uk/POLICY/roughguidetothecap200209.shtml

Hall, Ian (2001) 'Still the English Patient? Closures and Inventions in the English School', *International Affairs*, 77: 4, 931–942.

Handelman, Howard (1996) *The Challenge of Third World Development*, New Jersey, Prentice-Hall.

Haynes, Jeff (1996) *Third World Politics: A Concise Introduction*, Oxford, Blackwell Publishers.

Hedarty, Angela and Siobhán Leonard (eds) (1999) *Human Rights: An Agenda for the 21st Century*, London, Cavendish Publishing.

Helleiner, Eric (2000) 'New Voices in the Globalization Debate: Green Perspectives on the World Economy' in Richard Stubbs and Geoffrey Underhill (eds) *Political*

Economy and the Changing Global Order, Oxford, Oxford University Press, 60–70.

Hewitt, Tom, Hazel Johnson and Dave Wield (eds) (1992) *Industrialization and Development*, Oxford, Oxford University Press.

Hoffman, Stanley (1996) *The Ethics of Humanitarian Intervention*, Notre Dame, IN, University of Notre Dame Press.

Holsti, K.J. (1995) *International Politics: A Framework for Analysis*, New Jersey, Prentice-Hall.

Howard, Rhoda E. (1995) *Human Rights and the Search for Community*, Boulder, CO, and Oxford, Westview Press.

Hurrell, Andrew (1998) 'Society and Anarchy in the 1990s' in B.A. Roberson (ed.) *International Society and the Development of International Relations Theory*, London, Pinter.

Hutton, Will and Anthony Giddens (2000) *On the Edge: Living with Global Capitalism*, London, Vintage.

IATP (2002) *Food Sovereignty*, NGO/CSO Forum, Rome, 8–13 June.

ICTSD (2002) 'New US Farm Bill Upsets WTO Partners, Could Hurt Developing Countries' www.ictsd.org/weekly/02-05-15/story2.htm

IFAD (2002) 'International Organizations and UN Agencies' http://www.ifad.org

IFAD, FAO and WFP (2002) *Reducing Poverty and Hunger: The Critical Role of Financing for Food, Agriculture and Rural Development*, Rome, February.

IGC (2002) 'World Trade, Food Production and the Diverse Roles of Agriculture', NGO Background Papers. http://www.igc.org/csdngo/agriculture/agr_rspb.html

ILO (1976) *Employment, Growth and Basic Needs: A One-World Problem*, Report of the Director General of the ILO to the Tripartite World Conference on Employment, Geneva.

ILO (1977) *The Basic-Needs Approach to Development: Some Issues Regarding Concepts and Methodology*, Geneva.

Ingco, Merlinda (2002) 'Leveraging Trade, Global Market Integration and the WTO for Rural Development', The World Bank, Rural Development Department.

International Encyclopaedia of Social Science (1968) volume 14.

IPO (1979) 'Philosophical and Socio-cultural Implications of the New International Economic Order', International Meeting of Experts on the NIEO, Vienna, 2 April.

Jackson, John (2000) *The World Trading System: Law and Policy of International Economic Relations*, Cambridge, MA, MIT.

Jackson, Robert (1990) *Quasi-states: Sovereignty, International Relations and the Third World*, Cambridge, Cambridge University Press.

Jackson, Robert (1992) 'Pluralism in International Political Theory', *Review of International Studies*, 18, 271–281.

Jackson, Robert (2000) *The Global Covenant: Human Conduct in a World of States*, Oxford, Oxford University Press.

Jackson, Robert and Georg Sorensen (1999) *Introduction to International Relations*, Oxford, Oxford University Press.

Johnson, Keith (2002) 'Among Food Activists in Europe, Famine Sparks GMO Revisionism', *Wall Street Journal*, 3 September. www.foodsecurity.net/news/newsitem.php3?nid=1888&tnews=news

Jones, Dorothy (1992) 'The Declaratory Tradition in Modern International Law' in Terry Nardin and David R. Mapel (eds), *Traditions of International Ethics*, Cambridge, Cambridge University Press, 42–57.

Jonsson, Urban (1996) 'An Approach to Assess and Analyse the Health and Nutrition Situation of Children in the Perspective of the Convention of the Rights of the Child', paper presented in the WABA Forum, Bangkok, 2–6 December.

Joyner, Christopher (1997) *The United Nations and International Law*, Cambridge, Cambridge University Press.

Kaempfer, William, J. Markusen, K. Maskus and J. Melvin (1995) *International Trade: Theory and Evidence*, Singapore, McGraw-Hill.

Kamrava, Mehran (1993) *Politics and Society in the Third World*, London, Routledge.

Kaplan, Robert (1994) 'The Coming Anarchy', *The Atlantic Monthly*, February: 44–76.

Kapstein, Ethan (2000) 'Winners and Losers in the Global Economy', *International Organization*, 54: 2, 359–384.

Karol, David (2000) 'Divided Government and US Trade Policy: Much Ado About Nothing?', *International Organization*, 54: 4, 825–844.

Kent, George (2001) 'Food Trade and Food Rights', *United Nations Chronicle Online Edition*, Issue 3. http://www.un.org/Pubs/chronicle/2002/issue1/0102p27.html

Keohane, Robert (1995) 'Hobbes's Dilemma and Institutional Change in World Politics: Sovereignty in International Society' in Hans-Henrik Holm and Georg Sorensen (eds) *Whose World Order?: Uneven Globalization and the End of the Cold War*, Boulder, CO, Westview Press, 165–186.

Khor, Martin (2003) 'Developing Countries Prepare for Agriculture Battle at Cancun Ministerial', WTO Cancun Ministerial Meeting, TWN Report, September.

Knudsen, Tonny Brems (1999) *Humanitarian Intervention and International Society: Contemporary Manifestations of an Explosive Doctrine* (PhD thesis), Aarhus: Department of Political Science, University of Aarhus.

Koppel, Naomi (2003) 'Talks Collapse at WTO Meeting. Poor Nations Bind Together to Challenge Wealthy Nations', Associated Press, 15 September.

Korten, David (2000) 'Civilizing Society', The Annual FEASTA Lecture, Dublin, Ireland.

Kothari, Raj (2001) 'Effects of the Command Economy on Soviet Agriculture (1928–1968) http://econc10.bu.edu/economic_systems/economics/command%20econ/agriculture /soviet_ag

Kowalski, W.J. (2000) 'Anti Capitalism: Modern Theory and Historical Origins' www.personal.psu.edu/users/w/x/wxk116/antic

Krasner, Stephen (ed) (2001) *Problematic Sovereignty: Contested Rules and Political Possibilities*, New York, Columbia University Press.

Kwa, Aileen (1998) 'WTO and Developing Countries', *Focus on the Global South*, http://www.foreignpolicy-infocus.org/briefs/vol3/v3n37wto_body.html

Larson, Alan (2002) 'Freeing Trade to Combat Poverty', US Department of State http://usinfo.state.gov/journals/ites/0901/ijee/larson.htm

Latif, Iqbal (2001) 'What Is Anti-Capitalism Protest All About? The Debate Shifts to Qatar', *Business Recorder*, 18 May.

Lengyel, Miguel and Diana Tussie (2002) 'Developing Countries', *Making Global Trade a Tool for Development*, World Bank Group.

Lilliston, Ben (2003) 'WTO Breakdown Should Be a Wake-up Call for Real Reform', Institute for Agriculture and Trade Policy, Press Release, 14 September. www.iatp.org

Linklater, Andrew (1996) 'Marxism' in Scott Burchill and Andrew Linklater *Theories of International Relations*, London, Macmillan, 119–144.

Little, Richard (1998) 'International System, International Society and World Society: A Re-evaluation of the English School' in B.A. Roberson (ed.) *International Society and the Development of International Relations Theory*, London, Pinter, 59–79.

Little, Richard (1999) 'The English School's Contribution to the Study of International Relations', Conference paper, BISA, Manchester.

Little, Richard and Michael Smith (eds) (1991) *Perspectives on World Politics*, 2nd edn, Routledge, London.

Little, Richard and R.D. McKinlay (1986) *Global Problems and World Order*, London, Pinter.

Lundestad, Geir (1999) *East, West, North, South*, New York, Oxford University Press.

McChesney, Allan (2000) *Economic, Social and Cultural Rights*, Washington, AAAS.

McGrew, Anthony and Paul Lewis (eds) (1992) *Global Politics*, Cambridge, Polity Press.

McHale, J. and M. McHale (1977) *Basic Human Needs: a Framework for Action*, Center for Integrative Studies, University of Houston.

McLaughlin, Martin (2000) 'Progress Toward Food Security', *Center Focus*, Issue # 148, June–July.

Madeley, John (2000) 'Trade and Hunger: Extracts' www.grain.org/publications/dec002-en.cfm

Madeley, John (2002) 'Trade and the Poor', *The Guardian*, UK. www.igc.org/csdngo/agriculture/agr_madelay.html

Mapel, David and Terry Nardin (eds) (1992) *Traditions of International Ethics*, Cambridge, Cambridge University Press.

Marchal, Roland (2001) 'Somalia: A Difficult Reconstruction' in *The Geopolitics of Hunger 2000–2001*, London, Action Against Hunger, 43–50.

Marsh, Donald (2001) 'The WTO, Free Trade and Their Critics: The Need for Education', Washington Council on International Trade, Washington.

Maslow, A. (1971) *The Farther Reaches of Human Nature*, Harmondsworth, Penguin.

Matthews, Robert and Cranford Pratt (1985) 'Human Rights and Foreign Policy: Principles and Canadian Practice', *Human Rights Quarterly*, May: 159–188.

Mayall, James (1995) *The Community of States*, London, George Allen & Unwin.

Mayall, James (2000) *World Politics: Progress and its Limits*, Cambridge, Polity.

Mendoza, Miguel (2002) 'World Food Summit: Trade Liberalization and Food Security', WTO News, Rome.

Mernies, Jorge (2002) e-mail correspondence, Statistical Analysis Service, FAO, Rome.

Millar, Kate (2003) 'Campaigners Point Finger for WTO Failure at Rich Countries', Agence France Presse, 15 September.

Miller, J.D.B. and John Vincent (eds) (1990) *Order and Violence: Hedley Bull and International Relations*, Oxford, Oxford University Press.

Moon, Bruce (2000) *Dilemmas of International Trade*, Boulder, CO, Westview Press.

Moore, Mike (2000) 'The WTO Is a Friend of the Poor: Openness to Trade Alleviates Poverty Catch Up with Rich Ones', *Financial Times*, 19 June.

Moser, Ingunn and Vandana Shiva (eds) (1995) *Biopolitics: A Feminist and Ecological Reader on Biotechnology*, London, Zed Books.

Mullerson, Rein (1997) *Human Rights Diplomacy*, London, Routledge.

Murphy, Sophia (2002) 'Farm Bill Outrage Goes Global', *Foreign Policy in Focus* www.fpif.org/commentary/2002/0205farmbill_body.html

NAM (2002) 'The Non-Aligned Movement: Description and History' http://www.nam.gov.za/background/history.htm

Neumann, Iver B. (1997) 'R.J. Vincent' in I.B. Neumann and O.Waever (eds) *The Future of International Relations: Masters in the Making?* London, Routledge, 38–64.

Neumann, Iver B. and O.Waever (eds) (1997) *The Future of International Relations: Masters in the Making?* London, Routledge.

Newsom, David (ed) (1986) *The Diplomacy of Human Rights*, Washington, DC, University Press of America.

NFFC (2002) 'Via Campesina Seattle Declaration' http://www.nffc.net/trade1.htm

OECD (1998) *Open Markets Matter: The Benefits of Trade and Investment Liberalisation*, Paris, OECD.

O'Neill, Onora (1986) *Faces of Hunger: An Essay on Poverty, Justice and Development*, London, Allen & Unwin.

Oyejide, Ademola (2002), 'Special and Differential Treatment', *Making Global Trade a Tool for Development*, World Bank Group.

Parker, Nick (2003) 'Food Sovereignty: Global Rallying Cry of Farmer Movements', Oakland, CA, Food First.

Paterson, Matthew (1996) 'Green Politics' in Scott Burchill and Andrew Linklater *Theories of International Relations*, London, Macmillan, 252–274.

Peasant Meeting (2001) 'End Global Hunger: WTO Out of Agriculture', Press Release, 27 August, Bangkok, Thailand. www.info.com.ph/~globalzn/pr-peasantmeeting.htm

People's Food Sovereignty (2002) *Food and Agriculture Statement* www.peoplesfoodsovereignty.org/new/new.htm

Pettiford, Lloyd and Jill Steans (2001) *International Relations: Perspectives and Themes*, London, Pearson Education.

Pogge, Thomas (2002), *World Poverty and Human Rights*, Cambridge, Polity Press.

Poppendieck, Janet (1998) *Sweet Charity? Emergency Food and the End of Entitlement*, New York, Viking Penguin.

Reiter, Randy, M.V. Zunzunegui and Jose Quiroga (1986) 'Guidelines for Field Reporting of Basic Human Rights Violations', *Human Rights Quarterly*, November: 628–653.

Robertson, B.A. (ed.) (1998) *International Society and the Development of International Relations Theory*, London, Pinter.

Robinson, Mary (2002) 'The Right to Food: Achievements and Challenges', *World Food Summit, Five Years Later*, Rome, FAO.

Ruggie, John Gerard (1982) 'International Regimes, Transactions and Change: Embedded Liberalism in the Postwar Economic Order', *International Organization*, 36: 2, 379–415.

Rural Organisations (2002) *Declaration of Rural Organisations of Africa*, Third Regional FAO-NGO/CSO Consultation for Africa, 22nd FAO Regional Conference for Africa www.forumfoodsovereignty.org

Schott, Jeffrey (2002) 'Trade in the Post-Doha Global Economy: Reflections on the Doha Ministerial', Institute for International Economics. http://unsinfo.sate.gov/journals/ites/0102/ijee/schott.htm

Schulz, Michael, Fredick Söderbaum and Joakim Öjendal (eds) (2001) *Regionalization in a Globalizing World*, New York, Zed Books.

Scott, Jeffrey (2002) 'Reflections on the Doha Ministerial', Institute for International Economics. http://usinfo.state.gov/journals

Seddon, David (1982) 'The Basic Needs Strategy in Theory and Practice: a Utopian Response to World Crisis?', Discussion Paper number 119, School of Development Studies, University of East Anglia, Norwich.

Sen, Amartya (1995) 'Food, Economics and Entlitements' in Jean Dreze, Amartya Sen and Athar Hussain (eds) *The Political Economy of Hunger*, Oxford, Clarendon Press.

Sharma, Shefali (2003) 'Geneva Update from the 5th WTO Ministerial', Trade *Information Project*, IATP, Geneva.

Shaw, Malcolm (1997) *International Law*, Cambridge: Cambridge University Press.

Shue, Henry (1996) *Basic Rights: Subsistence, Affluence and US Foreign Policy*, 2nd edn, Princeton, NJ, Princeton University Press.

Shue, Henry (1999) 'Global Environment and International Inequality', *International Affairs*, 75: 3, 531–546.

Simmons, Pat (1995) *Words into Action: Basic Rights and the Campaign Against World Poverty*, Oxford, Oxfam Print Unit.

Simpson, Gerry (2001) 'Two Liberalisms', *European Journal of International Law*, 13: 3, 537–571.

Smith, B.C. (1996) *Understanding Third World Politics: Theories of Political Change and Development*, London, Macmillan.

Smith, Jackie and Timothy Patrick (2000) 'WTO: 101 Myths About the World Trade Organization', *Dissent*, 47: 2, 1–9.

Spitz, P. (1984) 'Right to Food for Peoples and for the People: a Historical Perspective' in Philip Alston and Katarina Tomasevski (eds) *The Right to Food*, Dordrecht, Martinus Nijhoff Publishers.

Srinivasan, T.N. (1984) 'Development, Poverty and Basic Human Needs' in Pradip K. Ghosh (ed.) *Third World Development: A Basic Needs Approach*, London, Greenwood Press.

Stiglitz, Joseph (2001) 'Protest and the Secret World of Financial Aid', *The Banker*, October.

Stubbs, Richard and Geoffrey Underhill (eds) (2000) *Political Economy and the Changing Global Order*, Toronto, Oxford University Press.

Suganami, Hidemi (1982) 'International Law' in James Mayall (ed.) *The Community of States*, London, George Allen & Unwin, 63–73.

Suppan, Steve (2002) *Food Sovereignty*, NGO/CSO Forum for Food Sovereignty, Rome, 8–13 June.

Take Action (7/2/02) 'Responding to the Mainstream Attitudes on the IMF & World Bank' http://www.50years.org/action/s28/responses.html

Taylor, Michael and Jody Tick (2001) 'Fulfilling the Promise: A Governance Analysis of the US Response to the WFS Goal of Cutting Hunger in Half by 2015', *RFF Report*, Executive Summary.

Thomas, Caroline (1997) 'Poverty, Development and Hunger' in John Baylis and Steve Smith (eds) *The Globalization of World Politics: An Introduction to International Relations*, Oxford, Oxford University Press, 449–468.

TOES (2002) 'Introduction to TOES' http://pender.ee.upenn.edu/~rabii/toes/ToesIntro.html

Tomasevski, Katarina (ed.) (1987) *The Right to Food: Guide through Applicable International Law*, Dordrecht, Martinus Nijhoff Publishers.

Tooze, Roger (1992) 'Conceptualizing the Global Economy' in Anthony McGrew and Paul Lewis (eds) *Global Politics*, Cambridge, Polity Press, 233–252.

Trade and Development (2002) 'User's Guide to the European Union's Scheme of Generalised Tariff Preferences' http://europa.eu.int/comm/trade/miti/devel/gspguide.htm

Tully, Andrew (2000) 'Economy: Poor Russian Harvest: A Recurring Nightmare?' www.rferl.org/nca/features/2000/07/F.RU.000717145839.html

UK Food Group (2002) 'World Trade Organisation and Food Security', UK Food Group and Sustain Organisation. www.sustainweb.org/pdf/wto.pdf

UN (1954) *Report on International Definition and Measurements of Standards and Levels of Living*, New York, United Nations.

UN (1972) *Declaration of the United Nations Conference on the Human Environment* http://www.unep.org/Documents/Default.asp?DocumentID=97&ArticleID=1503

UN (1974a) *Declaration and Programme of Action on the Establishment of a New International Economic Order*, UN General Assembly, Resolution 3201 S-VI.

UN (1974b) *Universal Declaration on the Eradication of Hunger and Malnutrition*, World Food Conference. http://www.unhchr.ch/html/menu3/b/69.htm

UN (1992a) 'Introduction', *Agenda 21* http://www.un.org/esa/sustdev/agenda21chapter39.htm

UN (1992b) 'Combating Poverty', *Agenda 21* http://www.un.org/esa/sustdev/agenda21chapter3.htm

UN (1992c) 'International Cooperation to Accelerate Sustainable Development in Developing Countries and Related Domestic Policies', *Agenda 21* http://www.un.org/esa/sustdev/agenda21chapter39.htm

UN (1992d) 'International Legal Instruments', *Agenda 21* http://www.un.org/esa/sustdev/agenda21chapter2.htm

UN (1993) *World Conference on Human Rights*, Vienna, 14–15 June. http://www.unhchr.ch/html/menu5/wchr.htm

UN (1995a) 'About the World Summit for Social Development' http://www.visionoffice.com/socdev/wssd.htm

UN (1995b) *Copenhagen Declaration on Social Development* http://www.visionoffice.com/socdev/wssdco-4.htm

UN (1995c) 'Programme of Action of the World Summit for Social Development' http://www.visionoffice.com/socdev/wssdpa-2.htm

UN (1995d) *The United Nations and Human Rights: 1945–1995*, New York, United Nations.

UN (2000) *United Nations Millennium Declaration* http://www.nepalicongress.org

UN (2001a) 'Brussels Conference Commits to Eradicating Poverty in World's Poorest Countries' http://www.unctad.org/conference/press/devbru24e.htm

UN (2001b) *Brussels Declaration* http://www.unctad.org/conference/main.htm

UN (2001c) *Duty and Quota Free Market Access for LDCs*, UN Geneva.

UN (2001d) 'Economic, Social and Cultural Rights: The Right to Food', *Commission on Human Rights*, Fifty-seventh session, 7 February.

UN (2002a) 'Extract from the Draft Report of the Main Committee of the World Summit on Sustainable Development' www.un.org/jsummit/html/documents/summit_docs.html

UN (2002b) *The Johannesburg Commitment on Sustainable Development* www.un.org/jsummit/html/documents/summit_docs.html

UN: Indicators on Population www.un.org/Depts/unsd/social/population.htm

UN (8/1/01) 'The Realization of Economic, Social and Cultural Rights: Globalization and its Impact on the Full Enjoyment of Human Rights', Economic and Social Council.

UN (7/2/01) 'Substantive Issues Arising in the Implementation of the International Covenant on Economic, Social and Cultural Rights', Committee on Economic, Social and Cultural Rights. http://www.unhchr.ch/tbs/doc.nsf/MasterFrameView/3d02758c707031d5

UN (28/8/02) 'Sustainable Development', World Summit on Sustainable Development. http://lnweb18.worldbank.org/ESSD/essdext.nsf/43DocByUnid/

UNCTAD (2001) 'Brussels Conference Commits to Eradicating Poverty in World's Poorest Countries', Third UN Conference on LDCs, 23rd and Final Meeting and Round Up.

UNCTAD (2002) *The Least Developed Countries Report*, UNCTAD Digital Library. http://www.unctad.org/en/pub/ps11dc02.en.htm

UNDP (2000) *Human Development Report* http://www.undp.org/hdr2000/english/HDR2000.html

UNDP (2001) 'Human Development: Past, Present and Future', *Human Development Report* http://www.undp.org/hdr2001/

UNHCHR (2001) 'The Effects of the Working Methods and Activities of Transnational Corporations on the Enjoyment of Human Rights', Sub-Commission on Human Rights Resolution 2001/3.

Veneman, Ann (2001) 'The World Must Unite to Fight Hunger and Poverty; Success Will Require an International Coalition', FAO Press Release, Rome, November.

Vidal, John (3/9/02) 'Warnings of Disaster Amid the Promise of Success', Earth Summit 2002, *The Guardian*.

Vincent, R. John (1974) *Nonintervention and International Order*, Princeton, NJ, Princeton University Press.

Vincent, R. John (1975a) 'The Idea of Concert and International Order', *Yearbook of World Affairs*, 31, London, Institute of World Affairs, 8–26.

Vincent, R. John (1975b) 'Military Power and Political Influence: The Soviet Union and Western Europe', *Adelphi Papers 119*, London, IISS.

Vincent, R. John (1977) 'Kissinger's System of Foreign Policy', *Yearbook of World Affairs*, 31, London, Institute of World Affairs, 8–26.

Vincent, R. John (1978) 'Western Conceptions of a Universal Moral Order', *British Journal of International Studies*, 4: 1, 20–46.

Vincent, R. John (1980) 'The Factor of Culture in the Global International Order', *The Yearbook of World Affairs*, 34, London, Stevens and Sons, pp. 252–264.

Vincent, R. John (1981) 'The Hobbesian Tradition in Twentieth Century International Thought', *Millennium*, 10: 2, 91–101.

Vincent, R. John (1982b) 'Race in International Relations', *International Affairs*, 58: 4, 658–670.

Vincent, R. John (1982a) 'Realpolitik' in James Mayall (ed.) *The Community of States: A Study in International Political Theory*, London, George Allen & Unwin.

Vincent, R. John (1983) 'Change in International Relations', *Review of International Studies*, 9: 1, 63–70.

Vincent, R. John (1986a) *Human Rights and International Relations: Issues and Responses*, Cambridge, Cambridge University Press.

Vincent, R. John (ed.) (1986b) *Foreign Policy and Human Rights: Issues and Responses*, Cambridge, Cambridge University Press.

Vincent, R. John (1986c) 'The Response of Europe and the Third World to United States Human Rights Diplomacy' in D. Newson (ed.) *The Diplomacy of Human Rights*, New York, University Press of America.

Vincent, R. John (1990a) 'Grotius, Human Rights and Intervention' in Hedley Bull, Benedict Kingsbury and Adam Roberts (eds) *Hugo Grotius and International Relations*, Oxford, Clarendon Press.

Vincent, R. John (1990b) 'Order in International Politics' in J.D.B. Miller and John Vincent (eds) *Order and Violence: Hedley Bull and International Relations*, Oxford, Clarendon Press.

Vincent, R. John (1992a) 'The Idea of Rights in International Ethics' in T. Nardin and D. Mapel (eds) *Traditions in International Ethics*, Cambridge, Cambridge University Press.

Vincent, R. John (1992b) 'Modernity and Universal Human Rights' in Anthony McGrew and Paul Lewis (eds) *Global Politics*, Cambridge, Polity Press.

Vincent, R. John (1994) 'The Place of Theory in the Practice of Human Rights' in Pamela Beshoff and Christopher Hill (eds) *Two Worlds of International Relations: Academics, Practitioners and the Trade in Ideas*, London, Routledge.

Vincent, R. John and Robert O'Neill (eds) (1990) *The West and the Third World: Essays in Honour of J.D.B. Miller*, Basingstoke, Macmillan.

Waever, Ole (1998) 'Four Meanings of International Society: A Trans-Atlantic Dialogue' in B.A. Robertson (ed.) *International Society and the Development of International Relations Theory*, London, Pinter, 80–144.

Wallerstein, Immanuel (1991) 'The Rise and Future Demise of the World Capitalist System: Concepts for Comparative Analysis' in Richard Little and Michael Smith (eds) *Perspectives on World Politics*, 2nd edn, London, Routledge, 305–317.

Watson, Adam (1987) 'Hedley Bull, State Systems and International Studies', *Review of International Studies*, 13: 2

Watson, Adam (1992) *The Evolution of International Society*, London, Routledge.

Website for data collection (e.g. annual population growth) http://daper.worldbank.org/daper/

WEF (2002) 'Agricultural Trade Task Force: Communique of Recommendations', New York. www.weforum.org/site/homepublic.nsf

Weid, Jean Marc (2002) 'A Civil Society Strategy to Overcome World Hunger', NGO/CSO Forum for Food Sovereignty, Rome, 8–13 June.

WFFS (2001) *Final Declaration of the World Forum on Food Security*, Cuba, 7 September.

Wheeler, Nicholas (1992) 'Pluralist and Solidarist Conceptions of International Society: Bull and Vincent on Humanitarian Intervention', *Millennium: Journal of International Studies* 21: 3, 463–487.

Wheeler, Nicholas (1996) 'Guardian Angel or Global Gangster: A Review of the Ethical Claims of International Society', *Political Studies*, 44, 123–135.

Wheeler, Nicholas (1997) 'The Dilemmas of Humanitarian Intervention', *International Political Science Review*, 18: 1, 9–25.

Wheeler, Nicholas (2000) *Saving Strangers: Humanitarian Intervention in International Society*, Oxford, Oxford University Press.

Wight, Gabriele and Brian Porter (eds) (1994) *International Theory: The Three Traditions*, London, Leicester University Press.

Windfuhr, Michael (2002) 'The Possible Role of An International Code of Conduct on the Right to Adequate Food', International NGO/CSO Planning Committee, Rome, 8–13 June.

Windfuhr, Michael (2003) 'The Code of Conduct on the Right to Adequate Food: a Tool for Civil Society', Hunger Notes, World Hunger Organisation. http://www.worldhunger.org/articles/global/foodashumrgt/windfuhr.htm

World Bank (1977) 'Basic Needs: An Issues Paper', Policy Planning and Program Review Department, 21 March.

World Bank (2001) *World Development Report 2000–2001* www.worldbank.org/poverty/wdrpoverty/report/index.htm

World Bank (2002a) 'Achievements and Challenges' in *World Development Report 2003*

World Bank (2002b) *Global Economic Prospects and the Developing Countries.*

World Bank (2002c) 'Launching Development Round Could Help Poor Countries Facing Global Downturn', News Press Release number 2002/111/S.

World Bank (2003) *Global Economic Prospects 2004* www.worldbank.org/prospects/gep2004/toc.htm

World Bank (7/2/02a) 'Data on Poverty: Data for the Analysis of Poverty Reduction' http://www.worldbank.org/poverty/data/ index.htm

World Bank (7/2/02b) 'IMF/World Bank PRSP Comprehensive Review' http://www.worldbank.org/poverty/strategies/review/

World Bank (7/2/02c) 'International Trade' http://www.worldbank.org/research/trade/index.htm

World Bank (7/2/02d) 'Infant, Child and Maternal Mortality' http://www.worldbank.org/data/dev/mortality.html

World Bank (7/2/02e) 'Overview of Poverty, Questions and Answers' http://www.worldbank.org/poverty/strategies/qanda.htm

World Bank (7/2/02f) 'Overview of Poverty Reduction Strategies' http://www.worldbank.org/poverty/strategies/overview.htm

World Bank (7/2/02g) 'Poverty Monitoring Database' http://www.worldbank.org/poverty/data/povmon.htm

World Bank (7/2/02h) 'Poverty/World Development Indicators' http://www.worldbank.org/data/dev/poverty.html

World Bank (7/2/02i) 'Trends in Poverty over Time' http://www.worldbank.org/poverty/mission/up3.htm

World Bank (7/2/02j) 'What is Poverty?' http://www.worldbank.org/poverty/mission/up1.htm

World Bank (8/4/02a) 'Income Poverty, the Latest Global Numbers' http://www.worldbank.org/poverty/data/trends/income.htm

World Bank (8/4/02b) 'Prospects for Poverty Reduction' http://www.worldbank.org/poverty/data/trends/prospect.htm

World Bank (8/4/02c) 'Prospects for Developing Countries and World Trade' http://www.worldbank.org/prospect/gep2001/chapt1.pdf

World Bank (8/4/02d) 'Prospects for Development' http://www.worldbank.org/prospects/gep2001/

World Bank (8/4/02e) 'Standards, Developing Countries and the Global Trade System' http://www.worldbank.org/prospects/gep2001/chapt3.pdf

World Bank (8/4/02f) 'Trade Policies in the 1990s and the Poorest Countries' http://www.worldbank.org/prospects/gep2001/chapt2.pdf

World Bank (28/8/02) 'Millennium Development Goals: Eradicate Extreme Poverty and Hunger' www.developmentgoals.org/Poverty.htm

Worldwatch Institute (2002) 'Forgive and Forget Won't Fix Third World Debt' http://www.worldwatch.org/alerts/010426.html

WPF (2002) 'Save the Earth Summit: a Sustainable World is Possible, Necessary and Urgent', *Declaration on the Rio + 10 Summit*, Johannesburg, 26 August–4 September.

WSRG (1995) 'In Search of World Society', Darmstadt/Frankfurt, *World Society Research Group Working Paper number 1.*

WTO (1994) Agreement on Agriculture, Uruguay Round.

WTO (2000a) *Agricultural Committee*, 14 November. http://www.wto.org/english/news_e/news00_e/ag_nov00_e.htm

WTO (2000b) 'US Presents Agricultural Market Access Proposal' http://usinfo.state.gov/topical/econ/wto99/ag1117.htm

WTO (2000c) 'US Pushes for Increased Transparency in the WTO' http://usinfo.state.gov/topical/econ/wto99/pp1010.htm

WTO (2000d) 'US Trade Policy and the Trading System' http://usinfo.state.gov/topical/econ/wto99/pp0413.htm

WTO (2000e) 'World Trade Organisation: Next Steps' http://usinfo.state.gov/topical/econ/wto99/pp0114.htm

WTO (2001a) *Annual Report to General Council* http://www.wto.org/english/tratop_e/agric_e/ann_rep2001_e.htm

WTO (2001b) *Doha Ministerial Declaration* http://www-heva.wto-ministerial.org/english/thewto_e/minist_e/min01_e

WTO (2001c) *International Trade Statistics* http://www.wto.org/english/res_e/statis_e/its2001_e/its01_toc_e.htm

WTO (2001d) 'United States, Europe and the World Trade System' http://usinfo.state.gov/topical/econ/wto99/pp0515.htm

WTO (10/12/01a) 'Agriculture and Developing Countries' http://www.wto.org/english/news_e/spmm_e/spmm47_e.htm

WTO (10/12/01b) 'Agriculture Explanation Summary' http://www.wto.org/english/tratop_e/agric_e/ag_intro07_summary.htm

WTO (10/12/01c) 'Distribution Services' http://usinfo.state.gov/topical/econ/wto99/distribution1214.htm

WTO (10/12/01d) 'Domestic Support' http://www.wto.org/english/tratop_e/agric_e/ag_intro03_domestic.htm

WTO (10/12/01e) 'European Communities, the ACP-EC Partnership Agreement' http://www.heva.wto-ministerial.org/english/thewto_e/minist_e

WTO (10/12/01f) 'Export Competition/Subsidies' http://www.wto.org/english/tratop_e/agric_e/ag_intro04_export.htm

WTO (10/12/01g) 'Fourth WTO Ministerial Conference' http://www-heva.wto-ministerial.org/english/thewto_e/minist_e/min01_e/min01_e.htm

WTO (10/12/01h) 'Grassley Comments on Progress by WTO Agriculture Committee' http://usinfo.state.gov/topical/econ/wto99/cg0327.htm

WTO (10/12/01i) 'Market Access' http://www.wto.org/english/tratop_e/agric_e/ag_intro02_access.htm

WTO (10/12/01j) 'Other Issues' http://www.wto.org/english/tratop_e/agric_e/ag_intro05_other.htm

WTO (10/12/01k) 'Procedures for Extensions under Article 27.4 for Certain Developing Country Members' http://www-heva.wtministerial.org/english/thewto_e/

WTO (10/12/01l) 'Proposals Received in Phase 1' http://www.wto.org/english/tratop_e/agric_e/negs_bkgrnd02_props1_e.htm

WTO (10/12/01m) 'Road to Qatar' http://usinfo.state.gov/topical/econ/wto99/cg0425.htm

WTO (10/12/01n) 'Significant Trade Barriers Remain After Uruguay Round' http://www.wto.org/english/news_e/pres01_e/pr222_e.htm

WTO (10/12/01o) 'Statement on the Administrations, 2000 Trade Policy Agenda' http://usinfo.state.gov/topical/econ/wto99/cg0303.htm

WTO (10/12/01p) 'Uruguay Round Reform Programme for Trade in Agriculture' http://www.wto.org/english/tratop_e/agric_e/ag_intro00_contents.htm

WTO (10/12/01q) 'USA, Europe and the World Trade System' http://www.usinfo.state.gov/topical/econ/wto99/pp0515.htm

WTO (10/12/01r) 'US-EU Summit Statement on a New WTO Round' http://usinfo.state.gov/topical/econ/wto99/pp0531.htm

WTO (10/12/01s) 'US Interests and Experience in WTO Dispute Settlement System' http://usinfo.state.gov/topical/econ/wto99/pp0620.htm

WTO (10/12/01t) 'US Trade Policy and the Trading System' http://usinfo.state.gov/topical/econ/wto99/pp0413.htm

WTO (10/12/01u) 'World Trade Organization: Next Steps' http://usinfo.state.gov/topical/econ/wto99/pp0414.htm

WTO (6/1/02) 'Net Food-importing Developing Countries' http://www.wto.org/english/tratop_e/agric_e/ag_intro06_netfood.htm

WTO (21/1/02a) 'Agriculture: Fairer Markets for Farmers' http://www.wto.org/english/thewto_e/whatis_e/tif_e/agrm3_e.htm

WTO (21/1/02b) 'Agriculture: Introduction' http://www.wto.org/english/tratop_e/agric_e/ag_intro01_intro.htm

WTO (21/1/02c) 'Agricultural Stake in WTO Trade Negotiations' http://wto.org/english/news_e/spmm_e/spmm53_e.htm

WTO (21/1/02d) 'In a Nutshell' http://wto.org/english/tratop_e/agric_e/negs_bkgrnd01_nutshell_e.htm

WTO (21/1/02e) 'Legal Texts, the WTO Agreements' http://www.wto.org/english/docs_e/legal_e/final_e.htm

WTO (12/4/02a) 'Agricultural Negotiations Backgrounder, Introduction' http://www.wto.org/english/tratop_e/agric_e/negs_bkgrnd05_intro_e.htm

WTO (12/4/02b) 'Phase 1, Non Trade Concerns: Agriculture Can Serve Many Purposes'
http://www.wto.org/English/tratop
WTO (14/01/04) 'Summary of 14 September 2003: Conference Ends without Consensus'
http://www.wto.org/english/thewto_e/minist_e/min03_e/min03_14sept_e.htm

Index

Abbott, K. 69, 72, 141
Africa: basic rights: right to food 58, 59, 60; Caribbean and Pacific 60, 61; Growth and Opportunity Act 59, 68, 87, 137, 141; international trade and hunger eradication 93, 101, 104, 111; North 9, 16; problem of hunger 11, 13, 16, 19, 24; *see also* Sub-Saharan Africa
Agency for International Development 74
Agenda 21 61–2, 65
Agreement on Agriculture 22, 27, 31; basic rights: right to food 56, 61, 66; international trade and hunger eradication 88–9, 94, 100, 110, 111
Agreement on Sanitary and Phytosanitary Standards 24–5
agricultural policies 26–31
AIDS 11
Ajami, F. 41
Alderson, K. 128
Algeria 60
Algiers conference of Non-Aligned Countries 35–6
Alston, P. 33, 36, 37, 50
American Bill of Rights 33
Andean Trade Preference Act 68
Angola 10, 14–15
Annan, K. 65, 76, 103
Argentina 90
Asia 9–10, 68; Central 16, 111; East 9, 11, 16; international trade and hunger eradication 91, 93; problem of hunger 10, 11, 13, 16; South 9, 11, 16, 18; South East 9
Aspen Institute 36
Australia 27, 90

Baehr, P.R. 34, 40
Bangladesh 10, 12
Barbados 67
Barcelona Declaration 60
Barkin, S. 132
Basic Needs approach 34–40
basic rights in international society: right to food 53–77; Doha Declaration 66–9; legalisation, degree of 69–77; poverty summits 61–6; World Food Summit and plan of action 53–61
basic rights project: Vincent 134–44; English School of International Relations 138–42; viability of basic right to food 134–8
Becker, E. 30
Bedau, H.A. 41
Bhagwati, J. 59, 97
Bill of Rights 33
biotechnology developments 18–19
Blue Box 27, 70, 71
Booth, C. 35
Botswana 67
Braun, J. 52
Brazil 12, 13, 30; international trade and hunger eradication 83, 90, 113
Bretton Woods system 81
Bridges 71
Brown, C. 82
Brussels Conference on Least Developed Countries 123
Brussels Declaration 64
Bull, H. 2, 43, 44, 45, 129–30, 138, 140
Bush, G.W. 59, 89, 125
Butterfield, H. 43

Buzan, B. 91, 103, 104, 129, 130, 132, 136, 139, 140; human rights: political origins 43, 46

Cairns Group 21
Canada 25, 27; basic rights: right to food 61, 67; international trade and hunger eradication 87, 94, 111
Cancun Summit 30, 66, 71, 72; basic rights project 136; international society and hunger elimination 116; international trade and hunger eradication 87, 94
Caribbean 9, 11, 16, 18, 60; Basin Trade Partnership Act 68; *see also* Africa, Caribbean and Pacific
Castells, M. 21
Center for Integrative Studies 36
Central America 13
Central Asia 16, 111
Centre 82
Chad 10, 14
China 63; international trade and hunger eradication 105–6, 111, 112; problem of hunger 10, 12, 13, 14, 16, 26, 30
Chomsky, N. 94
Chossudovsky, M. 109
Clapham, C. 103
Clay, E. 22
Clinton, B. 59
Club of Rome 82
Coconou Agreement 60
Cold War 38, 45, 105, 106, 126; East–West ideological division 33–4
Commission: on Human Rights 51, 74; on Sustainable Development 76
Committee: on Agriculture 100; on Economic, Social and Cultural Rights 51, 59, 74; on Food Aid 67; on World Food Security 57, 58, 59–60, 61, 74
Common Agricultural Policy 71, 89, 90, 136, 137
Communism 33
conflict 23
Congo, Democratic Republic of 15
Convention of the Rights of the Child 50
Copenhagen Declaration on Social Development 62, 123
Corn Laws repeal 80
corruption 14
Cote d'Ivoire 67

Council of Ministers 60
Covenant on Economic, Social and Cultural Rights 37–8, 51
Cox, R. 35
credit, access to 13–14
Cuba 67
Cyprus 60

De Haen, H. 9
debt, external 15
Declaration: on Environment and Development 61; and Programme of Action on the Establishment of a New International Economic Order 36; of Rural Organisations in Africa 110
Deen, T. 103
definitions 6–7
delegation 72, 74–5, 76–7
Delegation of Rural Organisations of Africa 101
Department: of Agriculture 74, 105; of State 74
depth of hunger 7
Development Box 92, 98, 99–100
DiazBonilla, E. 107
Diouf, J. 58, 90, 97, 104
discrimination against women 14
Dispute Settlement Body 72, 93
diversification 24
Doha Agreement 72
Doha Declaration 29, 89, 116; basic rights: right to food 53, 61, 66–9, 70–2, 77
Doha ministerial meeting 87; basic rights: right to food 65, 71, 76–7; problem of hunger 19, 28–9, 30
domestic support 27
Dominican Republic 67
Donnelly, J. 41
Dunne, T. 33, 43, 45, 46, 126, 127, 128, 139

East Asia 9, 11, 16
East–West divide 4, 33–4, 135
Eastern Europe 16, 111
economic growth effects from trade 64–5
EBA (Everything But Arms) 141
ECOSOC (Economic and Social Council) Resolution 120
Egypt 12, 30, 60, 67
Ehrlich, A. 113
Ehrlich, P. 113

Elliot, L. 13, 15
English School of International
    Relations 2–4, 32, 138–42; basic
    rights project 141, 142;
    international society and hunger
    elimination 118–19, 127–9; and
    Vincent 43–6
Equatorial Guinea 87
equitable access to rule-based trading
    system 93
equitable trade policies 92–9
Eritrea 12
Esipiu, M. 19
Ethiopia 12, 14
EuroMediterranean policy 60
Europe 34, 73, 126; *see also* Eastern
    Europe; European
European Commission 67
European Community 83
European Convention on Human
    Rights 120
European Council 60
European Union 130, 137; basic rights:
    right to food 53, 59, 61, 67, 68,
    70–1, 72; Council of Ministers 60;
    international trade and hunger
    eradication 87, 89, 90, 94, 97, 98;
    problem of hunger 19, 25, 27, 28,
    30
Everything But Arms initiative 60, 61,
    68, 87, 89, 137
existing system, maintenance of and
    new reforms 92–104; assessment
    101–4; development box, creation
    of 99–100; equitable trade policies
    92–9; Marrakesh Decision, reform
    of 100; sub-global arrangements
    100–1
export: competition 27; infrastructure
    24; subsidies 25
external debt 15

factors of production 64
first option 84
First World 38
Fischler, F. 70–1
Food and Agriculture Organisation:
    basic human rights: political origins
    50, 51; basic rights: right to food
    53, 58; basic rights project 138,
    141; international trade and hunger
    eradication 94, 96, 97, 98, 100,
    101, 104; problem of hunger 8–9,
    13, 15, 21

'Food and Agriculture Statement' 109
Food Aid Convention 22, 67
food distribution 12–13
food insecurity 6
Food Insecurity and Vulnerability
    Information and Mapping Systems
    8, 58
food, right to 50–2
food security 6
food sovereignty 108, 125
Food Sovereignty Declaration 109–10
food trade 26–31
former Soviet Union 34, 35, 105, 111,
    112
France 71, 111; Declaration of the
    Rights of Man 33
'Future of European Agriculture' 70

G-7 93, 111; Summit 85
G-8 Summit 59
G-15 93
G-20 30, 94
G-77 93–4
Galtung, J. 36, 37, 39, 40, 82
General Agreement on Tariffs and
    Trade 35, 141; international trade
    and hunger eradication 81, 83, 84,
    87; problem of hunger 21–2, 26, 28
Generalised System of Preferences 59,
    77
Genetically Modified Organisms 18–19
Germany 71, 111; Historical School 80
Gilpin, R. 79, 80, 83
Goldstein, J. 76
goods, prices of 64
government revenue 64
Gramsci, A. 82
Great Depression 91
Greek Stoics 32
Green Box 27, 29, 70, 71, 94, 99
Green, D. 20, 89
Green Movement 79, 82–3, 84–5
gross domestic product 23, 36–7, 65,
    117; international trade and hunger
    eradication 87, 91, 96, 97, 101
gross national product 82

Hagey Lectures 130
Haiti 10
Hamilton, A. 80
Havana Declaration 125
heavily indebted poor countries 15
Heckscher and Olin model 79, 81
Helleiner, E. 85

High Commissioner for Human Rights 51
Honduras 67
Human Development Report 63
human rights, basic: political origins 32–52; basic rights debate 40–3; East–West ideological division of the Cold War 33–4; emergence of basic rights 32–40; food, right to 50–2; North–South divide: basic needs versus New International Economic Order 34–40
human rights discourse 140
Hurrell, A. 126, 128

import restrictions 25
India 10, 12, 13, 30, 63
Indonesia 10, 12, 14, 26
Ingco, M. 88, 97
Interagency Working Group on Food Security 74
internal tariffs 24
International Alliance against Hunger 98
International Conference on Financing for Development 59
International Convention 110
International Covenant on Civil and Political Rights 50
International Covenant on Economic, Social and Cultural Rights 50, 51
international economy 139
International Fund for Agricultural Development 94
International Governmental Organisations 51, 57–8, 123
International Labour Organisation 35, 36
International Monetary Fund 15, 35, 51, 81, 100, 106
International Non-Governmental Organisatons 58
international political economy 2–3, 139, 140, 141, 142
international society and hunger elimination 115–33; key points summary 115–18; pluralism–solidarism 128–33; world society 127–8; world society as complementary feature or challenge to international society 118–20; world society as empirical side of Vincent's position on universality 125–7; world society as extension of international society 120–3; world society as hostile opposition to international society 124–5
international trade and hunger eradication options 78–114; existing system, maintenance of and new reforms 92–104; liberal trading system, current 85–92; radical change 105–14; theoretical background 79–85; Vincent's position, anticipation of 114
International Youth Forum 57
Iran 12
Ireland 71
Israel 60
Italy 111

Jackson, R. 131
Jackson, J. 81
Jackson, R. 77, 80, 82, 102, 103
Jamaica 67
Japan 25, 27, 29, 61; international trade and hunger eradication 83, 87, 90, 94, 98, 111
Johannesburg: Commitment 65; Plan of Implementation 75; Summit 18, 59, 65, 116
Johnson, K. 19
Jones, D. 77
Jonsson, U. 39
Jordan 60

Kaempfer, W. 79
Kaplan, R. 113
Kennedy Round 81
Kenya 67
Keohane, R. 112, 132–3
Kissinger, H. 48
Knudsen, T.B. 45, 128
Koppel, N. 30
Korea, Democratic Republic of 14, 29
Korten, D. 106, 109
Kothari, R. 105
Kwa, A. 13

land, access to 13–14
Landless Rural Workers movement 13
Larson, A. 87
Latif, I. 106
Latin America 9, 11, 16, 18, 73, 93
Least Developed Countries 22, 25, 87, 100, 102; basic rights: right to food 60, 63–4, 65, 67
Lebanon 60

legalisation, degree of 69–77; Doha
  Declaration 70–2; poverty-related
  summits 75–7; World Food Summit
  72–5
Lengyel, M. 21–2, 28
Lenin, V.I. 82
liberal trading system, current 85–92;
  assessment 89–92; description 86–9
Liberalism 79, 80, 81, 82
Lilliston, B. 30
Limits to Growth 82
Linklater, A. 82
Little, R. 35, 37, 43, 81, 139
low-income food-deficit countries 9,58
Luxemburg, R. 82

McHale, J. 35, 36–7
McHale, M. 35, 36–7
McKinlay, R.D. 35, 37, 81
McLaughlin, M. 106
Madeley, J. 111, 112
Malawi 19
Malaysia 26
malnutrition 7
Malta 60
Malthus, T. 113
Marchal, R. 15
market access 27
Marrakesh Decision 21, 22; basic
  rights: right to food 55, 56;
  international trade and hunger
  eradication 92, 98–9, 104; reform
  100
Marx, K. 82
Marxism 79, 81–2, 84; Classical 82;
  Leninism 82; Soviet 82; Western 82;
  see also neo-Marxism
Maslow, A. 39
Matthews, R. 41
Mauritius 67
Mayall, J. 128
Mendoza, M. 77, 86, 99
Mercosur 90
Mernies, J. 8
Mexico 12, 13
Middle Ages 33
Middle East 16
Millennium: Development Declaration
  64, 75, 76, 96, 116; Summit 59
Monterrey Conference 65
Moon, B. 28, 72, 80, 81
Moore, M. 86
Morocco 60, 67
Moser, I. 18

Mozambique 10
Mugabe, R. 13
Murphy, S. 89
Mutual Recognition Agreements 25

Nationalism 79, 80, 84, 139
Near East 9, 11
neo-Marxism 85, 139; third-worldist
  82
Net Food-Importing Developing
  Countries 22, 100
Neuman, I.B. 120, 126
New International Economic Order 33,
  34–40, 53, 124; international trade
  and hunger eradication 81, 82, 83,
  105, 106
'New Protectionism' 83, 84
new reforms *see* existing system,
  maintenance of and new reforms
New Zealand 26
Newly Industrialised Countries 83
Nigeria 10, 12
Non-Aligned Movement 35, 105
non-governmental organisations 5–8,
  14, 51; Forum 57; international
  society and hunger elimination 123,
  124; international trade and hunger
  eradication 84, 99, 109
North Africa 9, 16
North American Free Trade
  Association 68
North Atlantic nations 42
North–North divide 66
North–South divide 4, 34–40, 66, 79,
  80, 81, 106, 135
Norway 29

obligation 70, 73, 75
Official Development Assistance 96
'Old Protectionism' 83
O'Neill, O. 39
Organisation for Economic
  Cooperation and Development 27,
  31, 36, 132; international trade and
  hunger eradication 87, 88, 90, 95,
  97, 99, 101
'Other Economic Summit, The' 85, 111
overpopulation 12
Oyejide, A. 29

Pacific 9, 10, 16, 60; *see also* Africa,
  Carribean and Pacific
Pakistan 12, 67
Palestinian Authority 60

Parker, N. 6
Parliamentarians' Day 57
Paterson, M. 84
Patrick, T. 93, 94, 106
People's Food Sovereignty movement 109
Periphery 82
Peru 67
Pettiford, L. 83, 85
Philippines 13
pluralism 139; –solidarism 44–6, 128–33, 135, 137, 138, 140, 141, 142
political economy *see* international political economy
poverty 15–18
poverty summits 61–6, 75–7; economic growth effects from trade 64–5; government revenue 64; prices of goods and factors of production 64; transition costs and exposure to shocks 65–6
Pratt, C. 41
precision 70–1, 73–4, 75–6
prices of goods 64
problem of hunger 6–31; biotechnology developments 18–19; corruption 14; definitions 6–7; external debt 15; food distribution 12–13; food trade and agricultural policies 26–31; land and credit, access to 13–14; overpopulation 12; poverty 15–18; statistics 7–12; wars 14–15; women, discrimination against 14; world trade issues 19–26
production, factors of 64

Quad countries 60, 67, 95; *see also* Canada; European Union; Japan; United States
quality control measures 24–5
Quiroga, J. 41

radical change 105–14; assessment 111–14; description 105–11
Reducing Poverty and Hunger 94, 95
Reiter, R. 41
Renaissance 33
Ricardo, D. 79
right to food *see* basic rights
Rio Summit (1992) 76
Robinson, M. 51, 52
Rome Declaration on Food Security 54, 57, 83, 123

Rowntree, B.S. 35
Ruggie, J.G. 79, 81
rural poor 17

St Lucia 67
Scandinavia 71
Schott, J. 66, 70, 87
Seattle Ministerial Conference 28, 30, 91, 106, 124, 125
second option 84
security rights 47
Seddon, D. 39
Sen, A. 39
Senegal 67
Sharma, S. 30
Shaw, M. 34
Shiva, V. 18
shocks, exposure to 65–6
Shue, H. 32, 39, 41–2, 47–8, 140
Simmons, P. 41
Singapore Ministerial Conference 61
Smith, A. 79
Smith, J. 93, 94, 106
Snidal, D. 69, 141
solidarism *see* pluralism–solidarism
Somalia 15
Somavia, J. 63
Sorensen, G. 80, 82
South Africa 13
South America 90
South Asia 9, 11, 16, 18
South East Asia 9
South Korea 83
South Summit (Havana) 93
South–South divide 66
Spain 71
Special and Differential Treatment 29, 83, 99–100
Special Programme for Food Security 58
Sri Lanka 67
Stalin, J. 105
State of Food Insecurity and the World, The 8
statistics 7–12
Steans, J. 83, 85
Steiner, H. 33
Stiglitz, J. 86, 106
Stokke, O. 22
Stubbs, R. 81, 132
subglobal arrangements 100–1
SubSaharan Africa 59; international trade and hunger eradication 86,

88, 96, 97, 98, 103, 112; problem
of hunger 9, 10–11, 16, 18, 23–4
subsistence rights 47
Sudan 87
Suppan, S. 99, 100, 111
Sustainable Development Summits 61,
76, 83
Switzerland 26
Syria 60

Taiwan 13
Taylor, M. 74–5
Thailand 14, 26
third option 84–5
Third World 12, 22, 136; basic human
rights: political origins 35, 36–7, 38,
49; international society and hunger
elimination 124, 126, 133;
international trade and hunger
eradication 90, 91, 101, 106, 112
Thomas, C. 11, 12–13, 81, 83, 113
Tick, J. 74–5
Tomasevski, K. 50
Tooze, R. 79, 80
Trade Policy Review: Board 72;
Mechanism 72
Trade Related Intellectual Property
Rights Agreement 18, 93
transition costs 65–6
Trinidad and Tobago 67
Tully, A. 105
Tunisia 60, 67
Turkey 60
Tussie, D. 21–2, 28

Underhill, G. 81, 132
undernourishment 7
United Kingdom 35, 71, 80, 111; Bill
of Rights 33
United Nations 23, 110, 123; basic
human rights: political origins 39,
41, 51; basic rights: right to food
53, 57, 58; Children's Fund 36;
Committee on Economic, Social and
Cultural Rights 51, 59, 73, 74;
Conference 61; Conference on Least
Developed Countries 63, 116;
Conference on Trade and
Development 21, 23, 35, 123;
Department of Economic and Social
Affairs 76; Development Program
15, 76; Educational, Scientific and
Cultural Organisation 36;
Environment Program 141; General
Assembly 36, 51, 59, 74, 126;
Human Rights Declaration 33, 34,
35, 37; Millennium Declaration 63
United States 35, 49, 125, 130, 137;
basic rights: right to food 59, 60,
67, 68, 71, 72, 73, 74; Department
of Agriculture 19, 105; House of
Representatives 68; international
trade and hunger eradication 80–1,
83, 87, 89–90, 93–4, 97–8, 111;
problem of hunger 25, 27, 28, 30;
Senate 68
Universal Declaration: and the
Covenants 40; on the Eradication of
Hunger and Malnutrition 50–1; of
Human Rights 50
universality 125–7
urban poor 17
Uruguay Round 37; basic rights: right
to food 55, 56–7, 67; international
trade and hunger eradication 88–9,
90–1, 100, 101, 104; problem of
hunger 21–2, 27, 28

Venezuela 67
Via Campesina 109, 110
Vidal, J. 66
Vincent, R.J. 2–3, 4–5, 53, 69; basic
human rights: political origins 32–3,
36–41, 52; basic rights 43–50; and
the English School of International
Relations 43–6; 'Grotius, Human
Rights and Intervention' 120;
*Human Rights and Internaional
Relations* 44–5; hunger, problem of
6, 7, 12, 30, 31; 'Idea of Rights in
International Ethics, The' 121;
International Order 44;
international society and hunger
elimination 115–16, 118–24,
128–33; international trade and
options for hunger eradication 78,
91–2, 102, 104, 114; 'Modernity
and Universal Human Rights' 47;
'Rights in a cross-section of world
society' 121; and universality 125–7;
see also basic rights project: Vincent
vulnerability 7

Waever, O. 103, 104
Wallerstein, I. 82
wars 14–15
Watson, A. 43
wealth, unequal distribution of 24

Weid, J.M. 111
Wheeler, N. 33, 44, 45, 46, 129–30, 136, 139
Wight, G. 45
Wight, M. 43
Windfuhr, M. 52, 73–4
women, discrimination against 14
World Bank 138; basic human rights: political origins 35, 36–7, 51; basic rights: right to food 60, 64; international trade and hunger eradication 81, 87, 90, 97, 101, 106; problem of hunger 14, 15, 23, 25, 26
World Commission 110
World Development Report 96
World Food Conference 8, 50–1, 53, 57
World Food Program 14
World Food Summit 8, 59, 72–5, 135; basic human rights: political origins 51, 52; basic rights: right to food 58, 63, 76; Commitment 4 19; Declaration 51, 53–61, 73; international society and hunger elimination 116, 123; international trade and hunger eradication 89, 95; *see also* Seattle Ministerial Conference; World Food Summit Plan of Action
World Food Summit Plan of Action 51, 53–61, 73; Commitment 1 55; Commitment 4 55–7; follow-up 57–61
World Forum on Food Sovereignty (Havana) 108

World Human Rights Conference (Vienna) 40–1
World Parliamentary Forum 94, 109, 110
world society 44, 139
World Summit for Social Development 62, 116
world trade issues 19–26; external dimension 24–6; internal dimension 23–4
World Trade Organisation 51, 136, 140, 141; basic rights: right to food 55, 56, 66, 67, 68, 70, 71, 72; Committee on Agriculture 100; international society and hunger elimination 117, 120, 122–3, 130–2, 133; international trade and hunger eradication 84, 87–8, 90, 92–5, 98–9, 105–6, 108–14; Ministerial Conferences 28, 59; problem of hunger 18, 21–2, 23, 26, 28, 29; Singapore Ministerial Conference 61; *see also* Cancun; Doha
World Trade System 64
Worldwatch Institute 113

Yemen 87
Yugoslav Federal Army 14

Zambia 18–19
Zapatista movement 13
Zimbabwe 13, 137
Zunzunegui, M.V. 41